The Split Capital Investment Trust Crisis

Wiley Finance Series

The Split Capital Investment Trust Crisis

Edited by

Andrew Adams

John Wiley & Sons, Ltd

Other Wiley Editorial Offices

John Wiley & Sons Inc., 111 River Street, Hoboken, NJ 07030, USA

Jossey-Bass, 989 Market Street, San Francisco, CA 94103-1741, USA

Wiley-VCH Verlag GmbH, Boschstr. 12, D-69469 Weinheim, Germany

John Wiley & Sons Australia Ltd, 33 Park Road, Milton, Queensland 4064, Australia

John Wiley & Sons (Asia) Pte Ltd, 2 Clementi Loop #02-01, Jin Xing Distripark, Singapore 129809

John Wiley & Sons Canada Ltd, 22 Worcester Road, Etobicoke, Ontario, Canada M9W 1L1

Wiley also publishes its books in a variety of electronic formats. Some content that appears
in print may not be available in electronic books.

British Library Cataloguing in Publication Data

A catalogue record for this book is available from the British Library

ISBN 0-470-86858-9

Project management by Originator, Gt Yarmouth, Norfolk (typeset in 10/12pt Times)
Printed and bound in Great Britain by TJ International, Padstow, Cornwall
This book is printed on acid-free paper responsibly manufactured from sustainable forestry
in which at least two trees are planted for each one used for paper production.

Contents

List of Contributors

ANDREW ADAMS
University of Edinburgh Management School, Edinburgh, UK

ROBIN ANGUS
Personal Assets Trust and University of Edinburgh Management School,
Edinburgh, UK

JAMES CLUNIE
University of Edinburgh Management School, Edinburgh, UK

PIERS CURRIE
Aberdeen Asset Managers, London, UK

DANIEL GODFREY
AITC, London, UK

PETER GARDNER
Hansa Capital Limited, London, UK

DAVID HARRIS
InvaTrust Consultancy, London, UK

ANDREW McCOSH
Florida International University, Miami, USA and University of Edinburgh
Management School, Edinburgh, UK

JOHN McFALL MP
Chairman, Treasury Committee, House of Commons, London, UK

PETER MOLES
University of Edinburgh Management School, Edinburgh, UK

JOHN NEWLANDS
Newlands Fund Research, Edinburgh, UK

GEOFFREY WOOD
City University, London, UK

About the Contributors

ANDREW ADAMS

Andrew Adams is Senior Lecturer in Finance and Director of the Centre for Financial Markets Research at the University of Edinburgh. He is author or co-author of a number of books in the investment area and is co-author of the article "For whom the barbell tolls ..." [Appendix A]. His memorandum to the House of Commons Treasury Select Committee entitled "The split capital investment trust crisis: Underlying reasons and historical developments" is published as an appendix to the Committee's main report.

ROBIN ANGUS

Robin Angus is a director of two investment trusts and is a Visiting Fellow of the University of Edinburgh Management School. He is author of *Haec Olim: Exploring the World of Investment Trusts 1981–1991* and has written numerous articles on investment trusts and related themes. He is co-author of the article "For whom the barbell tolls ..." [Appendix A].

JAMES CLUNIE

James Clunie is Lecturer in Finance at the University of Edinburgh with a research interest in the pricing and risk assessment of split capital investment trusts. He was formerly Head of Global Equities at Aberdeen Asset Management and prior to that Head of Asset Allocation at Murray Johnstone International.

PIERS CURRIE

Piers Currie is Head of Investor Relations, Investment Trusts, at Aberdeen Asset Managers and was responsible for communication for the Aberdeen Group during the split capital investment trust crisis. He appeared before the Treasury Select Committee on Split Capital Investment Trusts.

DANIEL GODFREY

Daniel Godfrey is Director General of the Association of Investment Trust Companies and has been Chairman of the Personal Finance Education Group since 2000. He appeared before the Treasury Select Committee on Split Capital Investment Trusts.

PETER GARDNER

Peter Gardner is the Compliance Officer and Finance Director of Hansa Capital Limited, a London-based investment management company whose clients include Hansa Trust PLC, a London-quoted investment trust.

DAVID HARRIS

David Harris is Chief Executive of InvaTrust Consultancy. He was formally director of education and training at the Association of Investment Trust Companies and is a previous winner of the award "Best investment adviser in the UK". He is a director of three investment trusts, writes regularly for both the national and trade press and is a regular commentator on investment issues on both TV and radio.

ANDREW McCOSH

Andrew McCosh is the Alvah Chapman Eminent Scholar in Management and Ethics at Florida International University, Miami, USA. He is Professor Emeritus of Finance at the University of Edinburgh. He is also a Visiting Professor of Finance at the Cyprus International Institute for Management, Nicosia. He served as an Independent Director of the 16 mutual funds of the Lexington Family for seven years, and for two years was a director of the Pilgrim Funds. His most recent book is entitled *Financial Ethics* (Kluwer, 1999).

JOHN McFALL

John McFall MP is Member of Parliament for Dumbarton and is Chairman of the Treasury Select Committee that investigated split capital investment trusts.

PETER MOLES

Peter Moles is Lecturer in Finance at the University of Edinburgh and specialises in financial risk management. He is co-author of *Handbook of International Financial Market Terms* (Oxford University Press, 1997) and was formerly Director, Eurobond Syndication, at Chase Investment Bank.

JOHN NEWLANDS

John Newlands is an Edinburgh-based investment trust analyst with a particular interest in splits. Prior to forming his own consultancy in January 2003, he was investment trust analyst at the London stockbroking firm of Williams de Broë PLC. His industry report *Split Capital and Highly Geared Investment Trusts* (Williams de Broë, May 2000) was used as a reference document during the recent splits enquiry. He is also the author of *Put Not Your Trust in Money* (AITC, 1997), the official history of the UK investment trust industry, and co-author of *F&C – A History of Foreign & Colonial Investment Trust* (F&C, 1999).

GEOFFREY WOOD

Geoffrey Wood is Professor of Economics at City University, London and has been with the research staff of both the Bank of England and the Federal Reserve Bank of St Louis. He is the co-author or co-editor of ten books, which deal with, among other subjects, finance of international trade, monetary policy and bank regulation. Among his professional papers are studies of exchange-rate behaviour, interest-rate determination, monetary unions, tariff policy and bank regulation. He has also acted as an adviser to the New Zealand Treasury.

Foreword

The split capital investment trust crisis, which hit the radar screens in late 2001, has yet fully to unfold. But even if an ending in mid-2004 is still uncertain, the principal players and many of the causes of the crisis are reasonably well understood.

The story, as is so often the case in financial crises, is largely one of excessive expectations followed by disappointment. Many fund managers and their advisers in the sector saw the opportunity to make big fees by launching funds for which there was palpable demand, while overlooking the extent of the possible downside should things go wrong. There were also clearly excessive expectations on the part of many investors and their advisers seeking high returns without necessarily considering the inevitably higher risks.

Split capital investment trusts had over the years been good products, doing what they said on the tin. Zeros had provided steady, unspectacular, tax-efficient growth for the risk-averse without ever failing to meet their targets. Income shares had delivered high income, often with growth as well but occasionally incurring substantial capital losses as one might expect from geared shares that were clearly sold as higher risk. But now there was a fundamental failure of product design.

One element was the increase in levels of bank debt as interest rates came down. Although cheaper than using zeros for gearing, it added instability to the structure once banking covenants were breached, so that companies which were once being run for the benefit of shareholders now had to be run to protect the interests of creditors. Another element was the sometimes large investments in income shares of other companies that themselves invested in income shares of other companies that themselves invested in income shares and so on. This led to a loss of bearings as it became difficult if not impossible for managers to calculate their true levels of gearing, expenses or risks.

In the end, these failings brought a number of splits to their knees as the markets fell and many investors lost a substantial proportion of their wealth.

The Association of Investment Trust Companies' primary objective has been to protect the entire industry from potentially devastating reputational damage and regulatory backlash. Our approach has been to be visible, open and honest about the whole affair. We have not sought to defend the indefensible and we have accepted that we, along with many others, could have done more.

We played a major role in softening the recommendations of the Treasury Select Committee by ensuring that it was in a position to take an informed view, and we were able to turn around the most damaging of the proposed changes to the Listing Rules, originally set out in the FSA's Consultation Paper 164. Some of the proposed rules would have put existing investment trust "funds of funds" out of business and prevented any such structures being launched in the future.

We have also introduced the AITC's own *Code of Corporate Governance* to ensure that the industry emerges strengthened as a result of this crisis, but in a way that is flexible and non-prescriptive.

The overhang that remains at the time of writing relates to the FSA's disciplinary investigation and the question mark over whether investors will receive compensation.

The AITC has seen evidence to suggest that a limited amount of wrongdoing took place and has passed all such evidence to the FSA. It is our view that, if wrongdoing has occurred, those who have suffered financial detriment as a result should be restored to where they would be without the wrongdoing.

It is interesting to note that the more traditional zeros (those in investment companies without bank debt in their structure or cross holdings in their portfolio) have actually made money for shareholders over the past four years, which of course is exactly how they were billed for investors who wanted to take a low level of risk. Traditional ordinary income shares show, in some cases, substantial losses, but they are still paying dividends and live to fight another day.

This book provides a fascinating insight from the perspective of a wide variety of players in and observers of the crisis. The editor, Andy Adams, was one of the first commentators to draw attention to the risks that were emerging as the split capital products became increasingly stretched.

The irony is that split capital investment trusts remain an excellent concept and should still have a successful future ahead of them. I very much hope that, once issues of discipline and compensation are settled, they will be able to move on and once again provide a bespoke combination of risk and reward to different types of investor.

Daniel Godfrey
Director General
Association of Investment Trust Companies

Acknowledgements

We are very grateful to Christopher Brown, Hamish Buchan, Nicholas Lewis and Simon Moore for their many useful comments on drafts of the manuscript. As always, however, all errors remain our own.

1

Introduction

ANDREW ADAMS

1.1 AIMS OF THE BOOK

The crisis surrounding the UK split capital investment trust sector broke in late 2001. It led to a major Financial Services Authority (FSA) investigation and a House of Commons Treasury Select Committee enquiry that called as witnesses a number of well-known personalities from the investment trust industry. Some of these Treasury Select Committee hearings produced moments of great theatre that were widely reported in the mainstream press.

This book aims to provide an in-depth and authoritative analysis of the crisis. Although it is generally regarded as a difficult subject even for investment professionals, most chapters are suitable for the interested lay reader. An unusual feature of the book is the large number of contributors, each with expert knowledge of his chosen topic. This inevitably means that varying views are expressed but this I consider to be a strength of the book. It is important that different sides of the story are told if the reader is to obtain a balanced view of what happened.

The FSA investigation and the large number of interested parties with legal representation have made editing a book of this kind a considerable challenge. Some people have suggested that it is too early for a book on the splits saga. However, the alternative is to wait until the court battles are over, which could be years away. By then, many of the details of the crisis will have faded from memory. But there was more to this saga than a simple admonition that it represented "the unacceptable face of capitalism". While memories are fresh, it is useful to look beyond the casual soundbite and analyse the causes and effects of this serious crisis. There may be lessons to learn.

1.2 THE INVESTMENT TRUST INDUSTRY

An investment company invests in a portfolio of shares or other securities for the benefit of its own shareholders. It enables investors to purchase an interest in a professionally managed fund.

An investment trust company (also sometimes referred to as an "investment trust" or just "trust") is a UK investment company whose ordinary shares must be listed on the London Stock Exchange.[1] It is subject to the regulation of the Companies Act and the

---

[1] An investment company can become an investment trust company by complying with the requirements of Section 842 of the Income and Corporation Taxes Act 1988. One requirement is that the company must be listed on the London Stock Exchange. An investment trust company is exempt from tax on capital gains realised within its portfolio.

UK Listing Rules. It is not a product regulated directly by the FSA unlike a unit trust or an open-ended investment company (OEIC).

Ultimate responsibility for running the affairs of an investment trust lies with the board of directors, but day-to-day investment management and administration is normally delegated to a fund management firm.[2] This firm may also manage other investment trusts together with other types of fund, such as pension funds or unit trusts. The conduct of the fund manager in managing the portfolio of the investment trust is regulated by the FSA, as is its marketing activities.

In common with any other company, an investment trust has a fixed number of issued shares. To liquidate their holdings, investors must normally sell their shares to other investors.[3] An advantage of this "closed-end" structure is that the fund managers can invest for the best long-term interests of the trust shareholders without having to worry about a possible reduction in the underlying portfolio of assets in adverse market conditions. Such a problem can arise in the case of unit trusts or OEICs[4] because investors buy or redeem their investments directly with the managers, and if there are a significant number of redemptions the managers will be forced to sell assets in the underlying portfolio.

Again, in common with any other company, an investment trust can borrow money and thereby obtain the benefits and risks of "gearing". This can be done by issuing listed or unlisted loan capital or simply by borrowing from a bank. Ignoring the cost of borrowing, if the value of the underlying portfolio of the investment trust rises (or falls) by a certain percentage, the residual assets attributable to shareholders will rise (or fall) by a greater percentage. So, gearing exaggerates movements in the value of underlying assets from the investment trust shareholders' viewpoint.

Conventional trusts (i.e., trusts with only one class of share) generally invest almost entirely in equities, often with a heavy overseas exposure. "Generalist" investment trusts combine investment flexibility with the opportunity to diversify by spreading investments over several markets and sectors. "Specialist" investment trusts provide a vehicle for investment in some specialist area, such as a particular geographical region or a specific industry sector.

Split capital closed-end funds ("splits") may be defined as investment companies[5] or investment trust companies with more than one main class of share capital, offering different rights to income and capital.[6] They aim to match simultaneously the risk, income and tax preferences of different types of potential investor. Splits are usually designed to be wound up at some future date, with most splits having an original term of seven to ten years.[7] If the company is wound up, its assets are sold and the proceeds

---

[2] There are, however, a number of well-respected self-managed trusts.

[3] However, a number of trusts have a limited life. There may be a fixed redemption date but very often there are a number of optional wind-up dates. Furthermore, "buy-backs" in which a company buys its own shares and cancels them have been popular since 1999.

[4] Unit trusts and OEICs are "open ended" so that if a sufficient number of unit holders wish to sell their units it may be necessary to sell assets in the underlying portfolio to generate sufficient cash to meet the demand.

[5] Split capital investment companies may be domiciled offshore (e.g., in the Channel Islands). This can enable them to have certain advantages in respect of their tax and accountancy treatment.

[6] In everyday usage, the term "split" is often taken to include conventional trusts with high levels of bank debt. These we refer to here as pseudo-splits.

[7] They normally have a fixed wind-up date but for some splits there may be a range of wind-up dates and the life of others may be extended if a continuation resolution is passed. A number of "undated splits" were created in the splits boom in which the ordinary shares were undated. This was made possible by issuing zero-dividend preference shares (see Section 1.3) via a subsidiary company. It is the subsidiary which winds up, to be replaced by a follow-on subsidiary if the split structure is to be maintained.

Table 1.1 Size of the conventional trust and splits sectors

	End-1997 (£bn)	End-2000 (£bn)	End-2003 (£bn)
Conventional trusts	46.2	67.1	48.2
Splits	7.4	14.7	7.9
Total	*53.6*	*81.8*	*56.1*

Source: Cazenove/Fundamental Data.

are used to pay off the various classes of share capital after meeting the entitlements of holders of debt, if any. Shareholders always have the option to take cash, but in practice the directors and managers normally try to retain some of the funds under management by encouraging shareholders to roll over into an existing trust or by restructuring, rather than liquidation.

Table 1.1 shows the estimated total assets (including assets financed by borrowings) of the conventional trust and splits[8] sectors on three dates around the crisis period. It can be seen that the total assets of the splits sector doubled over the three-year period up to end-2000, but then roughly halved over the three-year period to end-2003.

1.3 TYPES OF SPLITS

There are two basic types of splits: "traditional splits" and "quasi-splits". However, many more complicated splits were launched, particularly over the period from 1999 to 2001, some of which have defied simple catagorisation.

Traditional splits

A simple "traditional split" has its ordinary share capital divided into two distinct categories: income shares and capital shares. Dualvest, the first split, launched in 1965, was of this type, as were many of the splits launched up to the late 1980s. They generally invested in a broad portfolio of UK equities with an above average yield and commonly had no borrowings.

Holders of the income shares of traditional splits are entitled to all or most of the distributed income and a predetermined capital value on liquidation. Thus, they receive a much higher income yield than that of the underlying portfolio. They are considered suitable for investors who require a high income, such as elderly people. Most income shares are entitled to a capital repayment when the trust is wound up, but some are more like annuities, with very little capital repayment.

Holders of the capital shares of traditional splits receive little or no income but are entitled to the remaining assets on liquidation after the income shares have been redeemed. So they obtain geared returns which depend on the growth of underlying assets up to the wind-up date. They are a risky type of share, which may appeal to high-rate taxpayers looking for potential strong capital gains.

---

[8] "Splits" in Table 1.1 means split capital and highly geared closed-end funds.

Quasi-splits

A "quasi-split"[9] always has zero-dividend preference shares (zeros) in issue but, in its most straightforward form, there is only one class of ordinary share capital, namely ordinary income shares (also known as income & residual capital shares). This type of structure was common from 1988, shortly after the first zero was invented, through to the late 1990s. Again, such splits generally adhered to prudent investment principles, holding a broad portfolio of UK or international equities, and did not incorporate additional complexities, such as bank borrowings.

Zeros are designed to pay a predetermined capital sum when the trust is wound up before any distribution can be made to ordinary income shareholders. They have no entitlement to income so that, importantly, there is no liability to income tax. Provided the underlying portfolio is widely spread and does not have overly demanding yield requirements, and there are no prior ranking charges (e.g. bank debt), the zeros in these simple structures are generally low risk. Such zeros are attractive to private investors who need a fixed sum at a future point in time and are able to use their annual exemption allowance to avoid paying capital gains tax. If sums of money are required at different points in time, an appropriate portfolio of zeros can be created. The zeros in these simple structures are suitable for such things as school fees planning and retirement planning.

Ordinary income shares offer high income plus all the remaining assets of a quasi-split trust at the wind-up date, after the zeros have received their capital entitlement. They are analogous to holding an equity portfolio partly financed through a prior claim (the zeros) repayable at wind-up.

More aggressively structured splits

A common variation of the above theme was to combine the traditional split and quasi-split concepts. In other words there could be three classes of shares: zeros, income shares and capital shares. When such a trust is wound up, zeros are (in the absence of borrowings) repaid first. So, other things being equal, the risk/return profile of the zeros is no different from that of zeros in a simple quasi-split. But, the income shares are likely to be more risky than in a simple traditional split because they rank after the zeros for capital repayment. The capital shares would have the lowest priority for repayment in either case.

In the buoyant markets of the late 1990s, it became fashionable to launch splits that used complicated capital structures, often with significant levels of bank debt and other devices, to make the shares appear attractive to investors. Some of them had a narrow thematic investment policy or invested in the high-yielding shares of other splits (hence "cross-holdings"). Their complexity made it almost impossible to "stress-test" the products adequately before launch. As always, one of the main driving forces behind the creation of these vehicles was the pursuit of fees by fund management firms and their broker/advisers. Some sections of the firms involved became highly profitable.

The shares in these aggressive structures often did not have the same well-known

---

[9] Some commentators use the term "quasi-split" to mean a conventional trust with high levels of bank debt. To avoid confusion, these highly geared conventional trusts will be called "pseudo-splits" (see Footnote 6).

characteristics as shares with the same title (e.g., zeros) issued by earlier simple splits. It was often very difficult to understand the investment attributes of the different shares, not least because sufficient information was not readily available to outsiders. Traditional risk statistics used to assess the risk of shares in a split often became dangerously misleading for the new splits. As a result, there was a general lack of understanding of the true risks involved. The obvious risk created by geared trusts investing in other geared trusts was generally missed by private investors and their advisers.

1.4 THE CRISIS AND ITS SIGNIFICANCE

Many analysts with specialist knowledge of splits felt that there was "an accident waiting to happen" by the end of 2000. But, it took a severe bear market to drive home the dangers of bank debt and cross-holdings to the majority of investors and their advisers. The impact of falling markets accompanied by equity dividend cuts led to collapsing market prices and dividend cuts for the income-bearing shares of many splits. The substantial cross-holdings then caused dividend cuts to compound themselves across a section of the splits sector, and share prices fell yet further. Even the market prices of a number of zeros fell sharply, a type of share which until then had generally been regarded as low risk. By the end of 2001, desperate measures were being taken by fund management firms and their broker/advisers to save many of the new splits, and the FSA started to take a much keener interest. Confidence in splits then collapsed. But the splits crisis will be remembered most for the Treasury Select Committee hearings in the second half of 2002 and for the financial losses suffered by private investors, some of whom are suffering real financial hardship as a result.

According to the Association of Investment Trust Companies (AITC), retail investors have lost over £700m[10] across all share classes in splits[11] that have gone bust. Of course, there are other shares in splits that are unlikely to recover their full launch value, but according to the AITC retail losses here stood at less than £500m[12] based on end-February 2004 share prices.

The crisis itself may arguably be over, allowing this book to be written, but it will be a long time before every compensation decision has been taken and we learn what disciplinary action, if any, the FSA has imposed on the firms and individuals it is currently investigating. While the principle of "caveat emptor" should never be forgotten, it is clear that both the Treasury Select Committee and the FSA believe that there has been some serious wrongdoing.

One obvious consequence of the crisis will be to reduce the complexity of future splits. But, as we will see in this book, the splits crisis will have a permanent effect on the whole investment trust industry in such areas as corporate governance, disclosure of information and the freedom of trusts to invest in other trusts. For better or worse, there is now a stricter regulatory environment for investment trusts.

---

[10] This figure is based on launch values and may underestimate the amount lost by retail investors as they could have bought their shares in the aftermarket at higher prices than launch value.

[11] The term "splits" here includes not only closed-end funds with more than one class of share capital and those with high levels of bank debt, but also closed-end funds investing in such funds ("funds of funds").

[12] Again, this figure is based on launch values and may underestimate the amount lost by retail investors as they could have bought their shares in the aftermarket at higher prices than launch value.

I should stress that most investment trusts are not splits, not all splits were a problem and the splits crisis was wildly out of character for the traditionally cautious investment trust industry. It is most unfortunate that the splits crisis has adversely affected the image of the investment trust industry as a whole, an industry which has served investors well for over 130 years. In my view, investment trusts remain an excellent vehicle for long-term investors.

The publicity surrounding the splits crisis has not helped the reputation of the savings industry. Along with other financial disasters, such as Equitable Life, endowment policy shortfalls, pensions mis-selling and precipice bonds, the splits crisis has discouraged people from saving sufficiently for their future. Given the urgent need for a rise in the UK savings ratio, so that people will be better able to provide for themselves when growing old, this could in the end prove to be the most significant aspect of the splits crisis.

1.5 OVERVIEW OF THE FIVE PARTS OF THE BOOK

This book is divided into five parts, each dealing with a different aspect of the crisis.

Part One (*The Crisis*) gives a historical background to the crisis, including the lessons from past booms and busts in the investment trust sector, and describes the main milestones in the evolution of the splits industry. The boom years of the late 1990s, the unfolding crisis and the underlying reasons for the crisis are also discussed.

Part Two (*Risk and Valuation Models*) is the most technical part of the book. It outlines theoretical models for the risk assessment and valuation of shares in splits, which will help in understanding their behaviour during the crisis. Less technically minded readers may find Part Two difficult whereas trust specialists may find it the most immediately useful part of the book.

Part Three (*Response to the Crisis*) discusses the media, regulatory and political response to the crisis. John McFall MP expresses some strongly held views formed from the Treasury Select Committee (of which he is chairman) enquiry in discussing the political response.

Part Four (*Management Issues*) tackles three key management issues which have been widely discussed in relation to the splits crisis. The contributors to this part of the book view the crisis from very different perspectives.

Part Five (*Looking Forward*) concentrates on the main lessons and implications of the crisis for the fund management industry, especially in the area of product innovation and marketing. The final chapter discusses the lessons for corporate governance of investment trusts, the Association of Investment Trust Companies, financial advisers, financial education, the financial press and the regulators.

Part One
The Crisis

2

Past Financial Crises

JOHN NEWLANDS

These parent "trusts" breed second "trusts"
To take their stock and right 'em
And these again breed other "trusts"
And so ad infinitum

(The old story of the fleas in a new shape,
Bankers Magazine, **96**, 1893)

2.1 INTRODUCTION

Financial fads and boom/bust cycles have a strange habit of repeating themselves every few years or decades. There are surprisingly few variations on the basic theme. Several features of the splits boom certainly fit the historical mould.

Markets are strong. A new idea comes along for investment, be it railroads, South American water companies, nitrates, emerging markets or the Internet. Investors are desperate to participate. Promoters are even more eager to make money. They do that by soaking up the demand through the launch of new funds.

Perhaps it's simply that markets *are* strong, in which case the precise investment area doesn't matter so much. In that situation the main thing is just to be in there. The classic tale of a 1980s' fund manager springs to mind. He can be heard shouting into a mobile phone the size of a house brick: "You bought Bass? I wanted BATS!" [Pause]. "No, no, never mind, I'll take them – it's gone up even more!"

Whatever the catalyst, there follows a rise and fall in investor sentiment, typically involving mouth-watering profitability for someone on the upside and eye-watering losses for someone else when the wheels come off. That was the pattern in the trust boom of 1888–90 and on several occasions since.

Sometimes there may even be a third stage to the boom/bust cycle. This happens when the original profit-makers on the way up decide things have fallen too far on the way down. They invest (or reinvest) themselves at a late stage. That way – assuming the investment is sound enough to survive and bounce back when things improve – they can win again.

This secondary success is, of course, easier said than done. Some UK investment managers tried to achieve it after the 1929 Wall Street Crash but went back in too early. Others, like Foreign & Colonial's legendary fund manager Michael Hart, got it right. Hart piled back into the UK market with newly borrowed money just after the "great storm" and market crash of October 1987 (McKendrick, 1993). Some of F&C's Board of Directors gained a few grey hairs overnight at the boldness of Hart's move – but the strategy paid off in style.

Rumour has it that this late-stage investment technique was tried in the splits crisis but in many cases it didn't work out. When some of the most distressed splits had fallen in value so far that ordinary shares issued at a pound could be bought in the market for, say, 15p, certain people poured millions of their own money into the bombed-out stocks. So the rumour goes, they even went so far as to stage presentations in City offices to the effect that "these geared ordinary shares are now cheaper even than annuities – it's ridiculous! The worm has turned. Never again will prices be so low."

The worm had turned – but it headed further underground. Wider investor sentiment remained at rock bottom and liquidity evaporated. Far from recovering, the same stocks fell from 15p to having no value at all. Had these gurus made a close study of the lessons of stock market history or even of investment trust history? It would appear not.

It is worth looking at some of the earlier investment trust "bubbles" to see whether the mistakes made in the splits crisis had indeed been made before. The four most significant of these booms took place respectively in 1888–89, 1927–28, 1972 and 1993–94. Bizarrely, a reference to over-demanding hurdle rates and aggressive capital structures can be traced even earlier, to a letter to the press from a concerned investor in June 1872.

2.2 THE TRUST BOOM OF 1888–89

It was only ... by eccentric balance sheet valuations that the enormous initial dividends were paid on these modern trust companies, with the result that in the nicely arranged match between founders and shareholders ... the founders romped home while the shareholders were nowhere.

(*Bankers Magazine*, **96**, 1893)

Déjà vu? The above quote refers to the "trust mania" of 1888–89, in which the public scrambled to subscribe for new investment trust after new investment trust. Each new issue seemed to offer a little more, but incorporated safety margins a little less, than the one before.

Investment trusts had first appeared in March 1868 (Newlands, 1997), as the next chapter describes, to bring wider share ownership to "the investor of moderate means" for the first time. The concept received a cautious welcome in the financial press and the sector grew quietly for almost 20 years, disturbed only by a landmark court case in 1878, which will be discussed in Section 3.5.

By 1887, there were 36 investment trust companies, which people tended to refer to simply as investment trusts, or "trusts", and still do so today. Shortly after that, the popularity of the sector took off, especially after George Goschen, the Chancellor of the Exchequer, reduced the nominal yield on Consols (government debt) from an already miserly 3% to $2\frac{3}{4}$%. The investing public became more and more keen to invest in a rising stock market and the 1888–89 trust boom had begun. As one observer put it at the time, "there developed a fascination in the word 'Trust' which worked wonders with a public who took very small pains to investigate, or to really ascertain, what it was they were trusting."

Promoters were not slow in coming forward to meet the soaring investor demand (where have we heard that before?) with the result that 15 new trusts were launched in 1888 and a further 35 in 1889. The range of company names dating to this period span all manner of industrial and geographical sectors. Titles include The Gas, Water & General Trust, Nitrate & General Trust and The Spanish Railways Investment Trust. There are other more familiar names, too, dating to the boom, like Edinburgh Investment Trust and Merchants Trust, both launched in 1889. Perhaps it is no coincidence that, right from the start, these long-term survivors had a broader investment remit than just the "sector of the moment".

Things were getting overheated but the rush to form new trusts continued, their issuers oblivious to the approaching stock market crisis. To make matters worse, unscrupulous characters jumped on the bandwagon, launching trusts of a dubious nature, in which a tiny number of holders of "founders' shares" received vast rewards after a fixed dividend had been paid on the ordinary shares. In an extreme case, The Trustees, Executors and Security Insurance Corporation paid c. £100,000 in one single year (1889) in dividends on a mere 100 founders' shares. These shares had a nominal value of £10 each but had only been part paid at £3. This at a time when a salary of £100 per year was described by William Gladstone as "the dividing line between the educated and the labouring part of the community" (McKendrick and Newlands, 1999). The effective dividend yield for the lucky founders, on their part-paid shares, was 33,333% in that single year.

These share schemes were just beginning to be exposed by the financial press when world events took a dramatic turn. Revolution broke out on the streets of Buenos Aires, triggering the most serious UK "market shock" of the late 19th century. The Barings crisis of 1890 had begun. (Aside: compare the last few lines with "the systemic risks of cross-invested splits and barbell trusts were just beginning to be uncovered when the September 11 terrorist attacks hit the US ...").

The reason for the 1890 crisis is worthy of a brief digression. The British merchant banking firm of Baring Brothers was so powerful and influential at the time that some referred to it as "the sixth great power" (Ziegler, 1988). On this occasion, however, the most recent of its numerous forays into South America – all highly profitable, to date – was almost to be the bank's undoing and the resulting shock waves ripped through the Square Mile.

South America was one of the key emerging markets of its day and Argentina, with its vast natural and mineral resources, was especially suitable for inward investment. Railways and water companies had a stolid utilitarian appeal to certain types of investor in the late 19th century, in much the same way that Railtrack and British Energy did in the 20th – at least until the wheels came off, quite literally in Railtrack's case.

Barings' decision to underwrite the Buenos Aires Water Supply & Drainage Company Loan to the tune of £25m was probably seen as another low-risk no-brainer. But, perhaps because of the growing awareness within the Argentine capital that the local government budget was hopelessly in deficit, the issue was massively undersubscribed.

Barings had guaranteed the water company's contractors payments in gold, while the value of the paper peso plunged during the revolution. At that point, things started to become painful for the venerable merchant bank. In shades of Nick Leeson, cabling London for cash over and over again in the same bank's other local difficulty a century later, Barings had to borrow more and more, at ever-increasing rates of interest, until even these borrowings were refused. In London, the news that Barings was about to go under caused the worst financial crisis since the Overend, Gurney bank collapse of 1866. Barings itself was eventually bailed out by something akin to an enforced whip-round by William Lidderdale, Governor of the Bank of England. But market confidence was shattered (Newlands, 1997).

In the investment trust sector, capital values fell, on average, by 60–70% during the 19th-century Barings crisis. Rather as with zero-dividend preference shares in 2001–03, the average drop in value in the aftermath of 1890 was derived from a blend of older, well founded trusts which weathered the storm, and grew thereafter, and more speculative trusts which lost everything. The 100% depreciation of these later funds, many of which had large, poorly diversified shareholdings in niche investment areas, not only pulled down the sector averages, but badly dented the reputation of "the Trusts" as a whole.

As *The Economist* of 2 May 1891 put it, fund promoters had "operated when securities were sustained by the glamour cast over them by a previous long-continued rise and combined together so as to carry that rise still further." This all sounds a little familiar.

Meanwhile, more prudently structured trusts, such as the Alliance Trust of Dundee, Foreign & Colonial and Scottish Investment Trust – all still thriving in the 21st century, incidentally, with tens of thousands of investors each – took a short-term hit but proved robust enough to fight another day.

When the dust had settled, *The Economist* of 1 August 1891, as ever demonstrating its uncanny knack of catching the mood of the time, observed that the boom just passed was "a melancholy illustration of the truism that inordinate profits and moderate safety are seldom if ever found in company."

2.3 THE 1920s' TRUST BOOM AND THE WALL STREET CRASH

By the early years of the 20th century, the words "investment trust" had regained an aura of respectability, and there were minor flurries (not quite booms) of fund launches between 1900 and 1914. These new funds were mainly invested in the "hot" sector of the day, be it copper (for electrical cables), rubber (for car tyres) or nitrates (for agricultural fertiliser). Many of the specialist trusts launched at that time are long-forgotten, but one or two, such as Scottish Mortgage, formed in 1909 to offer land mortgages for rubber plantations, developed into generalist funds and are still running today.

Everything stopped for the Great War, the effects of which on the City of London have been likened to "a bludgeon descending on a watch." The early 1920s depression which followed was, at least to begin with, scarcely an ideal climate for inviting public subscription to new investment funds. Gradually, as optimism improved with an upturn in the economy, investment trusts came back into vogue and no fewer than 78 new UK funds were launched between 1926 and 1929.[1] A sign of the growing importance of the sector was the publication for the first time, in 1927, of the *Laing & Cruickshank Investment Trust Yearbook*, a pocket-sized booklet which included 95 pages of trust data in 15 columns. This relatively compact document was the precursor to the 700 pages-plus megalithic tomes and online databases which analysts have to wade through today. Toward the end of the late 1920s' UK trust boom, there were so many funds that one ended up simply calling itself "The 1928 Trust".

The UK trust sector was on the face of it setting itself up for a fall once again. This volume of fund launches was a mere bagatelle, however, compared with what was happening on the other side of the Atlantic. The craziest investment trust boom in history was starting to unfold. Its origins can be traced to the reversal of fortunes that occurred during and after the First World War, before which the US had "investors, but no investing public" (Rottersman and Zweig, 1994).

In 1914, the US, still very much an emerging economy, was a net debtor nation to the tune of several billion dollars. At the outbreak of war this situation actually got worse for a time, because of a run on the US banks and an outflow of gold from the country. As the war developed, gold poured back into the US both to pay for supplies and munitions and for safekeeping for the duration of the conflict. By 1920 the US had become a three billion dollar *creditor* nation, with custody of one-third of the world's gold bullion and with Wall Street's power and influence vastly increased. Meanwhile, 20 million Americans had gained a taste for investment having bought liberty bonds from 1917 onwards. A new generation of smaller investors had been created. For a role model, fund promoters looked to the example of the UK investment trust.

By 1927 there were 49 US investment trusts but the boom was only just beginning. $600m worth of new funds were launched between March 1927 and April 1928 alone. By that month there were 179 US investment trusts managing a total of $1.35bn. By September 1929, the total figure had shot through the $3bn barrier, with more than $1.5bn being raised in that year alone, all in US investment trust companies. The later issues were, to quote one observer, "heavily laden with debt and preferred stock." Substitute bank loan for debt, and zero dividend preference shares for preferred stock, and remind oneself of the increasing prevalence of cross-holdings, and the comparisons with recent events are, once again, not hard to draw.

What made the situation even more dangerous – worse even than in the splits boom – was that many purchases were being made with brokers' loans, which toward the end were running at $400m per month. These trusts became known in the US as "high leverage" trusts, not without reason in view of subsequent events.

An almost lone voice warned that things were getting out of hand. In 1928 the US financial analyst Theodore Grayson wrote these prophetic words: "History tells us that about thirty-eight years ago British investment trusts went through a drastic era of house-cleaning and readjustment, and it will perhaps be the better for us that we have the house-cleaning at the beginning rather than several years from now ... it remains to be seen how such companies will weather the first severe period of depression" (Grayson, 1928).

---

[1] These were all investment trusts. Unit trusts had yet to be invented. The first British unit trust, or fixed trust as they were originally known, was the First British Fixed Trust on 22 April 1932, launched by Municipal & General (later M&G) Securities.

Other commentators chose to pour fuel on the fire. The *Magazine of Wall Street*'s September 1929 edition, for example, suggested that it was worth paying a huge premium to net asset value to climb aboard the bull market bandwagon. "If the past record of a manager indicates that it can average 20 per cent or more [growth per annum] on its funds," the magazine said, "a price of *150 per cent to 200 per cent* above liquidation value might be reasonable" (our italics). Nowadays, if an investment trust performs well and runs to a 5% premium the man on the Clapham Omnibus (make that the Docklands Light Railway) is advised "steady on, the trust's run ahead of itself. Wait until it falls to a discount again and then buy."

The rest, as they say, is history and by 1932 the Dow Jones Index had fallen from a peak of 386 to wallow at a miserable 41. Within two months of the Wall Street Crash approximately £8 billion had been wiped off the value of stock exchanges worldwide. How the mania developed, with investment trust pyramid schemes that multiplied gearing and risk to all-time high levels, is superbly described in J.K. Galbraith's classic analysis "In Goldman Sachs we trust" (Galbraith, 1955).

An instructive twist to the tale is that most UK investment trusts weathered the 1929–31 crash reasonably well, having avoided the worst excesses of the rush into unsafe investments. Many had also sold US securities in anticipation of a fall. But what really saved the day on this side of the water was that even by the late 1920s, a typical UK investment trust would have been invested almost in equal proportions between ordinary shares, preference shares and bonds. The last two asset classes tended to offset, or de-gear, the effects of any structural gearing taken on board by these trusts through the issue of their own preference or debenture stock.

The moral of this story is that it is not the influx of new funds which is likely to cause a crash. It is just that the easiest time to launch such vehicles is when markets are riding high – and no bull market lasts for ever.

2.4   THE 1970s' TRUST BOOM

The next thing that I want to touch upon is the huge expansion of the movement in the heady days of 1972 when well over £500 million of new money was raised. That gave the market a fit of indigestion from which it has barely recovered yet. It is not the first period of expansion which the investment trust movement has had in its lifetime. It happens about once a generation. Each one has been followed by an extended period of over-supply. People sometimes ask: "What is going to prevent managements from going out and doing the same thing in the next bull market?" My answer to that would be that the market simply would not absorb such issues again for a good many years ...

(Tom Griffin –
co-founder with Richard Thornton of GT Management –
Investment Trust Seminar, 1976)

Memories tend to be short in the financial sector. Thousands join young but a cursory examination of the age spread on the early morning "drain train" from Waterloo Station to Bank suggests that only a minority stay around through to retirement. True, some high-flyers remain at work in the City into late middle age. They probably don't have to crush onto the 7 a.m. tube any more. Instead, they leave Wimbledon even earlier, setting off by car at maybe six in the morning, to beat the traffic and park their prestige motor under Finsbury Square. On a good day they're home by 9 p.m. Others lie on a beach somewhere and run their own or someone else's portfolio. But whole waves of people seem to leave young, either because it didn't suit them or because they were made redundant in the post-1980s' cutbacks or because they simply couldn't stand it any more. Travellers through the far North of Scotland are often shocked to discover that there are more ex-City of London people than Highlanders hiring out canoes and running post offices.

Jobs for life with a single company are gone too and even those who stay around the Square Mile tend to change firms every couple of years. The result is an astonishing loss of corporate memory and maybe even a deliberate deaf ear to those wrinkled brokers standing in the corner of Eaton's Wine Bar who murmur "but have you ever seen a real bear market?" These claret-soaked veterans ought perhaps to have been given a better hearing. They were the people who had lived through the bear market of 1973–74. A few might even have recalled the investment trust boom immediately before it, in 1972, with the same impeccable timing of each of the great booms before and since.

The 1972 boom was triggered by a combination of strong market conditions and special tax concessions for investment trusts made in the 1972 Finance Act. It is an understatement to say that within a short time the market euphoria had evaporated. In the stock market collapse which followed, the FT-Actuaries All-Share Index (as it was then known) which had started at 100 in 1962 dropped from 221 to 66.8. It is hard to believe, but investor sentiment fell so far that in late 1974 the FT-30 Index was yielding 13% on a price/earnings (P/E) ratio of approximately four. Meanwhile, the well-meant (and hard-fought) tax concession for investment trusts had turned into a nightmare because it encouraged investors to sell their trust shares before anything else.

In short, the situation today is that investors pay capital gains tax on net gains realised when they sell their investment trust shares. No tax is payable by the trust itself on any gains made during its day-to-day share transactions. Back in 1972 a more complicated arrangement – the so-called "half and half" system – was instigated in that year's Finance Act. Trusts were taxed at half the normal rate of corporation tax on their day-to-day capital gains. By way of compensation for what would otherwise be double taxation, investors received a tax credit (is nothing new in the taxation world?) which reduced their own gains tax liability when they sold.

A cunning plan, except that when the vicious bear market struck, many investors wanted out. Because of the above tax credit situation they sold their trust holdings *first*. The combination of falling markets, loss of investor sentiment and tax concessions for trust share sales – all coming just after the latest trust boom – hammered trust share prices. By early 1975 discounts had widened out to a teeth-clenchingly wide sector average of more than 40%.

Some figures might put the scale of capital loss into context. In the 1973–74 stock market collapse, the FT-Actuaries All-Share Index fell by approximately 70%. Not every new trust was launched at the peak of the market, however, so let us err on the safe side and assume that the net asset values of the £500m wave of new trusts fell by "only" 60% during the bear market. The story gets worse because, as sentiment deteriorated, trust share prices fell even more than their underlying net asset value (NAV), to significant discounts of in some cases as much as 40% to their NAV. If we assume an average discount of 30%, then £500m of new monies put into the trust sector fell in net asset value to a low of £200m and share price market capitalisation to as little as £140m! On the face of it, £360m had been "lost" through launching new funds at the wrong time.[2]

The episode had all the hallmarks of a massive industry own goal. Yet there is another side to this particular story. In the 1972 trust boom, most of the new funds were mainly conventional, non-split trusts which went on to recover, eventually, when favourable markets returned. That same All-Share Index which had plunged into double figures in the 1970s went on to peak at 3265 on 4 September 2000 and despite market falls since then remained at well above 2000 at the beginning of 2004. The moral of the story is that trusts can take almost anything thrown at them and still produce notable long-term investment returns, if they are built to last.

This account of the 1972 trust boom began with a quote from sector veteran Tom Griffin, a chartered accountant who joined Foreign & Colonial as an assistant fund manager in 1956 and who would go on, with his colleague Richard Thornton, to found GT Management. Griffin's views, expressed in 1976, that the trust industry seems to enter bursts of expansion "about once a generation", then takes a hit followed by a lengthy recovery period, have stood the test of time. Though perhaps it is even simpler than that. Maybe it just takes that long for people to forget what can happen after bull markets peak.

Certainly, the timing of the 1972 fund launches had been a self-inflicted wound by the industry, and yet a similar thing happened in the trust boom of 1993–94.

2.5   THE TRUST BOOM OF 1993–94

The final trust boom on our list was not followed by a major financial crisis, as such. But it does demonstrate once more that given the right market conditions, fund management companies will bend over backwards to achieve as much issuance of new paper as humanly possible while investor demand remains strong. The brunt of the consequences of these managed funds "gold rush" periods, as we mentioned at the beginning of this chapter, tends to be borne by someone else.

By the beginning of 1993, a combination of factors had pushed the FTSE 100 Index into new territory at over 2800. "With the UK now out of the ERM [Exchange Rate Mechanism], the Conservatives elected for a fourth consecutive term, and the welcome improvements to PEP [Personal Equity Plan] legislation" (Newlands, 1997), markets looked like heading higher and demand for investment trusts – many standing at a chunky discount to net asset value – soared. The average trust discount narrowed from 16% in late 1992 to 6.8% at the end of 1993, and kept on tightening. The veteran Foreign & Colonial Investment Trust would even go to a 3% premium to net asset value and enter the FTSE-100 Index, which it did in late 1995.

Back in the trust promoters' "engine room", ideas were being urgently sought for fresh themes on which to base some massive new trust issues. The first of these came in December 1993 with the launch of Mercury World Mining Trust, which raised £426m. At the time, this was the largest ever investment trust new issue – but not for long.

Mining and metals might have been a popular choice of investment area but another was even more obvious. In the wake of a successful wave of UK government-run

---

[2] For some trusts the fall was even greater because the ordinary shares ranked behind other securities with a fixed final entitlement, such as debenture stock.

industry sell-offs, such as British Gas and the "Tell Sid" retail investment campaign, the time was ripe to launch funds which would invest in government privatisation issues. The idea was an instant hit – a "two-hit wonder", to be exact – and for a short time the public scrambled over themselves to subscribe. The trust industry was back in own goal territory.

Suffice it to say that Kleinwort European Privatisation Investment Trust (KEPIT) was launched in February 1994 with what its promoters believed to be an optimistic size cap of £500m. In the event, a staggering £880m was put up by investors and the balance of £380m had to be sent back. Mercury European Privatisation Trust (MEPIT) was launched just a month later, uncapped and raised £575m. Taken with other trust issues, nearly £5bn was subscribed for new investment trusts in 1993–94, even excluding 3i, the venture and development capital company, which opted for investment trust status at its £3.6bn flotation in July 1994.

Not for the first time in trust boom history, the timing proved unfortunate. In 1994, after three years of double-digit growth, global equity markets declined; the Mexican liquidity crisis arrived in December and the Kobe earthquake brought paralysis to Japanese markets. Perhaps not unreasonably in the circumstances, investor sentiment was not what it had been a couple of years earlier and trust discounts widened out once more, back into double figures. For KEPIT and MEPIT, it was even more difficult because European governments turned out to be slower than Britain to sell off state assets. Their own discounts widened out even more, and, while MEPIT soldiered on, KEPIT was unitised in November 1996, with 79% of its investors opting for a cash exit. Another painful lesson had been learned.

This time around, the industry had suffered what some called a "bout of indigestion". It was not a case of numerous trusts leaving their investors penniless and going to the wall. But it did demonstrate that the best time to invest is unlikely to be when optimism is at an all-time high. For investment trust investors at the top of the wave, this can mean buying something at launch for say 100p, which post-issue has a net asset value of 95p after expenses, and which promptly falls to a 10% discount in the market. Later investors can then buy the same share for perhaps 85p in the secondary market. Is this seen as less desirable by some, perhaps likening it to buying second-hand goods? Perhaps more basic financial education might not go amiss, even for the investors of the future while they are still at school.

The splits boom of 1999–2000, as other chapters of this book describe, had a further dimension: the quest for income at a time of low inflation, low equity yields generally and low interest rates. All sorts of fancy capital structures were devised to provide high starting yields but the downside was high annual growth targets – the so-called hurdle rates – just to preserve capital values.

To prove that there really is nothing new in the financial world, this chapter ends with a return to the 19th century and an account of an anonymous investor who took the promoters of a new investment trust to task for building in unrealistic capital growth assumptions from day one.

2.6   THE HURDLE-RATE WARNING OF 1872

In the autumn of 1878, a disgruntled private investor, Sir Henry Sykes, Bt, brought a court action against the Government and Guaranteed Securities Trust. He and other investors had subscribed for £100 certificates at the launch of the fund in 1872 but every penny had gone (McKendrick and Newlands, 1999). The fund's net assets, in short, had dwindled to nil and Sykes wanted his money back.

The case, which was decided the following year, and is decribed in more detail in the next chapter, is an important milestone in investment trust history, for two reasons. First, it brought into doubt the very legality of the early trusts, such as Foreign & Colonial, and thereby threatened the demise of the sector. Second, the trust's downfall owed much to a revolutionary capital structure, which included demanding asset growth rates just to give investors their initially promised returns. As other chapters of this book describe, high hurdle rates[3] and overstretched capital structures would be major contributors to the splits crisis just over 120 years later.

It is at this point that we go back to the launch of the Government and Guaranteed Securities Trust in 1872. The following piece of near-gobbledegook is an extract from the trust's prospectus:

> *The method of average investment introduced by the Foreign & Colonial Government Trust is extended ... [to include] the immediate distribution of each year's realised profit as bonuses in cash upon drawing ... and the progressive increase of such bonuses to compensate for delay in being drawn. The further available profit is to be devoted to the extinction of bonds in the order in which they are issued, at the rate of £200 per £100 bond.*

> (*Prospectus*, Government and Guaranteed Securities Trust, June 1872)

As far as can be made out, therefore, all capital gains were to be distributed to investors immediately. Nothing was to be put aside for a rainy day and investors with the earliest tranches of £100 bonds were almost bound to double their money and could then exit before the assets ran out. This sort of investment makes the precipice bonds of recent years look safe in comparison.

Before the trust had even got off the ground, someone simply calling himself "Scrutator" forecast that the scheme would never work:

> *Sir,*
> *The Foreign & Colonial Government Trust is evidently destined to have many imitations, but the latest which has appeared, that of "The Government and Guaranteed Securities Trust" ... seems to me the most fantastic of all.*
> *... I have devoted some hours to an attempt to unravel the details of this complicated scheme ... upon which an annual return must be obtained of £9 per cent, or the scheme cannot work ... [and as to the £200 redemptions per £100 certificate] ... it would be still more interesting to know upon what actuarial calculation this prospect, however distant, can be realised.*

> I am, Sir, your obedient servant
> SCRUTATOR
> (*The Times*, 12 June 1872)

What Scrutator was saying, in today's jargon, was that the trust's invested assets would have to achieve a hurdle rate of 9% per annum throughout the fund's life for it to work.

Sykes and a number of others must have ignored these prophetic words and piled in anyway, because these growth targets were not achieved, unsurprisingly perhaps given

---

[3] "Hurdle rate" is the required annual growth rate of gross assets to return the investor's capital in full.

the low interest rates and negligible inflation of the time. Where have we heard these words before?

Within a few years, the trust's certificates became unmarketable and the fund effectively went bust, hence the court case. Returning to the end of the tale, Sykes, who had invested £20,000, brought an action against one of the original trustees, Sir Cecil Beadon, hence the name of the case (*Sykes v. Beadon*, 1878). The action failed on the unusual grounds that the trust was "an illegal Association for the acquisition of gain".

The decision meant that all the early investment trusts like Foreign & Colonial (set up as a legal trust, as opposed to the trust company structure, which some other funds adopted) had to convert into limited companies or be forced to wind up. Everyone did this post-haste, the company format became standardised, and Boards of Directors were nominated for all the old legal trusts.[4]

In one of the many quirks which seem to surround the trust sector, once all these changes had been made, *Sykes v. Beadon* was reversed on appeal! But there was no going back. The investment trust company format was here to stay. The newly rationalised sector settled back ready for the next industry crisis, which, as we have seen, would come just over ten years later.

2.7 CONCLUSION

The above episodes show that for over a century, the investment trust sector has, every so often, experienced feast and famine on a massive scale. The long-term lessons of history were there to be seen.

One of the most galling things about the whole splits *débâcle* is that investment trusts, at their best, have for 135 years proved almost impervious to conflicts, crashes and crises on a global scale. Built, in capital structure terms, like the proverbial brick outhouse, they can withstand the worst conceivable conditions and be ready when the better times return. History has shown this time and again. Well-diversified managed funds, *including* those with split capital structures, can survive while big-name individual companies come and go.

It seems almost invidious to mention trusts by name but Aberforth Split, for example, produced positive returns for both its income shareholders *and* capital shareholders in the 2000–03 period during which the FTSE-100 Index fell by more than 3,000 points.[5]

Another point to ponder is that M&G, a fund management house frequently associated with a cautious, long-term approach to stock market investment, has been launching and managing investment trusts since 1971 and every single one has had a split capital structure. But these success stories are scarcely newsworthy when private individuals have invested in other funds with split capital structures and lost every penny.

---

[4] Each Foreign & Colonial director was required to vacate his office "on becoming bankrupt, on suspending payment, compounding with his creditors, or being found a lunatic."

[5] In late 2003, as this top-performing split began to approach its scheduled June 2004 wind-up date, its Board of Directors decided to recommend that the trust should "go early". Investors could roll forward their investment into an existing non-split trust, a unit trust or opt for a cash exit. Sadly, no split capital rollover option was offered at all.

A closer study of history might have caused splits designers to build in a few more safety features, as used in the successful split capital structures of those described above. Even the *FT*'s Lombard column expressed its jaundiced view of the *débâcle*:

The investment trust sector's despicable antics
Also sent right-minded citizens frantic
Split caps was the market that really did fester
With smooth sales talk aimed at the school fees investor
And pyramid structures that rivalled King Tut's
(The Egyptian Pharaoh who causes bad luck).
Bad luck was the factor that these merchants blamed
When their rickety structures came down in flames
But the truth of the matter was hungry for fees
These questionable folk with an aura of sleaze
Had built up cross-holdings so complex, yet bland,
That even an Einstein would ne'er understand
And so geared to a market that rose evermore
That disaster was certain as stocks dove through the floor.

(Lombard, *Financial Times*, 21 December 2002)

Harsh words that nonetheless reflect the disquiet of many. Yet, there is no reason the split capital concept, skilfully and prudently applied, should not continue to have a useful place in the investment industry of tomorrow.

At least the sector appears to have taken its medicine this time around, the horrible taste of which will hopefully never be forgotten, and to have moved forward once more. As *The Economist* of 23 May 1896 put it, "there is an evident disposition among those who conduct these undertakings, even of a less assured character, to 'forswear sack and live cleanly', the rise in market stocks having enabled them to realise stocks of doubtful permanent value, and thus put their house in order." Not much change there, then.

2.8   REFERENCES

Galbraith, J.K. (1955) *The Great Crash 1929*. Hamish Hamilton, London.

Grayson, T.J. (1928) *Investment Trusts, Their Origin, Development and Operation*. John Wiley & Sons, New York.

McKendrick, N. (1993) *The Birth of Foreign & Colonial*. University Printing Services, Cambridge, UK.

McKendrick, N. and Newlands, J.E. (1999) *F&C – A History of Foreign & Colonial Investment Trust*. Chappin Kavanagh, London.

Newlands, J.E. (1997) *Put Not Your Trust in Money – A history of the investment trust industry from 1868 to the present day*. Chappin Kavanagh, London.

Rottersman, M. and Zweig, J. (1994) An early history of mutual funds. *Friends of Financial History Magazine*, Spring.

Ziegler, P.S. (1988) *The Sixth Great Power, Barings, 1762–1929*. Random House, London.

3

Evolution of the Split Trust Sector

JOHN NEWLANDS

> *Adaptability is an integral part of City tradition and success ... Samuel Montagu's imaginative brainchild, Dualvest, a two-tier investment trust of which full particulars are published today, is a fine example of this.*
>
> (*The Times*, 6 May 1965)

3.1 INTRODUCTION

Splits have a history dating to 1965 – and a pre-history going back almost 100 years before that. A study of both phases is important to get to the roots of what happened in the 1990s' splits boom – and indeed how such a situation developed at all.

The fact that the origins of the split capital concept go back to at least 1873 is often missed, mainly because, as the previous chapter described, all forms of gearing and "less than straightforward" capital structures fell out of favour after the 1929 crash. The 1930s' Depression that followed hurt so much that it took over a quarter of a century for those stinging memories to fade. Or, to put it another way, it took that long for those with long memories to retire and a new generation of fresh-faced optimists to arrive on the investment management scene.

Putting longer term history to one side for the moment, though, split capital investment trusts, as we understand the term today, can be traced to the launch of Dualvest Limited, the prospectus for which was issued from the Broad Street offices of Samuel Montagu & Co. on 4 May 1965.

Not for the first or last time in financial sector evolution, the innovation came in rapid (and ingenious) response to a change in government legislation, in this case the 1965 Finance Act. The result of the new Act was that for some investors (mainly the wealthy) investment income became practically useless. For others, as today, income remained a lifeline. At the same time capital gains tax had arrived on the scene, but – rather as the thin end of the wedge – to begin with the impact was modest because the concessions were quite generous.

The solution, with hindsight, was staring City promoters in the face – let one type of shareholder have all the dividend income and let another keep the capital uplift.

Dualvest was the result, brilliant in its simplicity, comprising income shares and capital shares only, the returns for which were generated by a single underlying portfolio of investments. There were no extra bank borrowings, or other adornments – though, it has to be said, it did not take long for the tinkerings to start, in the wave of copycat trust launches which followed in Dualvest's wake. The basic idea worked well and some "traditional splits" still function successfully today, providing focused income or capital returns for those who need them, despite a very different stock market and fiscal environment from that in 1965.

This chapter describes the details behind Dualvest's launch and how the splits market – for some time the "hot sector" of its day – gradually grew and evolved during the next 15 years or so after 1965. Then, in the early and mid-1980s, splits started to fall out of favour as the taxation system for which the early "dual-purpose" trusts were designed disappeared. By the late 1980s, split structures gained in popularity once more but for a new reason – they made harder takeover targets than conventional trusts. There was a fringe benefit too – the discount to net asset value of the "sum of the parts" of most split trusts was much narrower than the 20%-plus average discounts which made many non-split trusts such tempting takeover targets in the first place. This encouraged some conventional trusts to become splits with the aim of eliminating the discount.

The next major development – the invention of the "school fees-friendly" zero-dividend preference share (the focus of many post splits crisis compensation cases) – occurred in 1987. Like the concept behind Dualvest, the idea was simple, clever and met a genuine investment demand. But, again like Dualvest, the idea worked best in its original, uncluttered form before the more "proactive" corporate financiers started playing around with the detail.

By the beginning of the 1990s splits had become an established component of the trust sector but still only accounting for c. £2bn, or just over 8%, of the then c. £24bn investment trust industry.

Splits continued to gather market share during the 1990s, expanding as equity markets worldwide climbed higher and higher. By the end of 1994, the splits sector had doubled in size from the start of the decade to some £4bn, or 10% of the sector as a whole. By the end of 1999, the assets managed by split capital trusts had more than doubled again to c. £9.6bn, or 12% of an investment trust sector which had itself expanded to a new peak of almost £80bn. Chapter 4 takes up the story from 1999 onwards; but further issue activity in 2000 and 2001 added at least £3bn more to split capital assets under management.

The various developments taking place while all this was going on included the introduction of the new Statement of Recommended [Accounting] Practice (SORP) for investment trusts in 1995, undated splits, the use of bank borrowings to gear capital structures, the "tweaking" of accountancy standards and the use of cross-holdings in other splits. These developments all affected the splits sector and the risks attached to it to varying degrees, while, of course, the Internet revolution and the TMT (technology, media and telecommunications) boom ran their own course too.

Before looking at these more recent developments, it is necessary to return to March 1868 and the birth of the investment trust industry itself. For only by looking at how the whole global managed funds industry of today got off the ground can the wider scene behind the split capital concept be set. Moreover, like all truly great inventions, the principle behind the diversified managed fund – invented in the form of Foreign & Colonial in 1868 – was, with hindsight, as straightforward as that of the wheel, the clockwork radio, and the hypertext link which allows us to negotiate the World Wide Web.

3.2   THE FIRST INVESTMENT TRUST

All hail, astonishing Fact!
All hail, Invention new –
The Joint Stock Companies Act –
the Act of Sixty-Two!

(*Utopia Limited*, Gilbert & Sullivan)

19 March 1868, the *Gentleman's Magazine* later recorded, was a rainy, cloudy day in London, and the reputation of the City was at its lowest level since the South Sea Bubble. The Joint Stock Companies Act of 1862, later immortalised in Gilbert and Sullivan's *Utopia Limited*, was supposed to have cleaned things up. Unfortunately, to begin with, it had the opposite effect.

On the face of it, the introduction of effective limited liability legislation was a good idea, especially given some of the disgraceful events that had preceded it. At last, small shareholders would not be thrown onto the streets and their wives and children put into the workhouses just because a company in which they had a few shares had gone into liquidation.

The trouble was that the 1862 Act led to a frenzied rush to launch new companies, their promoters safe in the knowledge that they could not lose more than their initial stake. The result was that out of several thousand companies launched in the wake of the Act, at least a third had gone bust within five years. Small wonder that the "Sid punters"[1] of the day steered well clear of stock market investment.

Philip Rose, who was Disraeli's solicitor, decided it was time to change Sid's mind. Rose came up with a new concept – the investment trust – which, he was determined, was going to restore investors' confidence by being so safe, so secure and so carefully managed that the most ardent sceptics would change their minds. Rose's brainchild, The Foreign & Colonial Government Trust, as the flagship of today's orthodox trust sector was then known, was launched from Rose's Westminster offices in March 1868 (McKendrick and Newlands, 1999).

F&C's ingenuity in founding the sector stemmed not from its ungeared, unsophisticated capital structure, but from its presentation of the new concept as the safest, most carefully managed investment vehicle ever invented. That was why F&C's 76-page prospectus was filled with words like "prudent", "cautious" and "reputable".

F&C's original portfolio consisted simply of 20 overseas government bonds. This spread of sovereign junk debt (in the parlance of today) provided an average yield of more than double that offered by the few low-risk alternatives available at the time – such as Consols yielding a fraction over 3%.

The idea lacked sophistication, but it worked. Not only did the development receive wide and favourable press coverage, it gave smaller investors confidence and faith, virtually for the first time. Mental barriers to stock market investment had, in short, been broken down. That is why the launch of F&C marks one of the greatest milestones in financial history.

---

[1] "Tell Sid" was the advertising slogan associated with certain government privatisation share issues after 1979. Thereafter the name Sid, or "Sid punter", became synonymous with the new generation of self-advised private investors.

Note one important distinction, however. F&C was formed not as a company, limited or otherwise, but as a legal trust. This situation would change in 1879 as will be seen.

3.3 THE SECOND MILESTONE

The next development in the trust sector's history came with the birth of the Scottish investment trust industry, in early 1873, almost simultaneously in Edinburgh and Dundee. The Dundee men got there first.

How he did it, no one really knows. But Robert Fleming, a 28-year-old former clerk who had left school at the age of 13 to work in a jute baron's back office for £5 per year, persuaded a group of Dundonian businessmen to support the first investment trust launched in Scotland. The Scottish American Investment Trust was formed in Dundee on 1 February 1873. Modelled on Foreign & Colonial, its capital structure also involved a legal trust, with a single class of security and no borrowings of any kind.

This is the same Robert Fleming whose surname graces the financial conglomerate of JPMorgan Fleming today and whose grandson, Ian, once described as the worst stockbroker in the world, created the fictitious spy character of James Bond.

3.4 EDINBURGH, 1873 – THE SPLIT CAPITAL CONCEPT IS BORN

The third milestone, and the most crucial in respect of this history, can be traced to April 1873 and the smog-filled streets of Edinburgh's New Town, where the ghosts of bodysnatchers Burke and Hare (not to mention a few ex-fund managers) are still said to roam at night.

In his offices in Hill Street, not far from Charlotte Square and the present-day location of a number of trendy French bistros, William Menzies, writer to the Signet,[2] was hard at work on the structure of a new investment company. He decided that its name would be The Scottish American Investment Company Limited, or SAINTS for short.

Why Menzies and Fleming chose virtually identical names for their two quite separate ventures is unclear, save that in the 1870s the words Scottish and American had the same appeal to investors as the terms technology and dot.com had in 1999. The similarity of titles continued for over 100 years, until the Dundee-launched vehicle was finally renamed Dunedin Income Growth in 1990.

Returning to William Menzies and SAINTS' formation in 1873, the 38-year-old Scots lawyer knew that he had two main classes of client, who can be summarised respectively as the risk-tolerant (e.g., wealthier individuals) and the risk-averse ("widows and orphans"). To meet their very different investment needs, Menzies chose to ignore the legal trust structure used by F&C and its early successors. Instead his brainchild, SAINTS, was formed from day one not just as a limited liability

---

[2] A senior solicitor conducting cases in the Court of Session (Scotland).

company, but one with a dual-purpose capital structure. That is why some would argue that SAINTS was the world's first split capital trust.

There were ordinary shares, which were part-paid, and these were significantly geared by the presence of a four-times-greater quantity of debenture capital, offering a fixed coupon of $5\frac{1}{2}\%$. The trust had no fixed life or pre-ordained wind-up date; but then again nor do several splits launched since 1997 – nor, for those with long enough memories, did New Throgmorton Trust when it was issued in 1966. The presence of the substantial debenture capital issue meant that SAINTS was launched with massive potential gearing (as opposed to actual, or net gearing – see below) of around 500%, despite not borrowing a penny from the banks as might happen today.

This level of potential gearing was made possible by the then relatively common practice of issuing the ordinary shares part-paid. The debt was thus secured against the uncalled portion, and shareholders could find themselves having to produce extra cash in times of difficulty. This type of arrangement lost its credibility after the 1890 Barings crisis described in Chapter 2.

In the case of SAINTS, the *actual* gearing was far less radical than the above 500% figure suggests, because of the trust's "debt-to-debt" structure in which the effects of the presence of debenture capital were offset by the trust's largely fixed interest portfolio of US railroad securities. The essential point is that more than one type of investor was being offered a tailored product by the same trust, just like Dualvest in 1965.

Ronald Weir, SAINTS' company historian, explains the thinking behind the dual offering (Weir, 1973):

> *Substantial capitalists who possessed sufficient cash to take a risk with only the security of the underlying investment could buy the Ordinary Shares, whilst people who wanted a safe and steady return on their money, yet at the same time at a higher yield than available elsewhere, could purchase Debentures with double security.*

The quote above encapsulates many of the features which can, when applied prudently and correctly, allow the split capital principle to work at its best.

3.5   THE FIRST MAJOR CRISIS – *SYKES v. BEADON*, 1878

After 1873 the limited company form became established as the preferred way to bring new trusts to the market. The result was that for several years the trust sector was made up of a mixture of legal trusts (like F&C) and trust companies (like SAINTS). This unsatisfactory situation ended following what was, with hindsight, a rather odd legal ruling in a court case, *Sykes v. Beadon*, 1878.

Briefly, Sir George Jessel, Master of the Rolls,[3] ruled that the old legal trusts were "illegal Associations for the acquisition of gain." F&C and the others were required to convert to the company form immediately, or be wound up. Mindful of lost funds under management, not to mention foregone directorships, etc., the old trusts turned themselves into companies, if not overnight then certainly with an urgency not always immediately obvious in the boardrooms of the day.

---

[3] The judge who presides over the Court of Appeal.

Then, when they had all made the great changeover, *Sykes v. Beadon* was overturned on appeal – but no one converted back into a legal trust. The trust company structure was here to stay.

What is interesting in the context of splits history is that F&C and most of the other former legal trusts took the opportunity to adopt a dual-capital structure at the same time as they converted to the company form. In F&C's case, this involved converting the old trust certificates into equal quantities of ordinary and preference shares. Not only did the "grandfather of the industry" have a subdivided capital structure in its early life, but so did much of the trust sector for 50 years, from 1879 until 1929.

3.6   1929 TO 1965 – BACK TO BASICS

As discussed in Chapter 2, gearing of any kind, including that created via complex capital structures, went completely out of favour in the early 1930s and did not come back into vogue until well after World War II. Adventurous trust structures became completely out of the question until such time as market conditions changed significantly for the better.

Nevertheless, the fact that these divided capital structures prevailed for so long provides food for thought. In fact, it suggests that the renewed popularity of split capital structures which occurred in the late 1980s and throughout most of the 1990s was not an aberration at all but a move toward the historical norm. Following the same train of thought, perhaps at various points in history it has been the departure from sound practice, and not the split capital concept itself, which has caused undue levels of risk.

Returning to the evolution of the trust sector, the austerity of the early post-World War II years, coupled with various economic crises and the government of the day's enormous nationalisation programme, caused a temporary setback before the halcyon (for investment trusts, at least) growth years of the 1950s and early 1960s.

Once the tide had turned, it became sensible – and at least before the reversal of the yield gap[4] in 1959, immediately justifiable on yield grounds alone – to borrow money to invest in high-grade equities. This enhanced returns (of both capital growth and income) as markets recovered and grew once more. Perversely, with such relatively easy pickings to be had, there was, as yet, no need to seek a sophisticated capital structure to make money. So even by the early 1960s the time was still not right for a splits comeback.

As markets rose, gearing declined. Debt cost more than the underlying investments could provide (the reverse yield gap) and there was no way of passing the higher costs across to capital, as we can today by using the SORP. The whole managed funds sector then hit the buffers with the passing of the 1965 Finance Act. Here's how Tony Arnaud (Arnaud, 1973), one of the leading industry figures of his day, described the tax situation before everything changed:

---

[4] The yield gap refers to the difference between the dividend yield on a typical UK ordinary share and the yield on a typical undated gilt-edged security. Historically, equities yielded more than gilts on the basis that they carried more risk. However, the yield gap "reversed" in the late 1950s and thereafter gilts yielded more than equities.

Before 1965 the investor lived in a fairly pleasant environment, except that his income was taxed at varying rates which tended to hurt more and more as the years went by. His capital was left untouched, at least until the introduction of the short-term capital gains tax, which in any event was an extension of the tax on income.

That cosy situation went out of the window with the passing of the new Act, introduced by the incoming Harold Wilson-led Labour government. Among the changes proposed were the introduction of corporation tax (including the levying of corporation tax on the day-to-day transactions of investment trust companies), long-term capital gains tax and the abolition of tax relief on underlying tax suffered by overseas companies in which they invested.

3.7 THE BIRTH OF DUALVEST

It was a chance conversation on the subject of estate planning which led to the creation of Dualvest, the first modern-day split. The idea developed following the realisation that, with the implementation of the 1965 Finance Act, income and capital were going to be taxed very differently.

Income was subject to a higher rate of $41\frac{1}{4}\%$ plus a surtax of up to $47\frac{1}{2}\%$ (i.e., up to an eye-watering total of $88\frac{3}{4}\%$, compared with the initial long-term capital gains tax rate of 30%). Things got worse: marginal rates of income tax reached a mind-boggling 98% during the 1970s. The net result was that while investment income continued to provide a lifeline for some investors, for others it was almost worthless.

A key consideration in this new investment and taxation climate was estate planning, and specifically the need to separate out income and capital returns. It was a paper written on the subject by Michael Behrens (of Samuel Montagu & Co.) which triggered the creation of Dualvest.

Stephen Cockburn, chairman of the Ionian Group, takes up the story. The quotation is reproduced in full because it relates just how the post-1965 split capital trust came about:

A conversation between Michael Behrens and the Hon. David Montagu about a simple but ingenious idea led to the launch of Dualvest; and Leda[5] was split by Ionian Bank later that year.

To begin with we didn't use the expression "split capital". We called it "Tandem" or "Father and Son" because it was seen as a particularly good vehicle for (minimising) estate duty. The old seven year rule still applied – quite simply if you gave it away you had to survive the seven years; and anyway there was always a resistance to giving things away because you never knew how your children were going to turn out.

(There was one famous Yorkshire estate and the chap gave it to his son. Two years later, he's in his Club and opens the Country Life and finds his house on the market! The son had lost all his money gambling and he was selling the family heirlooms and hadn't had the guts to tell his father.)

The point of the concept was that the father would keep and retain the income from the estate, ie the income shares; and the son or heirs were given the capital shares. So all the appreciation and therefore ultimately all the value was passed to them.

(Stephen Cockburn,
Interview, April 2000)

---

[5] Leda was a reconstruction of a conventional trust formed in 1962.

Dualvest Limited was the result and its prospectus was issued on 4 May 1965. The capital structure comprised nine million income shares of 10 shillings (50p), issued at par, plus the placing of two million capital shares of £1 each, again at par. There was no debt. Preliminary expenses were capped at £100,000; underwriting commission amounted to $1\frac{1}{2}$ (old) pence per share, and the director's remuneration was set at £750 per annum.[6]

The trust's brokers, legal advisers and auditors were, respectively, Panmure Gordon & Co., Clifford-Turner & Co. and Binder Hamlyn & Co; and its bankers were National Provincial and Samuel Montagu & Co. David Montagu himself was the trust's first chairman. The split capital sector had been born, and (as well as the quotation at the head of this chapter) *The Times* observed that:

> *This trust is clearly designed to meet the post-Finance Bill conditions ... Pensioners as well as pension funds will be attracted by the high yielding income shares. Those looking for capital growth – be they high tax-paying individuals or institutions – will look to the capital units ... The National Coal Board is taking a substantial slice of both.*

> (*The Times*, 6 May 1965)

3.8   SPLITS TERMINOLOGY

The above references to "Tandem" and "Father and Son" show that in the early years of splits, the terminology was far from standardised. One contemporary investment trust handbook (Messel & Co., 1966), for example, began in 1966 by referring to "two-tier investment trusts" but changed the title to "multi-purpose companies" in 1970. In 1973, Messel changed their terminology again and adopted the more widespread term "split-level trusts". Other firms used the term "split capital trusts" which eventually became the norm.

3.9   OTHER EARLY SPLITS

Anglo-International, the second split capital trust, was launched in August 1965, to be followed by Acorn Securities, Fundinvest and Leda later the same year. Seven more splits (Triplevest, Altifund, New Throgmorton, Anglo-Welsh, Rights and Issues, Channel Islands & International and Derby) were issued in 1966.

Most of these early splits followed Dualvest's example in having a straightforward capital structure comprising income shares and capital shares, but in some cases prior charges were added, in the form of unsecured loan stocks, debenture stocks, cumulative preference shares or convertibles. In the majority of cases, income shares were to be repaid at par on wind-up, with the capital shares receiving all surplus assets.

But it was not long before the complexity for which the split capital sector is renowned was brought into the equation. Anglo-International, for example, called its income shares dividend shares, but gave their holders a one-fifth participation of any surplus assets (in excess of 30 shillings per share) at wind-up.

---

[6] A fee of £750 p.a. in 1965 would broadly equate to a fee of £10,000 p.a. in 2004.

Altifund, another early split, opted for an arrangement all of its own. Both the income shares and the capital shares were issued at 50p which appeared, at first sight, to be simple enough. However, the income shareholders received 30/31ths of the trust's income during the trust's 20-year life, and a final redemption value of £1, not to mention any arrears on a 7% minimum dividend over the intervening two decades. Capital shareholders received 1/31th of the income each year, plus the trust's surplus assets at wind-up.

Other early splits gave income shareholders a degree of participation in future capital growth, but it was far less common for capital shares to have any entitlement to income.

The flow of new splits eased during the turbulent years from 1967 to 1970, especially after the bear market of 1969–70 (just as severe as the 1987 crash, and more sustained), before picking up again during the trust boom of 1971–72. This is how Messel's handbook described the boom:

> *The year from September 1971 has been notable primarily for the large quantity of new money raised by existing trusts (some £500m: £340m in equity money, £20m in debentures and £140m in foreign currency loans) and the flotation of no less than 40 new trusts – the largest money-raising campaign Trusts have ever embarked on ... the only unfortunate effect is that the average discount of the movement at around 15 per cent is much wider than would otherwise be expected at such a time.*
>
> (L. Messel & Co., 1972)

Splits were now hot property. Indeed, some of the early split launches proved so popular that they were heavily oversubscribed, attracting newspaper headlines like "By Jove, it's a new issues bonanza" and "Capital start for the Danae twins", both of which appeared in the *Evening Standard* in early 1972. The Danae issue was an extraordinary 68 times oversubscribed, the trust's income shares racing to a 25% premium over the issue price, while Jove's capital shares quickly jumped to 29.65p from their 10p issue price.

By now split trusts, from a standing start seven years earlier, would account for approximately one-tenth of the entire trust sector in numerical terms, although when assessed by total asset value they remained relatively insignificant, at only around 3% of the industry.

Table 3.1 shows how the split capital sector was made up in 1976.

Table 3.1   The split capital investment trust sector in 1976

Acorn Securities	Fundinvest
Altifund	Jove
Ambrose	Leda
Anglo-International	M & G Dual
Brandts (William)	M & G Second Dual
Channel Islands & International	New Throgmorton
City & Commercial	Rights and Issues
Danae	Rosedimond
Derby	Save and Prosper Linked
Dualvest	Throgmorton Secured Growth
English National	Tor
Equity Consort	Triplevest

Source: AITC (with thanks).

Figure 3.1 Investment trust sector discount, 1970s.
Source: Datastream.

In the meantime, the vicious 1973–74 bear market had struck and created another investment trust boom/bust cycle, as documented in Chapter 2. This time, the investment trust industry found itself in the midst of a triple-whammy effect, in which markets were falling, discounts were widening and, to cap it all, hard-pressed investors were finding it tax-efficient to sell their trust shares before other equities. The one good feature was that no splits were due to be liquidated at that time. Figure 3.1 shows how the sector average discount moved during the 1970s.

Not surprisingly, it became difficult to launch any new trusts during the second half of the 1970s. Then, as if the sector didn't have problems enough, predators, mainly in the form of nationalised industry pension funds, started to move in. Several conventional trusts suffered hostile takeover bids, taking large chunks of money out of the sector. The combined effect of takeovers, unitisations, liquidations and mergers took 11% out of the investment trust sector's total assets in 1976–77 alone.

By the end of the 1970s, there were 24 split trusts, capitalised at a total of some £240m. This amounted to just under 3.5% by value of the 165-strong, £6.9bn trust sector as a whole.

3.10 TAX CHANGES AFTER 1979

The abolition of corporation tax liabilities on the day-to-day transactions of trusts, the removal of exchange controls and other improvements after the Conservatives took over as the government in 1979 gave the trust industry as a whole a kick-start, just as the 1980s' boom years gathered momentum.

For splits, it wasn't quite such good news. The slow convergence in tax rates on income and capital gains meant that the original motivation for launching traditional splits (those with straightforward income and capital shares) like Dualvest had dimin-ished. It would be some time before splits emerged from the doldrums. There were few new launches in the first half of the 1980s and shrinkage started to occur as some of the older splits reached the end of their fixed lives.

In January 1981, Acorn Securities became the first split trust to run its full course. The income shareholders were repaid in cash; and the capital shareholders were offered either 133p per share in cash, or two ways to roll forward their investments into other managed funds. Dualvest itself, the oldest split of all, was unitised in February 1987, almost 22 years after it had been formed.

3.11   NEW BOOST TO THE ATTRACTIONS OF SPLITS

The next boost to the split sector's apparently fading attractions came from an un-expected direction. As markets soared in the mid-1980s, conventional trusts performed well in asset terms; but discounts were slow to narrow and were still averaging more than 20% by 1986 (see Figure 3.2). This left the sector wide open to hostile bids.

The combination of buoyant market conditions and wide discounts made conven-tional trusts juicy targets for predators once more – one of whom, a certain Robert Maxwell, successfully took out the £329m Philip Hill Investment Trust in 1986. Another large trust, the £669m TR Industrial & General, was taken out by the British Coal Board Pension Fund in 1988.

To counter this threat to their survival, a few long-established conventional trusts opted to "split-level" their capital structure. For not only did splits offer some protec-tion against unwanted bids, they offered the chance to narrow, or even to eliminate, the dreaded discount. This development (the split-levelling of existing trusts) gave splits a new lease of life. This is how the theory was explained by Robin Angus at the time:

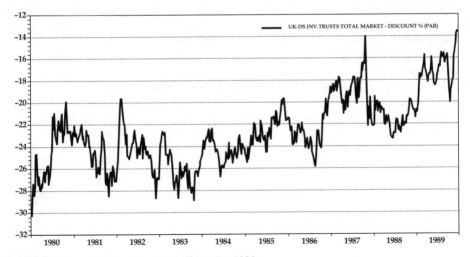

Figure 3.2   Investment trust sector discount, 1980s.
Source: Datastream.

A bundle of goods sold individually is likely to command a higher price than the same bundle of goods sold as a bundle. Someone at an auction may want to buy a mangle. Someone may want to buy a Dresden shepherdess. Someone may want to buy the Complete Works of Shakespeare. But it is unlikely that someone will want to buy all three. So, if one repackages a trust's portfolio ... to enable each type of return to be sold separately, it is highly likely ... that the sum of the entitlements will command a higher price than the unseparated job lot.

(Robin Angus, *Haec Olim*, 1991)

The trend began in earnest in June 1987, when the then 106-year-old River & Mercantile Trust opted to become a split – a move which the *FT*'s Philip Coggan called "a leap into the unknown".

In the meantime, the appeal of the old traditional split format waned still further when the maximum rates of tax on income and capital gains were aligned at 40% in the 1988 Finance Act.

It had also become recognised, as a number of these traditional splits matured over the years, that the basic division into income shares and capital shares had the disadvantage of producing less and less gearing as time went by. For example, capital shares which might have been relatively highly geared, high-risk instruments at a trust's launch, had typically grown over the years to the point at which further rises in the market as a whole would produce only a modest enhancement in the value of the capital shares. A further potential disadvantage of having income and capital shares in the capital structure of the same trust was that investment managers could be faced with the conflicting objectives of generating high income while creating capital growth.

The introduction of the first zero-dividend preference shares (zeros) applied what has been described as "permanent structural gearing" to the ordinary (and any other category of lower ranking) shares. The pioneers of the new share class were Scottish National and River Plate & General, which converted into split trusts within ten days of each other, just a few weeks before the 1987 Crash.

Both these trusts had a number of advisers. But credit for the introduction of the zero must be awarded to Nicholas (Nic) Lewis, of Lewis & Co. Lewis had seen both the zero-dividend coupon bond and the zero-dividend preference share used outside the investment trust sector and recognised the potential for introducing structural gearing while requiring no outflows of either capital or revenue until the wind-up date of the trust. The concept, in short, was brilliant in its simplicity and, at least to begin with, highly effective in its execution.

River Plate's Board of Directors described the development thus:

In September 1987, on the Board's recommendation, the company's capital structure was changed to that of a split-level investment trust, which eliminated the discount to assets of the share price. At the same time the company raised, by way of a placing of Zero Dividend Preference Shares, £14 million net of expense of the issue ... these measures were both an indication and reinforcement of the robust position of the company.

(River Plate & General, *Company History*)

Scottish National (SNAT) pursued a similar route, but with a unique, multi-pronged capital structure, sometimes described, with feeling, as an analyst's nightmare. With income shares, capital shares, stepped preference shares, zero-dividend preference shares and warrants, SNAT in its original (post-1987) form remains one of the most complex split trusts ever devised. And although SNAT's overall capital structure was never copied, the zero-dividend preference share which it and River Plate introduced went on to become an established component of the managed funds sector.

The timing, on the other hand, could hardly have been worse. SNAT and River Plate restructured just before the events of October 1987, in which capital shares in particular, to quote a contemporary critic, were "savaged in the Crash". But, crucially, good-quality splits, whether of the traditional variety or including a zero, as described below, rode the great storm of 1987 and lived to fight another day, unlike some of their more aggressively constructed brethren some 13–14 years later.

3.12   THE HYBRID, OR QUASI-SPLIT CAPITAL TRUST

The attractions of zeros and the diminished popularity of capital shares after the events of 1987 led to a new standard format for splits: the so-called hybrid, or "quasi-split capital investment trust". Quasi-splits have only two classes of share: zero-dividend preference shares and highly geared ordinary income shares. And, as these second generation splits were conceived in 1987, that was it, as far as the capital structure was concerned. The idea of introducing bank borrowings ranking ahead of the zero would take another ten years.

The investor had two very different options: buy the zeros, offering a relatively secure fixed return (but no dividend income), or buy the highly geared ordinary share with an enhanced dividend and a greater exposure both to risk and to potential reward. In offering these two separate types of investment from a vehicle with a single underlying portfolio of assets, the designers were echoing the plain thinking behind the launch of SAINTS a century or more earlier (see Section 3.4). In some ways, with the introduction of zeros (but still with a very sound underlying portfolio of investments), splits had gone back to their Victorian roots.

This relatively straightforward "ordinary shares plus zeros" model remained the norm for new split trusts for a decade, running alongside the older, traditional splits plus a number of others, some with features drawn from both types of split structure. By 1997 the birth of a new generation of splits was about to occur. The ramifications would not be felt until 18 months into the new millennium.

3.13   1997 – BEGINNINGS OF THE NEW SPLITS ERA

While fewer than 60 splits were formed during the 1960s, 1970s and 1980s combined, more than 100 were created or restructured during the 1990s. How did this come about?

Figure 3.3 gives some clues as to why the attractions of splits, especially those with high-yielding ordinary shares, grew and grew. The chart's three fluctuating lines cover a whole raft of incidents and crises from the 1987 Crash, to the UK's foray into the ERM, to the Gulf War (Newlands, 2000).

Whatever else had been happening on the world stage, there was a seemingly relentless long-term decline in yields in both fixed interest and equity markets. Despite this, the demand from investors for high investment returns remained undiminished. Fund promoters were as quick to recognise this demand as their forebears had been in the

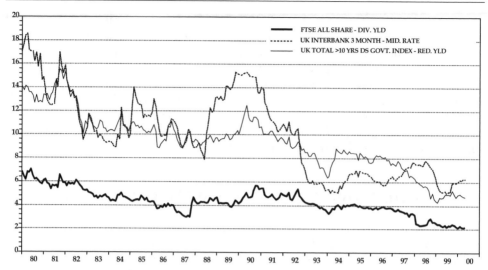

Figure 3.3 The long-term decline of equity and fixed interest yields.
Source: Datastream.

rising equity markets of the late 1880s and on other occasions since. What is more, a number of technical developments and structural devices made it possible for new splits to be launched with ever-higher starting yields. Together with the proven attractions and perfect past repayment record of zeros, the design and launch of new splits became not only highly profitable for their promoters but started to take on the characteristics of a one-way bet. Or so it seemed at the time, before the markets turned.

3.14   TECHNICAL DEVELOPMENTS AND STRUCTURAL CHANGES

The first development to have a major impact on the way that splits were designed was the new SORP for investment trusts, introduced by the Association of Investment Trust Companies (AITC) in 1995.[7] In particular, the SORP recommended that the managerial and interest costs incurred in the running of a trust should be allocated between capital and revenue "in accordance with the board's expected long-term split of returns" ... in the form of capital gains and income, respectively, from the relevant investments of the trust. So, if the Board of Directors expects 25% of a trust's total return to come from capital, it should charge 25% of management expenses and 25% of interest costs to the capital account.

Historically, all such costs had been allocated entirely to the revenue account, which reduced the sum available for distributable dividends, although it did have the benefit of not eroding capital values. Now, though, if a trust's board judged that the underlying portfolio had a balanced investment objective between income and growth then costs

---

[7] SORPs are recommendations on accounting practices for specialised industries or sectors. They supplement accounting standards and are issued, not by the Accounting Standards Board (ASB), but by industry or sectoral bodies recognised by the ASB, such as the AITC.

should be split 50/50 between revenue and capital. If they judged that it was *entirely* growth-oriented then most, or all, costs could be allocated to the capital account, leaving the revenue account intact and capable of servicing higher dividend payments as a result.

This was generally good news for trust designers whose remit was to devise more and more attractive offerings for the primary market. "Attractive" in this context (noting Figure 3.3) meant creating very high starting yields on the ordinary shares in which case the success of a new trust issue was assured.

The inventive use of the SORP was just the beginning. The objective, however, was always the same: to make each trust issue more attractive than the one before. Other devices brought in to trust structures included the innovation of undated splits, bank borrowings to gear capital structures, off-shore registration to permit the "tweaking" of accountancy practices and, last but not least, investment in other splits as a source of high income, all of which are discussed in greater depth in Chapter 4.

Every time a fancy new way was devised to ramp up the starting dividend yield on the income-bearing shares, whether by passing more and more costs to the capital account or by investing in higher and higher yielding underlying securities, the risks were increasing too. Those underlying portfolio assets had to work harder and harder – and meet the so-called hurdle rate – while all the time that same portfolio was being required to generate more and more income for distribution.

3.15   ABERDEEN NEW PREFERRED BREAKS THE MOULD

Some "new splits" had one of the above new features and some had others. But the 1997 reconstruction of Aberdeen Preferred into Aberdeen New Preferred, devised by David Thomas, chief investment trust designer at Brewin Dolphin & Co., in consultation with Chris Fishwick of Aberdeen Asset Managers, was the first occasion on which so many of the above devices were incorporated in a split capital/highly geared trust at once. That is why the reconstruction of "AbPref", as the trust was known colloquially, is such a milestone in the evolution of splits.

AbPref had undated ordinary shares – normally, something of a contradiction in terms for a split trust containing dated securities, such as zeros. Thomas achieved this by having the zeros issued via a subsidiary company, so that when the zero reached its repayment date, only the subsidiary had to be wound up. (The downside of this ploy became apparent later, when bank covenants began to be breached, because subsidiaries counted as liabilities thus restricting the ability to pay dividends in many cases.) AbPref also had bank debt ranking ahead of the zero – another factor which increased risk, whether it was recognised at the time or not, and an inflation-linked debenture thrown in for good luck too.

And while AbPref is no more, despite (or, some would argue, because of) a further reconstruction in late 2001, credit must be given for the ingenuity, if not the execution, of some of its innovative features as devised by David "Dotty" Thomas.

3.16 KEY FIGURES IN THE HISTORY OF SPLITS

The investment trust sector is by its very nature understated and introvert and so are many of the figures who shaped its development. Few people in the street would recognise the name of Michael Hart, for example, one of the most forward-thinking fund managers of the post-war era. Similarly, Nic Lewis, "inventor" of the zero-dividend preference share, is not widely known within the investment community, never mind outside it.

That is why it is almost invidious to name individuals and any list will be glaring, in some quarters, in its omissions. Going all the way back to 1868, London solicitor Philip Rose devised the entire managed funds concept which led to a multi-billion global industry today, yet there isn't even a small blue plaque in Victoria Street, Westminster, where his offices were based.

Five years later another solicitor, William Menzies, in Edinburgh, came up with the design of SAINTS which arguably makes Menzies the "father of the splits industry". If that is going a little too far back, then David Montagu and Michael Behrens must jointly take that honour for thinking up the concept behind Dualvest's launch in 1965.

What happened to the industry in the 1960s and thereafter would simply not have been possible without some outstanding technical innovation and "thinking outside the box". It would probably take another book to address this subject properly, but among the unsung heroes are Richard Green, formerly a partner at James Capel & Co. and later with Williams de Broë and finally Teather & Greenwood before his retirement in 2003.

Green, and other figures, such as John Gray (and later David Thomas) of Messel & Co. and John Hales of Cazenove & Co., helped to drag the sector out of the dark ages by, for example, learning to use early mainframe computers to automate calculations, produce regular statistical data and achieve a greater degree of accuracy than ever before. Later Green, together with his colleague Simon Moore, would produce one of the most advanced trust modelling computer programmes in the sector.

Meanwhile, in Edinburgh in the late 1960s, a team of Scottish analysts was developing what began as the Wood Mackenzie daily net asset value service but ended up as the source of a range of trust data supplying both the *Financial Times* and the AITC. Three of the key players were Peter Derby and later Hamish Buchan, both of whom worked for Wood Mackenzie & Co., and Ian Rushbrook, then at Ivory & Sime.

Then there is David Thomas himself, who recruited me into the industry and who, with his colleagues Jonathan Maxwell and Peter Bell, devised so many of the complex features which came to be associated with new splits and trust reconstructions during the 1990s.

It has to be said that while Thomas is the most widely recognised architect of the new wave of splits, there were a number of others and other corporate teams, devising and promoting funds with similarly aggressive capital structures.

Names which spring up time and again as key figures in the modern day splits story include Chris Fishwick of Aberdeen Asset Managers, John Szymanowski of UBS Warburg, Rolly Crawford and Ken Dalziel of Collins Stewart and Tony Reid, founder of BFS investments. There are other figures whom we have not mentioned, whose role was perhaps just as important. Maybe one day their full story will be told.

3.17   CONCLUSION

Split capital trusts in their modern form date to the launch of Dualvest in 1965 but the split capital concept itself can be traced back to 1873.

It should be no surprise that split capital structures have evolved. One of the reasons the trust industry thrives today, despite warnings, even as long ago as 1868, of its imminent demise, is its ability to change with the times.

Sometimes, however, as in other apparently unconnected areas like motor racing or aerospace technology, design concepts are pushed just too far. Whatever stress-testing has been done proves, in the event, not to have been enough. Something breaks under unforeseen duress, leading to catastrophic failure. And sometimes what has happened may be judged to have been avoidable, the result of negligence or greed, or both. Hard knocks are taken, lessons are learned and the world moves on. But, for some reason, in the financial sector some of the most painful lessons get forgotten and have to be relearned the hard way.

Split capital structures still have their place if the prudent application of their principles becomes the required standard for the future. The answer is not to stifle initiative and innovation, but to encourage it – while ensuring that a light but strong framework of checks and controls, whether regulatory or self-imposed by the industry, is in place. The material for such a framework should be drawn to a very great extent from a study of the expensive lessons of financial history.

3.18   REFERENCES

Angus, R. (1991) *Haec Olim: NatWest Investment Trust Annual Review*. County NatWest, Edinburgh.

Arnaud, A.A. (1973) *Investment Trusts Explained*. Woodhead-Faulkner, Cambridge, UK.

McKendrick, N. and Newlands, J.E. (1999) *F&C: A History of Foreign & Colonial Investment Trust*. Chappin Kavanagh, London.

Messel & Co. (1966) *Investment Trust Handbook*. L. Messel & Co., London.

Newlands, J.E. (2000) *Split Capital and Highly Geared Investment Trusts*, Williams de Broë, London.

River Plate & General (1987) *Company History*. River Plate & General, London.

Weir, R. B. (1973) *A History of the Scottish American Investment Company Limited*. SAINTS, Edinburgh.

4

The Crisis Unfolds

ANDREW ADAMS

> *As reverse leverage did its work, investment trust managements were much more concerned over the collapse in the value of their own stock than over the adverse movements in the stock list as a whole. The investment trusts had invested heavily in each other. As a result the fall in Blue Ridge hit Shenandoah, and the resulting collapse in Shenandoah was even more horrible for the Goldman Sachs Trading Corporation.*
>
> (J.K. Galbraith, *The Great Crash 1929*, p. 145)

4.1 INTRODUCTION

There was a booming new issue market in splits over the three-year period 1999 to 2001, with over 80 launches,[1] more than in the previous ten years. Many of them were far riskier than investors, particularly private investors, realised. This chapter describes in outline the boom and bust of a section of the splits sector and the underlying reasons for the crisis. Particular attention is given to the role of zeros, a higher proportion of which were held by private investors as compared with other classes of shares in the new splits. Many of the subsequent compensation claims have related to zeros.

4.2 AGGRESSIVE STRUCTURES

The quest for income among investors resulting from the marked fall in interest rates over the second half of the 1990s, provided an opportunity for the issue of innovative income products. The aggressive pursuit of fees on the part of certain fund management companies and broker/advisers in a buoyant market drove them to use various devices toward the end of the 1990s to maintain the initial yields on income shares[2] and thus create starting yields that were unattainable elsewhere in the market. Raising equity through the issue of ordinary income shares also enabled them to sell zeros to the

---

[1] Includes highly geared closed-end funds and "rollovers" into splits – see Annexes 1 and 2 at the end of this chapter.
[2] Henceforth in this chapter, the term "income shares" is taken to mean income-bearing shares, including traditional income shares and ordinary income shares.

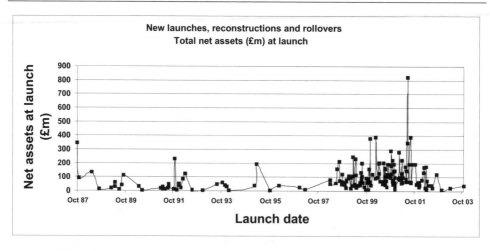

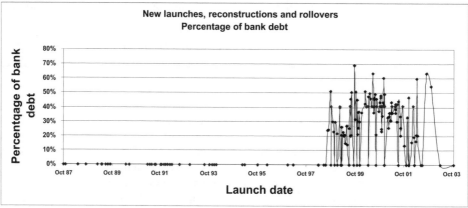

Figure 4.1   The build-up of bank debt in the splits and highly geared sector.

Sources: Trust Associated Ltd, London Stock Exchange Official List announcements, prospectuses, Thomson Financial Datastream, Report & Accounts.

investing public. The more ordinary income shares they created, the more zeros they could issue.

During the period of falling interest rates, the gross redemption yield[3] on a typical zero remained high, at say 9% p.a., whereas bank debt finance could be arranged at perhaps 6.5% p.a. So, bank debt became increasingly useful to finance gearing and accordingly started to build up in the splits sector in 1999 (Figure 4.1) alongside the growth in zeros.

But the inclusion of bank debt in a split's capital structure meant that, in the event of a breach of covenant, the bank had the right to demand early repayment (in full or in part, with breakage costs), restructuring of the underlying portfolio or dividend suspensions/reductions. Furthermore, the lower gearing of trusts after the enforced repayment

---

[3] Broadly speaking, "gross redemption yield" is the internal rate of return per annum if the security is held to redemption, before any tax.

of bank debt makes it more difficult for them to maintain dividends on their income shares and also to recoup losses if the market rises.

Significant proportions of the income shares in the new issues of splits were typically placed with other splits (hence "cross-holdings"). As a result of splits investing in the income shares of other splits (thus helping them to meet their own yield requirements), a so-called "magic circle"[4] developed consisting of fund managers whose splits held shares in one another. Initially, this consisted of just a handful of fund management groups subscribing for shares in each other's trusts, but it widened as others joined in during the splits boom. In a memorandum to the Treasury Select Committee, the Association of Investment Trust Companies (AITC) reported that it had heard numerous rumours and anecdotes about collusion where managers and sponsoring brokers were alleged to have agreed to support each other's new issues (HCTC, 2003a, Ev. 28). The AITC subsequently received complaints for making such a public statement.

A large proportion of annual management fees and bank loan interest in the new structures was generally allocated to the capital account rather than the revenue account. This was an accounting treatment that produced high headline yields for the income shares but also meant that over time capital would be eroded. It often went against the Statement of Recommended Practice (SORP) for investment trusts (see Section 3.14) although many of the aggressively structured funds were offshore companies and for them the SORP's writ did not apply. Such companies tended to charge even more to the capital account than UK investment trusts – sometimes as much as 100%.[5]

4.3   BARBELLS

The devices discussed in Section 4.2 were often combined with a thematic investment strategy in the so-called "barbell" investment trusts. Barbell trusts held two distinct portfolios of investments – a growth portfolio and an income portfolio. In pictorial form this asset structure can look like the barbell used in weightlifting. This is because assets are held at either end of the income/growth spectrum, with nothing in the middle. The income portfolio typically consisted of bonds (with varying degrees of risk) and high-yield investment trust securities (including the ordinary income shares of other splits). The "growth" portfolio (Figure 4.2) was typically invested in a sector or market that was popular at the time of issue. The most obvious portfolio risk of many barbell trusts arose because they invested in a single fashionable specialist "growth" area like technology with considerable specific risk. However, high-yield bonds and high-yield investment trust securities can also be risky, and if the bonds were issued by companies in the same "growth" area, this increased the overall risk further. Management companies and broker/advisers seemed to have overlooked these risks.

The liabilities side of the balance sheet of a barbell tended to include a significant amount of bank debt. The share capital typically consisted of zeros,[6] ordinary income

---

[4] The term "magic circle" in this context is a colloquial usage which became common in the press and elsewhere toward the end of the 1990s and simply means split capital trust managers whose trusts hold shares in one another.

[5] Offshore companies can even charge expenses other than management fees and bank loan interest to the capital account.

[6] Although barbells launched before August 2000 rarely issued zeros at launch, they were sometimes introduced to the capital structure later in restructuring deals.

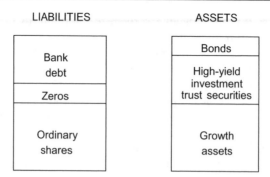

Figure 4.2   Structure of a typical barbell.

shares and in some cases other classes of share. Some private investors clamoured for the new ordinary income shares offering "high income with a touch of equity" while others were attracted by the high gross redemption yield and tax advantages of the zeros.

Those who sponsored the barbell issues argued that the portfolio structure enabled them to offer an income product backed by growth (low-yielding) stocks. Thus, they argued, it offered diversification for the splits sector away from value stocks to growth stocks. But they were much less stable structures than many professional financial advisers and retail investors realised, and were designed for a bull market.

The first barbell trust, Technology & Income, was launched in July 1999. Its growth portfolio consisted of low-yielding technology shares and its income portfolio consisted of high-yielding bonds. Of the £197.2m (net of expenses) raised, £90m was bank debt. There was heavy investor demand for the shares. Annexes 1 and 2 at the end of this chapter show that over 30 barbells were created during the following two years.[7]

Two barbells launched at the height of the technology boom in February–March 2000, European Technology & Income and Framlington NetNet.Inc, were of some significance as we will see later. They raised a total of £391m and £98m, respectively. Both had significant levels of bank debt and a split share capital structure but with no zeros issued at launch. European Technology & Income's investment policy at inception was to invest 50% in European technology shares and 50% in bonds. Framlington NetNet.Inc's investment policy was to invest 50% in Internet shares and 50% in high-yielding split capital shares.

4.4 BIG FEES

Both the fund management companies and their broker/advisers were remunerated on the basis of fees on gross assets. Initial and annual fees looked reasonable at issue; but, with a significant amount of bank debt, these fees were much larger than appeared at first sight. This became clear if fees (and other expenses) were expressed as a percentage of net assets attributable to equity[8] shareholders who in fact bear all the initial and

---

[7] The definition of "barbell" is that given in Cazenove & Co. (2001b): namely, a closed-end fund with bank debt representing at least 35% of total assets and having no more than 65% of assets at inception invested in a "growth" asset class.
[8] The term "equity shares" includes income-bearing shares and capital shares, but not zeros. (Capital shares are entitled to the surplus assets on wind-up after repayment of other classes of shares.)

annual costs. And if the underlying assets declined after launch, fees (and expenses) could become excessive (unless they were waived) from the equity shareholders' viewpoint. This, in turn, could affect the security of any zeros in the capital structure and the zeros would also not benefit from the high-dividend distributions to holders of income shares.

Consider first the initial fees. It was usual for broker/advisers to charge a fee of 1% on all monies raised. This sounds unexceptionable. But if a new trust raised £100m, of which £50m was bank debt and £40m was raised by placing shares with related parties (including other splits), broker/advisers received their £1m fee (1% of £100m) for finding new shareholders (independent financial advisers, private client stockbrokers and other institutions) subscribing only £10m. So it can be argued that on the money they have actually raised, they were paid a fee of no less than 10%!

Other issue expenses, including a significant element of marketing costs, typically boosted total issue expenses to about 2.25% of the gross capital raised, including bank debt, and sometimes very much more. If equity shares represented 50% of the gross capital subscribed, this meant that expenses would approach 5% of the equity shares' starting net asset value.

Next consider the annual management fees, typically 1% of gross assets. Such fees looked reasonable at first glance and fund management firms would argue that they manage the whole portfolio of assets. However, gross assets include assets financed by bank debt and zeros, as well as equity share capital. So, at the beginning of the life of a split, if equity shares represented 50% of the gross capital subscribed, equity shareholders were typically paying annual management fees of 2% of the assets actually attributable to them. This introduces a potential conflict between the interests of managers and equity shareholders. Managers are better off the more debt there is but equity shareholders may be worse off.

That is not the full story. Total expenses were greater than management fees alone. Fitzrovia, a company that specialises in monitoring expenses of funds, estimates that on average only two-thirds of expenses for investment trusts are represented by management fees. Hence, total expenses typically amounted to an annual 3% of assets attributable to equity shares – a massive hurdle to clear just to maintain the net asset value.

Finally, if the underlying portfolio of assets included holdings in other investment trusts, there would be management fees upon management fees, unless fee waivers had been arranged.[9] And taking this further, if a trust invests in a trust which itself invests in another trust, there could be a further layer of management fees, and so on.

To sum up, unless there was sufficiently strong growth in the underlying assets, shareholders' funds in the new structures would haemorrhage through large fees and through the charging of the majority of interest and expenses to the capital account.

4.5 LACK OF INFORMATION

The prospectus for a new issue is a long and complicated document. While prospectuses for the new structures may have included all information required by the Listing Rules,

---

[9] Trusts usually exclude from the value of their portfolio the value of holdings in other trusts managed by their managers, when calculating their management fees.

important information concerning risk and fees were not always shown "upfront". Indeed, some important information may not even have been required to be given. For example, if zeros were to be issued, a "wipe-out rate"[10] was generally given for the income shares but not for the zeros. But, for the new "geared" zeros ranking after bank debt, this was a vital piece of information. Investors might have interpreted its absence as meaning that the zeros could not be wiped out.

There was generally insufficient information available on crucial matters, such as bank covenants on borrowings, and on investments in other splits. This was due partly to the splits being new structures, with no models/case law as to what should be disclosed. After the initial launch, the precise terms of banking covenants were not readily available, despite being important to shareholders because the terms of the covenant could determine the investment actions of the managers. One wonders in retrospect how market makers could make a price in securities known to rank behind high levels of bank debt without knowing the trigger point at which the bank could effectively take control of the portfolio.

As regards investments in other splits, the Listing Rules required trusts to disclose their "top ten" holdings once a year in their Report & Accounts and many split trust managers voluntarily provided monthly fact sheets, which included an update of the "top ten". But this was not as helpful as it appears. One trust's ten largest holdings might have amounted to over 50% of its portfolio by value while those of another trust might have represented less than 10%. It was possible for splits to have a large number of undisclosed holdings in other splits.[11]

The Report & Accounts was the main source of information on any split's portfolio, cash position, debt and cross-holdings. However, not only did the extent of disclosure vary considerably, but the Reports & Accounts of different splits were also in respect of different year-ends. This made comparisons between splits difficult, particularly since the degree of disclosure in Interim Reports (the next obvious source of information) also varied widely.

4.6 THE ZERO MARKET EXPANDS

Table 4.1 shows the very substantial increase in the number and volume of zeros issued from around 1998 onwards. This is then broken down into geared, ungeared and options,[12] to reveal the growing importance of "geared" zeros since 1998.

Partly due to their complexity, there was considerable ignorance in the market as regards the risk of zeros, particularly among private investors and their advisers. While the good name of zeros suggested to private investors that the predetermined returns were all but guaranteed, they were not. The "geared" zeros of the new structures issued from 1999 were very different from the zeros that had gone before. They ranked *after* a sizeable layer of bank debt and were often backed by volatile assets, including holdings in other highly geared trusts.

---

[10] "Wipe-out rate" is the annualised rate of decrease in gross assets that would just lead to no capital payment (or wipe-out) on wind-up for a particular class of shares.

[11] Only holdings that represented more than 3% of a class of shares of another company had to be declared.

[12] The term "options" in this context means option-based zero-like instruments issued by an investment company which had only one class of shares.

Table 4.1 Number and initial value of zeros issued each year*

	Totals		Geared		Ungeared		Options	
	Count	£m	£m	Count	£m	Count	£m	Count
1987	2	78.0	78.0	2	0.0	0	0.0	0
1988	2	68.0	63.5	1	4.5	1	0.0	0
1989	7	169.6	106.4	4	63.2	3	0.0	0
1990	0	0.0	0.0	0	0.0	0	0.0	0
1991	12	178.9	0.0	0	178.9	12	0.0	0
1992	8	154.6	0.0	0	154.6	8	0.0	0
1993	10	143.4	38.7	2	104.7	8	0.0	0
1994	5	44.1	36.4	3	7.7	2	0.0	0
1995	5	67.7	9.0	1	58.7	4	0.0	0
1996	5	193.7	90.5	3	103.2	2	0.0	0
1997	5	173.9	5.8	1	168.1	4	0.0	0
1998	14	435.0	219.4	9	215.6	5	0.0	0
1999	31	841.5	658.5	25	163.0	5	20.0	1
2000	23	358.6	331.1	22	0.0	0	27.5	1
2001	36	883.0	637.6	29	129.0	4	116.5	3
2002	7	236.5	196.3	5	0.0	0	40.3	2
2003	5	47.4	0.0	0	19.1	1	28.2	4
Sum	*177*	*4,073.9*	*2,471.1*	*107*	*1,370.3*	*59*	*232.5*	*11*

Sources: Trust Associated Ltd, London Stock Exchange Official List announcements, prospectuses, Thomson Financial Datastream, Report & Accounts.
* The figures include new zeros, rollovers and reconstructions as well as further issuance of existing zeros.

When a trust issued zeros ranking behind a hefty slice of bank debt and held a volatile portfolio of underlying assets, there was a significant chance that the predetermined capital sum at maturity would not be paid. As a result, there was effectively a reintroduction of the conflicts of interest that the original quasi-splits of the late 1980s had partly been designed to avoid (see Section 3.11). Allocation of charges (both interest and management fees) to the capital account and large income payments to the ordinary income shareholders continuously deplete the asset base for the zeros, unless sufficient growth of the underlying assets is achieved. It is, of course, the duty of the directors to balance the competing interests of different classes of shareholder, but zero shareholders may tend to be discriminated against for the following reasons:

• Zero shareholders lack the same management performance monitoring that ordinary income shareholders possess through their dividend entitlement. Payment dates for ordinary income shareholders are twice a year, not once at the end of the life of the trust.

• Zeros do not carry a vote, unless their entitlements are being altered.

Some have argued that there might also be a temptation for fund management companies to try to exert influence on their trust Board to treat the ordinary income shareholders more favourably so as to maintain the income flow to other splits in order that they, in turn, could continue to pay out their own forecast dividends. However, in its response to the Treasury Select Committee's report, one company,

Aberdeen Asset Management, stated: "Aberdeen boards and Aberdeen as managers at all times balanced the interests of all shareholders" (HCTC, 2003b, p. 30).

On the other hand there were some "windfall benefits" for zero holders as a result of the Companies Act restrictions on dividend payments and legal opinions regarding whether it was appropriate to pay dividends when zeros were uncovered, neither of which were anticipated at the time of launch.

There was considerable complacency as regards the risks of zeros right up to July 2001 and beyond, partly due to the perfect repayment record of zeros issued by splits between 1987 and 1998. These were issued in generally rising markets and had no bank debt in their structures. In reality, however, like was not being compared with like. Geared zeros had a very different risk profile from the earlier zeros that had created this perfect repayment record. Few financial advisers understood that zeros now varied much more in quality than previously and there was little concern regarding the limited information available on cross-holdings and banking covenants. Many investors were putting money into securities that they and their advisers did not understand. It was only when specific warnings about the risks inherent in some zeros started to appear in the press (around the end of July 2001) that many financial intermediaries woke up to the risks of lower quality zeros. Up to that point, they were inclined to regard all zeros as being of similar quality.

There was also a rise in the number of new unit trusts investing in zeros in the years 2000 and 2001, along the lines of Exeter Zero Preference Fund, which had been launched in 1991 and which had been a strong performer. Predominantly, private investors hold the units in these funds. One of the funds, Aberdeen Progressive Growth, launched in August 2000, was heavily marketed through to the summer of 2001. The objective of the fund was to provide capital growth from investment primarily in zero-dividend preference shares. It was advertised as being low risk and was promoted under the banner: "The one year old who lets you sleep at night." But for many who purchased units in the trust, their investment would later turn out to be a nightmare.

4.7 MOUNTING CONCERN

In early November 2000, the directors of European Technology & Income were forced to carry out a restructuring as the trust's bank covenant became endangered. About £42m (after expenses) was raised from a share placing, including £30m of zeros. It was not obvious why there was sufficient demand for these new shares but, as a result of the placing, the cash flows to income shareholders (i.e., the dividends from their income shares in European Technology & Income) were maintained. Although the underlying income portfolio of European Technology & Income was invested in bonds and not in other splits, other splits had invested in the company; so, it still raised the question of systemic risk within the splits sector. The stated aim of the placing was to increase the technology content of the underlying portfolio back to 50%. But then, later in the same month, the board repaid £40m of the bank loan after its gross assets had fallen further, having already repaid £25m in July 2000.

The European Technology & Income forced restructuring in the autumn of 2000 was the first concrete evidence of the problems that the aggressive trust structures could create. It triggered Robin Angus and myself to consider writing an article to increase investor awareness of the issues and risks involved.

The AITC also acted in November 2000 by starting to publish information on underlying portfolios in its *Monthly Information Release* (MIR), although very few splits provided the required information initially because either they were unwilling to provide it or they did not have the systems in place to carry out the analysis. The revised MIR gave a breakdown of the percentage of underlying assets in: bonds, investment trust income shares, investment trust income & residual capital shares, other investment company shares, UK equities, international equities, and cash or cash equivalents. This followed concern that had been building up at the AITC concerning the lack of information available to investors on trusts' underlying portfolios.

In January 2001, after talks with its bankers, Framlington NetNet.Inc introduced £8m of synthetic zero-coupon financing[13] and repaid £5m of bank debt. The trust had already raised a new equity injection of £3.7m (net of expenses) in October 2000, keeping most of the proceeds in cash to boost its banking ratios (so-called "cash offset" arrangements). Subsequent to its launch in March 2000, figures for the portfolio distribution between Internet shares, the income shares of other splits, and any cash or bond holdings, were not readily available. In particular, after the January 2001 restructuring, this information was not made available to the market.

At a meeting between Peter Moffatt (Director of Investment Business, Guernsey Financial Services Commission) and Robert Aitken (Head of Department – Investment Firms, Financial Services Authority) at the FSA on 30 January 2001, which covered a range of issues, Peter Moffatt mentioned his concerns about incestuous investment in split capital investment trusts. He was given to understand that the FSA had already identified concerns about the sector (HCTC, 2003a, Ev. 227–228).

From February 2001, where investment trust prospectuses disclosed an intent to generate income by investing in the income shares of splits, the Guernsey Financial Services Commission required the following additional risk warnings (HCTC, 2003a, Ev. 228):

Prospective investors should be aware that many of the split capital investment trusts or companies in which the company may invest will themselves have cross-holdings in the same split capital investment trusts and companies. This may be considered to give rise to a systemic risk should there be difficulties within the sector.

On 20 February 2001, Hamish Buchan,[14] an independent analyst at the time, visited the FSA to discuss the quality or lack of quality of information provided in new issue prospectuses of new investment trusts. He also expressed his concern about the potential problems building up in sections of the split capital and highly geared trust sector, particularly regarding the income shares of barbells, stressing the high charges to the capital account and the high growth rates of underlying assets required to maintain the initial assets. He went armed with a draft of the forthcoming article "For whom the barbell tolls ..." by Robin Angus and myself, which would be published on 2 April 2001.

---

[13] This was achieved by using derivatives rather than the issue of zeros. The synthetic zero financing was at a rate of 6.51% p.a. until 2008. But the covenants that the counterparty negotiated were not made available to the market.
[14] Hamish Buchan is now a Deputy Chairman of the AITC.

The Personal Investment Authority (PIA), now subsumed within the FSA, gave a warning in March 2001 about certain income products (PIA, 2001). This was the first time that the UK regulatory authorities had made any pronouncements on the risks of split capital investment trusts. The PIA had considered the marketing literature of a range of splits. This had raised concerns about the way that the risks of ordinary income shares had been described. As a result, the PIA issued guidance for firms wishing to market the products. In my view, the guidance placed too much reliance on hurdle rates (Chapter 6). There was no mention of zeros. Nevertheless, the warning was an indication of the growing concern building up as regards splits.

In March 2001, the directors of Framlington NetNet.Inc announced that the company had repaid £41m of its borrowings and was left with net assets of only £7.8m, a far cry from the £57.8m net assets at the time of its launch only a year earlier. But there were also many other highly geared trusts in difficulties as equity markets fell.

4.8 "FOR WHOM THE BARBELL TOLLS ..."

An article entitled "For whom the barbell tolls ..." (Adams and Angus, 2001) was published in the April 2001 edition of *Professional Investor*, the journal of the UK Society of Investment Professionals. (The article is reproduced in full in Appendix A at the end of the book, pp. 227–232). Although the journal has limited circulation, it is closely read among fund managers, investment analysts and the broking community. The article warned about risks inherent in the then still fashionable "barbell" investment trusts, arguing that:

> *The risks created by geared trusts investing in other geared trusts are very real. Substantial price declines in the ordinary shares of some individual barbell trusts might all too easily become a self-feeding downward spiral as the net asset values of the ordinary shares of other trusts that held them fell in their turn. Confidence in barbell trusts in general could thus ebb away, causing still further price declines in their ordinary shares.*

The article concluded:

> *Because barbells are complicated and difficult to understand, they should put more emphasis on communicating their investment characteristics to investors. In particular, there is an urgent need for the significant risks and expenses involved to be spelt out more clearly in their Prospectuses and Report & Accounts.*

Although the article contained very strong warnings about the dangers of barbell investment trusts, particularly for retail investors, the main emphasis was on the implications for ordinary income shares rather than zeros. It asked the question:

> *How many holders of the ordinary shares of barbells really expect to receive back significantly less than the money they have subscribed?*

Meanwhile, corporate activity continued as aggressively structured funds, particularly barbells, started to get into difficulties. Perhaps more surprisingly, new issues of aggressively structured funds continued. There was still little concern about zeros in the press and both the AITC and FSA continued to treat zeros as a single low-risk asset category.

Peter Moffatt (Guernsey Financial Services Commission) sent a letter dated 9 April 2001 to Robert Aitken (FSA) in which he referred to their meeting in January 2001 and the topic of high-income shares of splits. He said in the letter that he was "still concerned at the potentially incestuous nature of this business" and that "we have been stepping up our required risk warnings as a consequence" (HCTC, 2003a, Ev. 229).

The Investment Regulatory Organisation (IMRO, now part of the FSA) also reported in April 2001 on a project it had started in February 2001 to assess the risk concentration of holdings of splits and to establish whether any regulatory action was required. IMRO's conclusion was that the risk concentrations did not indicate a problem for the splits sector as a whole, but the exercise would need to be repeated periodically to maintain a watching brief on the sector (HCTC, 2003a, Ev. 148).

4.9 BARBELLS UNBALANCED

The report entitled "Barbells Unbalanced" by stockbrokers Cazenove & Co., which was sent out to clients on 25 July 2001, had a negative effect on the market valuation of split trust securities, including zeros. The 32-page report concentrated entirely on barbells and their problems.

It started with a repeat of analyst Chris Brown's prophetic words about barbells' asset portfolios in Cazenove's *Investment Trust Companies Research – Annual Review*, dated 10 January 2001 (Cazenove, 2001a):

> *We remain nervous about some of the barbell portfolios underlying these funds. The growth portfolio is often highly volatile, while the income portfolio has more capital risk than many investors think. Not only could the proportion invested in other splits fall sharply if the underlying hurdle rates are not met, but the high yielding (née junk) bonds that are popular in some structures are quasi equity. The worst case scenario for investors is therefore a growth portfolio that does not grow and an income portfolio that suffers defaults and capital loss. In this instance high headline yields do little to mitigate the overall losses that will be suffered.*

There was not much discussion of zeros in the report but it did emphasise that zero shareholders should be aware that volatile assets are very bad news, stating that:

> *They have all the downside risk, but with only limited upside.*

The report concluded:

> *Despite their popularity, we have shown that there are some serious problems with the barbell structure. Our biggest concern is the risk of systemic collapse in the highly geared sector due to high levels of investment in other split capital and highly geared funds. The catalyst could be further defaults by trusts which might then have to sell their trust holdings. Unless there is demand for these, this will cause prices to fall, which in turn could lead to further defaults by other highly geared funds holding splits and further sales. It is easy to see how a downward spiral could develop, exacerbated by high gearing.*

4.10   CHANGE IN MARKET SENTIMENT

On 25 July 2001, the same day as *Barbells Unbalanced* was sent out to Cazenove's clients, European Technology & Income announced the suspension of the monthly dividend on its income shares. With the possible exception of Framlington NetNet.Inc, this was the first time that a barbell had paid a lower dividend than indicated at launch; it came as a shock to the market. After that, there was a fall in the price of income shares and a number of splits with cross-holdings started to suffer financial difficulties as most cross-holdings were in income shares.

On 23 August 2001, the directors of European Technology & Income announced that they were in discussions with Technology & Income, another barbell managed by Aberdeen Asset Management, which might lead to an offer being made for all classes of shares in their company. A further announcement was to be made in due course.[15]

A fall in the market following the tragic events in New York and Washington on September 11th 2001, caused further very sharp falls in the majority of income shares of splits. Perhaps more importantly, "geared zeros"[16] suffered sharp falls (Figure 4.3). This brought home the fact that the zero market had become far from homogeneous. It was necessary to distinguish between "investment grade" zeros and zeros of bank-geared and/or cross-invested splits. Managers of splits whose portfolios contained a mixture of quality stocks and lower quality illiquid shares in splits often had to sell the former to reduce gearing, leaving them with a portfolio of much lower quality than had originally been intended.

The banks were now in a difficult position. They did not wish to trigger a crisis in which they would be major losers. So the banks allowed troubled splits to offset cash holdings against their bank debt and gave them time to arrange restructuring deals.[17] There was a brief spate of such restructurings in the autumn of 2001. However, these deals often involved splits making further investments in each other's newly issued paper, a short-term "fix" that only served to make the cross-holdings problem worse. The vast majority of new "income" securities were sold to other splits or other funds whose managers also managed splits.[18] Moreover, many of these transactions were carried out by stock swaps at mid-market prices. Given the illiquidity and very large spreads of these shares, mid-market prices were a purely theoretical value at which to transfer holdings.

Giving evidence to the Treasury Select Committee, Daniel Godfrey, Director General of the AITC said (HCTC, 2003a, Ev. 201–202):

> *We have also been told there were instances towards the end of the launch glut where trusts were beginning to run into trouble and there was not so much cash available from the other funds to invest in new funds but when they went out to do the marketing, they were told, "We cannot give you cash but we can give you these shares in other splits as a swap for your new issue," and the broker would say, "Do you want these shares?" and the fund manager would*

---

[15] The offer document did not come out until 29 November 2001 due to weak markets and was extremely complicated. Ironically, Technology & Income, which had "rescued" European Technology & Income, had its own listing cancelled on 26 November 2003.

[16] The term "geared zeros" includes zeros ranking behind bank debt or long-term loan capital.

[17] Some argue that by failing to take firm action at an early stage, the banks made matters worse for many zero shareholders.

[18] In its evidence to the Treasury Select Committee Enquiry on 11 July 2002, the AITC said that "as much as 70% of the income shares issued in 2001 were bought by split funds and other funds whose managers also managed splits" (HCTC, 2003a, Ev. 31).

Index of geared zeros

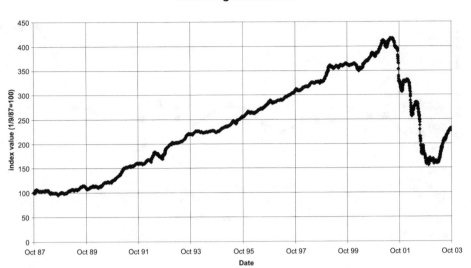

Index of ungeared zeros

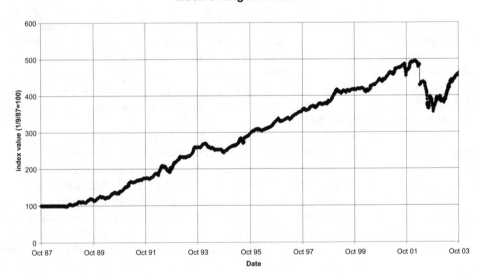

Figure 4.3   Performance of geared v. ungeared zeros.
Source: Trust Associates Ltd (with thanks).

> *say, "Yes," and as a result of that the starting portfolio may have looked quite different to the model on which the sponsoring broker, the accountant and even the board had signed off and may have been of lower quality than had initially been ...*

High-yielding preferred income shares were common in the "mini" reconstructions in the autumn of 2001. In my opinion, the income rights of some of these shares meant

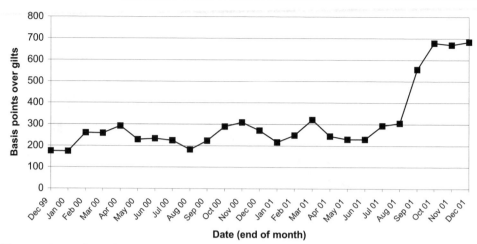

Figure 4.4   Median of "points over gilts".

that there was a transfer of value from zero shareholders to the subscribers to the new preferred income shares.

By the end of 2001, concerns were mounting that, in order to repay the banks, splits in breach of their covenants might be forced to sell illiquid holdings in the income shares of other splits, thereby initiating the kind of self-feeding downward spiral that Adams and Angus (2001) and Cazenove & Co. (2001a, b) had warned about. Meanwhile, splits holding the ordinary income shares of other splits that cut their dividends were compelled to cut dividends on their own ordinary income shares as a result of the lower income they received. So, the existence of substantial cross-holdings caused dividend cuts to compound themselves across large numbers of splits. Dividend cuts also caused the share prices to fall, thus reducing the portfolio valuations of other trusts that themselves held these shares.

A surge of complaints from the investing public led the FSA to issue a discussion paper on split capital closed-end funds in December 2001. The FSA requested views on three subjects: disclosure, governance and mis-selling. It also announced that it was investigating allegations of collusive behaviour by the managers of certain trusts.

Figures 4.4 and 4.5 summarise the apparent change in market sentiment toward zeros over the years 2000 and 2001, using the yield risk premiums[19] ("points over gilts") of all zeros with an outstanding term to redemption of more than one year.[20] Fundamental Data provided the "points over gilts" data. Figure 4.4 shows that the median of "points over gilts" broadly remains within the range 200–300 basis points up to the summer of 2001.[21] While there was little change in the median of "points over gilts" during the first half of 2001, there was a dramatic increase in the median over the second half of 2001. Figure 4.5 shows that there was also a dramatic increase in the inter-quartile range of "points over gilts" over the second half of 2001, suggesting much greater differentiation

---

[19] The yield risk premium ("points over gilts") is simply the gross redemption yield of the zero less the gross redemption yield of a benchmark gilt with a similar term to redemption.

[20] Zeros with a term to redemption of less than a year were excluded to avoid the results being distorted.

[21] Note that there is some deterioration in the quality of zeros over time as zeros of the more aggressively structured splits are introduced.

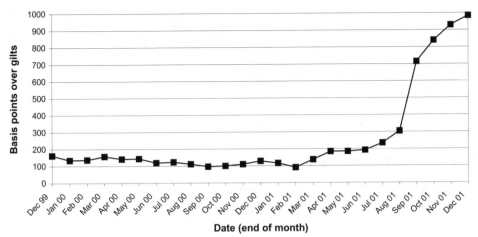

Figure 4.5   Inter-quartile range of "points over gilts".

between higher quality and lower quality zeros, a reflection of the pre-1999 and post-1999 structures.

4.11   ABERDEEN'S HALF-DAY FORUM

This conference entitled *The Regulation of Split Capital Closed End Funds* was held at The Insurance Hall, London on 1 February 2002. It was sponsored by Aberdeen Asset Management and supported by the AITC. There was a lot more interest in the conference than expected so the venue had to be changed to a larger hall at the last minute. Even then it was packed out with around 150 delegates attending, including journalists, lawyers and directors of trusts. Its timing was significant – two weeks before the deadline for submissions to the FSA Discussion Paper 10.

The conference started with a presentation by Rolly Crawford, Head of Investment Trusts at Collins Stewart, on the origins of splits and the background to the current issues. In a wide-ranging talk he argued that mistakes had been made but nobody set out with a view to losing money for investors. A number of lessons had been learned but it was unlikely that greater regulation would solve the problems of the sector, other than sensible moves to greater disclosure.

Comments and questions were then invited from the floor. Richard Moon, a fund manager, immediately stood up and, in an atmosphere of stunned silence, quoted figures he had obtained from a "specialist consultant". A group of 48 trusts had been studied which had more than 25% of their total assets invested in the income shares of other splits. Cross-holdings had been separated out of these trusts so that the position could be understood on a consolidated basis, without the confusion of cross-holdings. On this basis, the debt was a substantially higher proportion of assets, as cross-holdings were excluded.

Mr Moon concluded:

The statistics give me a very clear message. This is not just a little market hiccup. We are in the early stages of an unfolding financial crisis of major and dynamic proportions. It's going to get much worse and spread like a cancer throughout the investment trust area. It's going to affect thousands, probably tens of thousands of people, and cost billions of pounds. I believe that when the financial history of this era is written, the three great scandals will be, in order of magnitude, although it's too soon to say for sure:

1. Pension mis-selling.
2. Equitable Life.
3. And now, the Split Trust scandal.

In fact in terms of cash losses, although not in numbers of people, this may end up as a greater catastrophe than the Equitable. That's my view.

In his reply, Rolly Crawford said:

I think the doomsday scenario that you are suggesting may or may not come true, and a lot of it will depend on where markets go.

Mr Moon's blunt comments suggested that the problems within part of the relatively small splits sector were capable of inflicting reputational damage on the wider fund management industry.

Subsequent sessions at the morning forum included disclosure, governance, financial promotion and allegations of mis-selling and structural issues, much of which was relevant to potential submissions by the conference delegates to the FSA's Discussion Paper 10. A clear message that came over was the need for financial education and improved standards of reporting in the financial press.

4.12 SUSPENSIONS AND LIQUIDATIONS

The shares of Quilter Global Enhanced Income were suspended on 3 April 2002. This was the first split to have its shares suspended and was only the first of many. Perhaps more significant was the announcement on 18 April 2002 of the controlled liquidation of Gartmore Monthly Income. It seemed likely at the time that this would result in the first zero not being repaid in full on the due date.

Things got very much worse for the splits sector in July 2002 with the announcement of a further nine suspensions. With the significant number of cross-holdings within the sector, share suspensions now became a vicious circle. By the end of 2002, 19 splits or highly geared funds had been suspended.

Table 4.2 gives a list (up to November 2003) of splits and highly geared funds whose shares were suspended because the value of their assets had fallen below the value of bank debt.

Severe falls (−70.2% over the year to 28 August 2002[22]) in the unit price of Aberdeen Progressive Growth unit trust, which had been promoted as "the one year old who lets you sleep at night" demonstrated that it was in fact highly risky in certain market conditions. Most of its zero holdings had bank debt ranking in priority and a number of holdings had collapsed in price. In consequence, the unit trust's manager, Aberdeen Asset Managers, announced in June 2002 that it intended to use its own cash reserves to provide a so-called "uplift package" to all 7,000 investors in the fund so that they receive back no less than their initial investment at some unspecified date in 2005.

---

[22] Source: TrustNet.

Table 4.2 Suspensions of splits and highly geared funds

Trading suspended	Manager	Suspended	Zeros
Quilter Global Enhanced Income	Quilter	03/04/02	No
Framlington Health & Income	Framlington	28/06/02	No
BC Income & Growth	BC	08/07/02	Yes
Media & Income	Aberdeen	10/07/02	Yes
Geared Income	BFS	15/07/02	Yes
Leveraged Income	Aberdeen	17/07/02	Yes
Aberdeen High Income	Aberdeen	18/07/02	Yes
Britannic Global Income	Britannic	25/07/02	Yes
Geared Opportunities Income	ISIS	25/07/02	Yes
Martin Currie High Income	Martin Currie	25/07/02	No
Yeoman	BC	29/07/02	Yes
Exeter Enhanced Income	Exeter	06/08/02	No
LeggMason Investors American Assets	LeggMason	08/08/02	No
Framlington Split Income	Framlington	09/08/02	Yes
CI Income	Collins Stewart	14/08/02	Yes
LeggMason Investors Strategic Assets	LeggMason	19/09/02	Yes
Aberdeen Preferred Income	Aberdeen	25/09/02	Yes
Dartmoor	Exeter	27/09/02	No
LeggMason Investors Income & Growth	LeggMason	08/10/02	Yes
New Star Enhanced Income	New Star	29/07/03	Yes
Quarterly High Income	Morley	05/08/03	Yes

Source: Cazenove (with thanks).

In February 2002, the FSA announced formal investigations into what was now being described as the splits "scandal" in some circles. This was followed by an FSA policy statement in May 2002. Soon after that, the Treasury Select Committee announced that it was to conduct its own enquiries, in which the FSA and leading splits industry figures would be called to give evidence. Media interest soared, as discussed in Chapter 8.

4.13   CONCLUSION

The aggressive pursuit of fees by certain fund management companies and broker/advisers drove them to launch new funds that exploited the retail demand for high yield in the environment of the falling interest rates of the late 1990s. This led in many cases to substantial bank debt financing, high charges to the capital account and investment in the ordinary income shares of other splits, to generate the required initial yield and meet demand for new split issues as interest rates fell. Thus, the need for ever-more demanding starting yields for ordinary income shares and gross redemption yields for zeros caused management companies and broker/advisers to devise increasingly aggressively structured funds, which did not fully take account of possible stock market conditions. It cannot be out of the question that a number of management companies and broker/advisers may have overlooked, or miscalculated, the risks involved and that a contributing factor might have been the fact that they would be remunerated on the basis of gross assets (including assets financed by bank debt).

At the same time, there was a lack of understanding of the true risks involved in the new aggressive structures on the part of almost everyone from directors of splits to

IFAs, and possibly even the inventors of the products. There was considerable complacency as regards the risks of geared zeros right up to July 2001, partly due to the perfect repayment record of zeros issued by splits between 1987 and 1998, which had no bank debt in their structures. Few financial advisers understood that zeros now varied much more in quality than previously. And few realised that what was critical here was not the fact that the share was a zero but the quality of its asset backing and the size of the borrowings ranking in priority to it. There was little concern regarding the limited information available on cross-holdings and banking covenants.

There was a collapse of confidence in splits in the opening months of 2002 followed by suspensions and liquidations. Even the prices of some zeros, which had often been sold as low-risk investments to private investors, collapsed. It seemed increasingly likely that fund management companies, financial advisers and brokers would be involved in major compensation battles.

4.14 REFERENCES

Adams, A.T. and Angus, R.J. (2001) For whom the barbell tolls ... *Professional Investor*, **11**(3), April, 14–17 [see Appendix A of current book].
Cazenove & Co. (2001a) *UK Investment Companies Research – Annual Review*, 10 January.
Cazenove & Co. (2001b) *Barbells Unbalanced*, 25 July.
FSA (2001) *Discussion Paper on Split Capital Closed End Funds* (December). Financial Services Authority, London.
Galbraith, J.K. (1975) *The Great Crash 1929*. Pelican Books, London.
HCTC (2003a) *Split Capital Investment Trusts* (Third report of session 2002–03, volume II: Minutes of evidence and appendices, February). House of Commons Treasury Committee.
HCTC (2003b) *Response to the Committee's Third Report: Split Capital Investment Trusts* (Fourth special report of session 2002–03, April). House of Commons Treasury Committee.
PIA (2001) *Regulatory Update 85* (March). Personal Investment Authority, London.

Acknowledgements

I am grateful to Simon Moore of Trust Associates, Christopher Brown of Cazenove and Hamish Buchan for providing certain charts and tables for this chapter.

Annex 4.1 New issues of split capital and highly geared funds (from 1998) – money raised, after expenses, at time of launch

Launch (month/year)	Company	Manager	Equity (£m)	Zeros (£m)	Debt (£m)
4/98	Leveraged Income Fund (S)	Graham	38.5	40.0	
7/98	Martin Currie High Income	Martin Currie	23.8		25.0
10/98	Exeter Enhanced Income Fund	Exeter	38.4		26.7
11/98	Guinness Flight Geared Income & Growth (S)	Guinness Flight Hambro	25.8	15.1	18.2
12/98	Monthly High Income (S)	Commercial Union	37.7	40.1	
2/99	Acorn Income Fund	Collins Stewart	11.5		8.0
2/99	Enhanced Zero	Aberdeen	59.2		40.0
3/99	Gartmore High Income (S)	Gartmore	19.0	10.0	10.0
3/99	Govett Enhanced Income (S)	Govett	41.7	45.4	22.7
4/99	Edinburgh Income & Value (S)	EFM	23.0	15.1	11.2
5/99	BFS Small Companies Dividend (S)	BFS	14.2	6.3	3.7
6/99	Premier High Income (S)	Premier	18.2	15.4	5.7
7/99	Close FTSE 100 (S)	Close	38.4	40.8	54.4
7/99	Govett European Enhanced (S)	Govett	30.0	32.6	16.3
7/99	Technology & Income (S, B)	Aberdeen	107.2		90.0
8/99	Zero Preference Growth (S)	BFS	14.4	15.0	30.0
11/99	Exeter Equity Growth & Income Fund (S)	Exeter	28.8	15.0	15.0
12/99	Close FTSE 100 Income & Growth Fund (S)	Close	20.6	18.8	
12/99	Murray Japan Growth & Income (B)	Murray Johnstone	44.3		38.5
2/00	European Technology & Income (S, B)	Aberdeen	191.0		200.0
3/00	Framlington NetNet.Inc (S,B)	Framlington	57.8		40.0
4/00	European Monthly Income (S, B)	Aberdeen	100.6		95.0
4/00	Global High Yield Bond Fund	Morley	25.1		170.7
4/00	Johnson Fry Income & Growth	Johnson Fry	73.3		52.0
5/00	Quilter Global Enhanced Income	Quilter	20.9		51.0[a]
6/00	Edinburgh Pacific & Income (B)	EFM	31.8		21.9
6/00	Property Acquisition & Management (S)	Collins Stewart	57.3	10.0	146.7
7/00	BFS Asian Assets (S, B)	BFS	104.7		59.5
7/00	Global Opportunities (S, B)	Morley	85.7		72.7
7/00	HL Income & Growth	Hargreaves Lansdown	39.0		26.7
7/00	Premier Pacific Income Fund (B)	Premier	24.1		20.8
7/00	Progressive Geared Income (B)	Progressive	43.5		30.0
8/00	Framlington Health & Income (B)	Framlington	69.3		48.0
9/00	Exeter Smaller Companies Income Fund (S, B)	Exeter	56.7	8.8	38.9
10/00	American Monthly Income (S, B)	Aberdeen	143.3	22.5	130.0
10/00	Investec European Growth & Income (S, B)	Investec	63.7	8.8	50.0
10/00	LeggMason Investors American Assets (B)	LeggMason	96.2		89.3
10/00	US Growth & Income Fund (B)	BC	57.8		40.0
11/00	CI Income Fund (S)	Collins Stewart	40.7	10.5	17.5
11/00	Gartmore Absolute Growth & Income (S, B)	Gartmore	36.2	10.0	32.0
12/00	Britannic Global Income (S, B)	Britannic	68.6	18.8	60.0
12/00	Exeter Financials Fund (B)	Exeter	10.1		7.0
12/00	Framlington Global Financial & Income Fund (B)	Framlington	57.8		40.0
3/01	BC Income & Growth Fund (S, B)	BC	47.8	15.0	35.0
3/01	Framlington Split Income (S)	Framlington	52.8	15.0	30.0
3/01	Investec High Income (S, B)	Investec	26.7	8.4	19.6
3/01	Morley Absolute Growth	Morley	107.9	17.0	96.0[b]
4/01	BFS US Special Opportunities (S, B)	BFS	47.8	15.0	35.0
4/01	LeggMason Investors Strategic Assets (S)	LeggMason	68.5	13.0	45.5
5/01	New Star Enhanced Income (S, B)	New Star	47.5	9.0	31.5
5/01	Property Income & Growth Fund (S)	BC	77.0	27.0	72.0
6/01	Blue Chip Value & Income (S)	Collins Stewart	39.7	10.0	28.5
6/01	Jupiter Financial & Income (S, B)	Jupiter	71.6	18.8	56.2
6/01	Real Estate Opportunities (S, B)	Aberdeen	274.9	75.0	471.9[c]
7/01	BFS Managed Properties (S, B)	BFS	83.5	26.0	86.0
8/01	Britannic UK Income (S)	Britannic	213.8	45.0	130.0
8/01	Equity Partnership Investment Company (S)	Equity Partnership	53.9		13.7
8/01	Pavilion Geared Recovery (S)	Pavilion	28.5	15.0	15.0
9/01	Royal London UK Equity & Income (S)	Royal London	95.5	20.0	80.0
12/01	Aberforth Geared Capital & Income (S)	Aberforth	34.2		34.2
12/01	European Value & Income Fund (B)	Collins Stewart	9.3		6.4
12/01	Premier Recovery (S)	Premier	28.3	12.5	

2/02	Ecofin Water & Power Opportunities (S)	Ecofin	101.5		70.0
4/02	Zero Dividend Recovery Fund	Collins Stewart	11.5		4.0
		Total	*3,712.1*	*740.7*	*3,315.6*

Source: Hamish Buchan (with thanks).
[a] Includes £18.2m of convertible unsecured loan stock.
[b] Includes £22.6m of mezzanine finance.
[c] Includes £124.9m of convertible unsecured loan stock.

S = Split share capital.
B = Barbell, defined as a closed-end fund with bank debt representing at least 35% of total assets and having no more than 65% of assets at inception invested in a "growth" asset class.
"Equity" includes income-bearing shares and capital shares, but not zeros.

Annex 4.2   Rollovers into split capital and highly geared funds (from 1998) – new money raised, after expenses

Month/year	Company	Manager	Equity (£m)	Zeros (£m)	Debt (£m)
4/98	INVESCO Geared Opportunities (S)	INVESCO	9.4	4.1	21.1[d]
7/98	BFS Income & Growth (S)	BFS	68.1	63.5	
7/98	Dresdner RCM Income Growth (S)	Dresdner RCM	5.8	0.0	
9/98	Murray Extra Return (S)	Murray Johnstone	26.3	16.8	18.0
10/98	Gartmore SNT (S)	Gartmore	11.6	34.8	
11/98	INVESCO Recovery 2005 (S)	INVESCO	11.2	4.1	10.0
12/98	BFS Overseas Income & Growth (S)	BFS	36.2		21.0
1/99	Jupiter Enhanced Income (S)	Jupiter	43.6	44.4	
1/99	Yeoman (S)	BC	12.3	0.0	20.0
4/99	Quarterly High Income (S)	Commercial Union	61.6	29.5	24.0
5/99	New Fulcrum (S)	Maunby	9.5	1.7	7.7
7/99	Martin Currie Enhanced Income (S)	Martin Currie	15.8	9.6	15.1
8/99	Framlington Second Dual (S)	Framlington	41.6	10.1	21.5
10/99	Guinness Flight Geared Income & Growth (S)	Investec Guinness Flight	33.9	3.6	29.3
11/99	BFS Absolute Return (S, B)	BFS	62.0	28.8	57.8
11/99	Gartmore Split Capital Opportunities (S)	Gartmore	37.9	13.9	19.2
11/99	Jupiter Dividend & Growth (S)	Jupiter	102.2	100.0	140.0
12/99	Edinburgh High Income (S)	EFM	24.1	8.1	20.3
8/00	Govett European Technology & Income (S, B)	Govett	31.5	9.2	36.9
8/00	Media & Income (S, B)	Aberdeen	59.2	12.1	89.2
9/00	Income & Growth (S)	Aberdeen	20.9		15.0
10/00	BFS UK Dual Return (S)	BFS	51.0	7.6	89.9
11/00	European Growth & Income (S, B)	Aberdeen	58.5	20.6	85.0
2/01	Edinburgh Leveraged Income (S)	EFM	44.2	0.0	27.4
2/01	Gartmore Monthly Income (S, B)	Gartmore	40.9	0.0	72.0
2/01	Geared Opportunities Income (S)	Friends Ivory & Sime	47.5	0.0	30.7
3/01	Exeter Selective Assets (S)	Exeter	50.5	37.2	25.0
3/01	Murray Emerging Growth & Income (S)	Aberdeen	31.6	21.9	23.1
4/01	Govett Asian Income & Growth Fund	Govett	31.2		25.9
6/01	Investors Capital (S)	Friends Ivory & Sime	30.7	15.1	105.0
10/01	M&G Income Investment Company (S)	M&G	0.1	0.0	25.0
1/02	Schroder Split Investment Fund	Schroder	0.4	0.0	12.1
3/02	JP Morgan Fleming Income & Capital (S)	JP Morgan Fleming	0.4	2.8	33.0
4/02	M&G Recovery Investment Company (S)	M&G	0.1	1.5	25.0
5/02	Smaller Companies Value (S)	Scottish Widows	7.6		8.1
		Total	*1,119.4*	*501.0*	*1,153.3*

Source: Hamish Buchan (with thanks).
[d] Convertible unsecured loan stock.

S = Split share capital.
B = Barbell, defined as a closed-end fund with bank debt representing at least 35% of total assets and having no more than 65% of assets at inception invested in a "growth" asset class.
"Equity" includes income-bearing shares and capital shares, but not zeros.

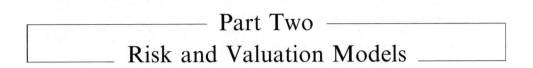

Part Two
Risk and Valuation Models

5

The Impact of the Structures

PETER MOLES

> *"Contrariwise,"* continued *Tweedledee, "if it was so, it might be; and if it were so, it would be, but as it isn't, it ain't. That's logic."*
>
> (*Alice Through the Looking Glass* by Lewis Carroll)

5.1 INTRODUCTION

This chapter examines the pricing and behavioural relationships between the different claims in a split capital investment trust. In particular, we aim to show the impact of financial engineering on the securities issued by a split and the complex nature of the securities offered to investors. To illustrate this, a contingent claim[1] valuation approach is adopted that uses simple binomial option pricing.[2] This allows us to model changes in the value of the underlying investment portfolio in response to changes in the market and its effect on the trust's securities.

Under the simplifying assumptions of the binomial model, the value of the portfolio can only increase or decrease by a given rate over a specified time period (a step), so the portfolio value can only take two possible values for each step. While this is clearly unrealistic, it simplifies the analysis and reduces the number of possible values for the portfolio when the split is wound up. The model requires that the paths for the portfolio recombine in order to limit the number of possible future values. If the portfolio value rises in a given step and then subsequently falls again in the next step – or does the opposite – it returns to the original value. In addition, the possible future values for the portfolio are not path-dependent (i.e., the values do not depend on the sequence of price changes).

The model for the future behaviour of the investment portfolio ignores the question of cross-holdings. Holding shares in trusts which are themselves geared creates complications that are not easily incorporated in the simple approach used here. As detailed in Section 6.2, cross-holdings significantly raise the risk to investors. However, the new Listing Rules (Section 9.11) impose a severe limit on cross-holdings, so they will not be a significant problem in future.

---

[1] "Contingent claim" is a generic name given to an option or security that has a feature of choice.
[2] For details of the binomial option pricing method, see Cox et al. (1979).

Table 5.1   Pricing variables for contingent claim valuation

Variable	
Current value of portfolio	100
Time to winding up the fund	4 years
Risk-free rate of interest	5% p.a.
Volatility	30% p.a.
Portfolio dividend yield	6% p.a.
Total expenses	1.5% p.a.
Pricing step	1 year

The numerical analysis is based on an existing[3] split capital investment trust whose underlying investment portfolio has a current market value of 100. One-year steps are used. The trust will be wound up and the proceeds distributed to claim holders after four years (i.e., after four steps in our model). The return to investors in the trust will depend on the future value of the investment portfolio at the end of the four years. The return to claim holders in the trust will be, in aggregate, a combination of capital appreciation (or loss) and the dividends from the holdings in the portfolio, after deducting expenses. For modelling purposes, the yield on the underlying portfolio is fixed at 6.0% p.a. and the volatility of the underlying portfolio is 30% p.a. The volatility figure may have been considered inappropriately high before the crisis unfolded, but nevertheless may be considered reasonable if there are significant cross-holdings. The risk-free rate of interest is assumed to be a constant 5% p.a. for the four years.

Total annual expenses are assumed to be 1.5% of gross assets and it is further assumed that these expenses are taken entirely to the revenue account. The model could be adjusted to allow for other allocations of expenses between the revenue account and the capital account. Many splits take part of their annual expenses, and in some cases all these expenses, to the capital account, which boosts the running yield on their income-bearing shares.

The pricing variables and the parameters of the binomial option-pricing model used to illustrate the consequences of the trust's capital structure on the value of its claims are summarised in Table 5.1.

5.2   FUTURE VALUES FOR A TRUST WITH A PRIOR CLAIM

We first look at a trust that has two types of claim: a prior claim with a redemption value of 50 at maturity and a residual claim. The prior claim is taken to be a pure discount security, such as an issue of zero-dividend preference shares. The residual claim (geared ordinary shares) receives a dividend stream (after expenses) plus whatever is left over at maturity after the prior claim has been paid.

The effect of prior claims in the capital structure is shown in Figure 5.1. Note that the

---

[3] As it is an existing trust, initial expenses deducted from the fund at the time of launch are not relevant to this study.

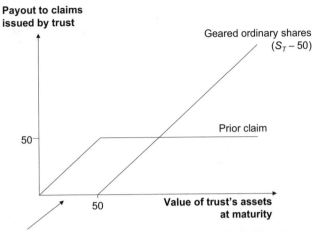

Payout to claims issued by trust

Geared ordinary shares
$(S_T - 50)$

Prior claim

50

50

Value of trust's assets at maturity

If the assets of the trust are worth less than 50 at maturity, the holders of the geared ordinary shares get nothing and the prior claim holders get whatever is left.

Figure 5.1   Effect of prior claim on payout to holders of geared shares at maturity.

payout for the geared ordinary shares is functionally the payout of a call option on the underlying portfolio with a strike price of 50. For a discussion of how prior claims create an option on repayment, see Brealey and Myers (2003, chap. 18).

The future unknown values of the underlying investment portfolio for each year, derived from the binomial model, are shown in Figure 5.2.[4] With an annualised volatility of 30%, after four years the terminal capital value can range from a maximum of 332.0 down to a minimum of 30.1. If the trust were a conventional trust with no prior claim, ordinary shareholders would simply receive the entire value of the trust at the end of year four. But with the prior claim, at maturity the ordinary shareholders in the geared trust receive the maximum of $(S_T - 50)$ or zero, where S_T is the portfolio value at maturity. The repayment of the prior claim in its entirety can only take place if the portfolio value is 50 or greater. If the terminal portfolio value is less than 50, the prior claim holders receive whatever value remains in the fund and the ordinary shareholders receive nothing.[5] This occurs in the lowest case of the example in which prior claim holders receive 30.1 rather than the promised 50.

The payouts from the fund at maturity for the five possible outcomes, given the simplifying assumptions, are shown in Table 5.2.

5.3   VALUING THE CLAIMS

If the prior claim is risk-free, its current value is simply the present value of the amount due at maturity using the risk-free discount rate. This gives a present value of 41.1. However, if the prior claim is subject to default, its present value will be less than this

---

[4] The model assumes that in any given year the value can only increase by a rate U or decrease by a rate D in a predetermined manner although at any point in time we do not know whether the value will increase or decrease at the next step. So, after four years there are five possible values for the portfolio. This is obviously unrealistic. More realism can be achieved by increasing the frequency of steps in the model (say, monthly).

[5] Limited liability protects the ordinary shareholders from having to make up the shortfall.

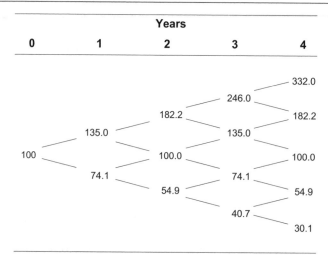

Figure 5.2 Future portfolio value. The initial portfolio value of 100 either increases at the rate U or decreases at the rate D. The values for U and D depend on the volatility (i.e., the uncertainty of the future value of the portfolio). Higher volatility means a wider spread of values in the future. U and D are computed as $U = \exp(\sigma\sqrt{\Delta t})$ and $D = \exp(-\sigma\sqrt{\Delta t})$, where σ is the volatility and Δt is the length of the step (in this case one year). With a volatility of 30% and one-year step, the value of U is 1.350 and D is 0.741. Note that if the volatility is only 20% then U is 1.221 and D is 0.819. The higher the volatility, the greater the range of possible future values.

default-free value reflecting the possibility that the promised payment may not be made in full. In option terms, the ability of a firm to default is a put option, which will be exercised if the value of the investment portfolio is below the redemption value of the prior claim. At any point in time the value of this risky prior claim will be:

$$\text{Value of risky prior claim} = \text{Value of risk-free prior claim}$$
$$- \text{Value of default option} \tag{5.1}$$

At the wind-up date the promised payment is 50 but in the lowest outcome the value of the portfolio for distribution is 30.1, meaning that prior claim holders will receive 19.9 less than their promised maturity payment. In the language of options, prior claim holders have written (sold) a put option to the ordinary shareholders. Using the simple option valuation approach discussed earlier, the value of this put option is shown in Figure 5.3. The present value of the option is 2.0 using the binomial option pricing model we have adopted.

Table 5.2 Payout at maturity to the split's securities based on fund performance

Portfolio value at maturity	Payout to	
	Prior claim	Geared shares
332.0	50	282.0
182.2	50	132.2
100.0	50	50.0
54.9	50	4.9
30.1	30.1	0.0

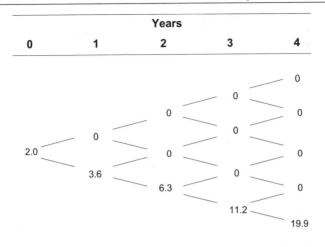

Figure 5.3 Value of default put. Working in a backward induction process starting with the known values at year four when the option is either exercised or abandoned, the present value of the option is then calculated step by step. To do so, we need the probabilities of the price changes. At any point prior to the maturity date, looking forward there are two possible outcomes for the portfolio value on which the put value depends. By assuming investors are indifferent to risk (in a process known as the risk-neutral valuation method), the expected return on the underlying portfolio is taken to be the risk-free rate (less any dividend yield). For year four, the lower two nodes are 54.9 and 30.1, respectively. Hence, the expected value of the portfolio is $p54.9 + (1 - p)30.1$, where p is the probability of a price rise. We also know the value of the portfolio at year three, which is 40.7, and the present value of the expected value at the end of year four for the two lowest nodes. Over the year, the portfolio is expected to grow at the risk-free rate less the portfolio dividend yield, so the expected value at the end of year four will be 40.3. We can now solve for the probability p, which is 0.41, and hence the probability of a decline is 0.59. In the same way, the expected value of the option at the given period at each of the intermediate points is simply the probability-weighted sum of the two possible future values. This expected value then has to be discounted to give the prior year value. For example the expected value at the end of year three is simply $(0.41 \times 0 + 0.59 \times 19.9) = 11.7$. Discounting this expected value at the risk-free rate of 5% p.a. gives the three-year value of 11.2. The other values are derived in the same way.

Subtracting the present value of the default option from the present value of the prior claim at the risk-free rate gives a value of 39.2. Given this value, the promised redemption yield on the prior claim subject to default is 6.30% p.a. – 1.30% pick-up over the risk-free rate. The calculations are given in Table 5.3. The value of 39.2 depends on the assumptions of the model. Factors that are not taken into account in the model but which might have a bearing on the required return to prior claim investors include:

- Liquidity risk, which reflects the ease with which investors can sell their claim at or close to its market value. For the investor planning to hold the prior claim to maturity, liquidity risk may not be an important factor.

- Restructuring risk. For instance, the risk that there may be unanticipated changes to the investment portfolio.

- Volatility risk. The prior claim includes an embedded default option and when volatility rises, the value of the option increases thereby reducing the value of the risky prior claim.

Table 5.3 Value of prior claim with default option

Value element	
Present value at risk-free interest rate	41.1
Less default option	2.0
Value of prior claim	39.2
Redemption yield	6.30%
Yield over risk-free interest rate	1.30%

Due to rounding, individual items may not add up to the total.

- Risk that the directors of the trust do not fulfil the promises made in the prospectus and change the trust's investment portfolio or investment strategy, or otherwise alter the risk characteristics of the trust.

- What might be called "risk risk" (namely, not understanding the risk/reward characteristics of the security or the trust structure). Such additional uncertainty will lower the price of the prior claim, suggesting an additional yield spread over and above that required to compensate investors for the risk of default.

Other things being equal, zero-dividend preference shares should offer a higher redemption yield than zero-coupon bonds for contractual reasons. Lenders will require the trust to agree borrowing covenants, which are designed to protect their interests. Zero-dividend preference shares do not generally have this protection and, in addition, will rank behind any borrowings.[6]

Having determined the present value of the prior claim, the value of the geared ordinary shares will be the residual amount of the trust's net assets less the present value of the future expenses. This value is made up of the present value of expected future dividends and the present value of the capital element. Using the same option valuation approach as applied to the default option, the present value of the capital element on the shares, treated as a call option, is 40.1 and the dividend element is 15.5.[7] Therefore, the current values of the claims in the trust are as shown in Table 5.4. Note that the aggregate value of the trust's claims is lower than 100, which is the market value of the portfolio. This is due to the deduction of the present value of future annual expenses.

The promised dividend yield on the ordinary shares is 4.5/55.6 = 0.0809 or 8.09%, much higher than the yield (after expenses) on the ungeared shares of 4.5/94.8 or 4.75%. Of course, this is not achieved without increasing the risk.[8]

---

[6] In theory the existence of bank debt which includes covenants that gives banks powers to control management action should increase protection for zeros, but this has not happened in practice.

[7] In the model, the value of the dividends is determined as a fixed percentage of the portfolio value. Hence, if the portfolio rises in year one, the dividends to be paid will be 4.5% of 135, or 6.1. Equally, if the portfolio value falls, the dividend will be worth only 3.3. Using the same valuation process as applied to the capital element of the geared shares, the present value of the expected dividend stream is 15.5. Since holders of the geared shares are entitled to this future income, this is reflected in their value.

[8] We can think of the total risk of the geared shares as being the risk in the investment portfolio (investment risk) and now an additional risk from partly financing the assets by using a prior claim which has precedence over the shares. This latter risk is known as financial risk. So, geared shares are subject to both investment risk and financial risk.

Table 5.4 The value of the claims of a trust with a prior claim

Claim element		Value	
Geared ordinary share		55.6	
Of which:	Capital element		40.0
	Dividend stream		15.6
Prior claim		39.2	
		94.8	

Conceptually, all corporate claims can be considered a combination of a safe investment with a guaranteed return and a risky element that will depend on the future performance of the company. Hence, the risky prior claim in the trust can be regarded as partly a safe investment (that which the holder is guaranteed to receive at maturity, whatever happens) and an exposure to the performance of the investment portfolio. The bear market from 2000 to 2003 demonstrated that, for some trusts, the prior claims had a very high exposure to the (negative) performance of the investment portfolio.

With an additional amount of prior claims, the geared ordinary shareholders will do very well when the portfolio value rises but also very badly if the opposite should happen. The additional gearing also raises the risks for prior claim holders as they have greater exposure to the performance of the portfolio. This is reflected in a higher redemption yield. With the maturity amount of the prior claim increased to 60, the present value of this prior claim without default risk is 49.3, the value of the default option is 5.0 and the value of the prior claim is therefore 44.3, implying a redemption yield of 7.88%.

Higher volatility means greater uncertainty concerning the future portfolio value and, hence, the range of possible future outcomes will widen. This can arise from increases in market volatility or changes in the fund's investment philosophy that increases the volatility of the portfolio (e.g., by investing in the more risky shares of other splits). The exposure of prior claim holders to the future performance of the investment portfolio increases. Since additional uncertainty about the future value of the investment portfolio means greater potential losses, higher volatility reduces the value of the prior claim. Figure 5.1 shows that the maximum payoff of the prior claim is capped. With higher volatility there is a greater risk that the portfolio value will end up below the amount required to meet the obligation on the prior claim. From the point of view of the ordinary shares, the downside is limited but the upside is unlimited, and an increase in volatility means greater upside potential.

An important result of this analysis is that additional volatility in the investment portfolio reduces the value of the risky prior claim and raises the value of the ordinary shares. This dependency between the assets and claims creates a conflict of interest between ordinary shareholders and prior claim holders.

5.4   VALUE OF SHARES IN A TRADITIONAL SPLIT

In a traditional split, the income shares are promised all of the distributed income and a fixed payout at maturity, with the residual value at maturity going to the capital shares.

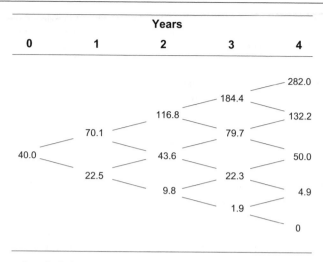

Figure 5.4 Value of capital shares as an option. For explanation see Figure 5.3.

If the fixed payout for the income shares is 50, the capital shares are functionally equivalent to a call option on the portfolio value with an exercise price of 50. At any maturity value for the fund below 50, the capital shares are worthless. At maturity values above 50, the capital shares are worth $(S_T - 50)$. As shown in Figure 5.4, using the contingent claim valuation approach the present value of the capital shares is 40.0. In the absence of any other liabilities, the income shares are functionally equivalent to holding a pure discount prior claim instrument and the dividend annuity stream. Hence, part of the income share's current value will be the present value of the capital repayment due at maturity while the balance will be the present value of the future dividend income stream. The value of the capital element for the income shares is 39.2 (that is the same as the prior claim security in Section 5.3) and, by subtraction, the future dividend element is worth 15.6. Note that there is the potential for dividing and recombining the capital and income elements through financial engineering.[9]

Given the above, the components of the split capital trust's market value can be broken down as shown in Table 5.5. It is worth noting that the running yield on the income shares is 8.21% rather than the 4.75% (after expenses) on the ungeared shares. The 3.46% yield pickup is the reward for surrendering any capital appreciation over and above the 50 due on redemption, if the portfolio performs well. The running yield is higher than the 8.09% on the geared ordinary shares discussed in Section 5.3. Note too that the income shares can repay less than the full redemption value and in that respect have the same embedded default option as the prior claim example in Section 5.3.

---

[9] For instance, it is possible to split the income and capital appreciation elements into their component parts. Separating off the underlying portfolio's income stream creates a pure income share (known as an annuity share). Hence, in this structure, holding a zero-dividend preference share and an annuity share creates an income share. Or an income share could be split to make an annuity share and a zero-dividend preference share.

Table 5.5 The value of the claims of a traditional split trust

Claim element		Value	
Capital shares		40.0	
Income shares		54.8	
Of which:	Capital element		39.2
	Dividend stream		15.6
		94.8	

5.5   TRADITIONAL SPLIT WITH PRIOR CLAIM

What if we combine a pure discount prior claim (e.g., zero-dividend preference shares) as in the earlier example of Section 5.3, with the traditional split capital structure of Section 5.4? In this case, assume the prior claim has the promised maturity value of 50, as in Section 5.3, but the ordinary shares are now divided into income shares with a redemption value of 25 and capital shares with a variable payoff at maturity equal to the maximum of $(S_T - 25 - 50)$ or zero. So, the capital shares rank last in repayment. This is a typical subordinated structure: first in priority is the prior claim, then the income shares and finally, if there is enough value left, the capital shareholders receive a payment. If the portfolio value is less than 75 on wind-up, the capital share investors receive nothing. At values above 50 but below 75, the income shares receive part of the promised redemption value and at values below 50 the prior claim holders receive less than their full entitlement. From the perspective of the capital shareholders, the required performance of the investment portfolio has been raised since, in order to receive any payment, they now require a value of more than 75 at maturity rather than the 50 in the earlier example.

Using the same valuation approach as described in the earlier sections, we can now determine the current values of the different elements. The prior claim will have the same value of 39.2 as in Section 5.3. Reworking the valuation of the geared ordinary shares from Section 5.4 using our contingent claim methodology, but now with the higher required payoff, gives a value for the capital shares of 27.5. The value of the income shares will be 28.1 of which, as before, 15.6 is the present value of the dividend stream. Since in this new example the entitlement of the income shares to capital has fallen, but they are still entitled to the dividends from the trust, the proportion of the value represented by the dividend stream has risen. With this more complicated trust structure, the current values of the different claims are as given in Table 5.6.

Engineering the claims in this way between prior claim, income shares and capital shares increases the headline-projected returns to the residual claim holders – but it does add to the risk. The income shares can be promised a dividend yield of 16.0% rather than 4.75% (after expenses), but income shareholders will only be paid their full entitlement if the trust has a value of 75 or more at maturity. A higher promised yield has meant taking on more risk to the capital element of the shares.

Table 5.6 The value of the claims of a traditional split trust with a prior claim

Claim element		Value	
Capital shares		27.5	
Income shares		28.1	
Of which:	Capital element		12.5
	Dividend stream		15.6
Prior claim		39.2	
		94.8	

5.6 EFFECT OF THE DIFFERENT STRUCTURES ON PROJECTED RETURNS

How might investors be attracted to these highly geared structures? Making an assumption about the expected growth in the investment portfolio – say, it is projected to grow at 15% per annum – the portfolio value after 4 years will be 174.9. Capital shareholders would be looking at a projected return of 38.1% p.a. from their current value under this assumption. The capital structure has geared their returns. With a constant dividend yield of 4.5% (after expenses) on the underlying portfolio, the effects of the different structures on the projected returns can be summarised as in Table 5.7. Note that were the expected return on the portfolio only 5% p.a., capital shareholders would only get a return of 14.0% p.a. If the portfolio declined by 5% p.a., capital shareholders would be facing a negative return of 30.4% p.a. and only get back 23.5% of the current value of their shares. So, assumptions about the return on the portfolio greatly affect the *ex ante* attraction of the capital shares.

By building in more risk, the structure can produce higher "headline" running yields and projected returns. For yield-hungry investors who perhaps do not understand or care about risk, this has obvious appeal.

Table 5.7 Effect of gearing and trust structure on projected returns assuming 15% p.a. increase in capital value and a constant 4.5% dividend yield (net of expenses)

Structure	Securities	Income yield (%)	Capital return (%)	Internal rate of return (%)
No gearing	Ordinary shares	4.7	16.6	21.9
Trust with prior claim (Section 5.3)	Prior claim		6.3	6.3
	Geared ordinary shares	8.2	22.4	31.0
Traditional split with prior claim (Section 5.5)	Prior claim		6.3	6.3
	Income shares	16.0	(2.9)	20.2
	Capital shares		38.1	38.1

5.7   VALUE SENSITIVITY

This section highlights the effect of changing the pricing variables on the value of a split's claims. Using the complex capital structure example from Section 5.5, which included a pure discount prior claim, income shares and capital shares, a simple sensitivity analysis of the key market variables is now undertaken. These variables are outside the control of investors and fund managers. The simple binomial pricing model for valuing the different components is used in the calculations. The results of this analysis are shown in Table 5.8. What the analysis clearly shows is that issuing multiple classes of securities by an investment trust creates the following behavioural characteristics:

- Additional volatility is good for the residual claim securities with their option-like characteristics. The opposite applies to fixed claims, such as debt, zero-dividend preference shares and income shares, which have implicitly embedded written options. The converse also applies. Reducing volatility benefits fixed claimants, but at the expense of residual claimants.
- All else equal, an increase in interest rates benefits residual claim securities, but adversely affects fixed rate claims. A fall in interest rates has the opposite effect.
- Enhancing the dividend yield on the portfolio benefits income claims at the expense of capital claims (including zeros and capital shares). Reducing the dividend yield benefits capital claims at the expense of income shares.
- A rise in the market value of the investment portfolio increases the value of the residual claims more than the prior claims, due to gearing effects. At the same time, the value of the default option is reduced, as now it is less likely to be exercised. Conversely, when the market value of the portfolio falls, these effects are reversed.

Table 5.8   Sensitivity analysis

Claim element		Current values	Volatility +1%	Risk-free rate +1%	Dividend yield +1%	Portfolio value +1%
Capital shares		27.5	28.1	28.8	25.3	28.2
Income shares		28.1	27.7	28.1	30.6	28.4
Of which:	Capital element	12.5	12.1	12.5	12.0	12.7
	Dividend stream	15.6	15.6	15.6	18.6	15.7
Prior claim		39.2	39.0	37.9	38.9	39.2
		94.8	94.8	94.8	94.8	95.8
Percentage change in claim						
Capital shares			2.0	4.8	−7.9	2.4
Income shares			−1.3	0.0	9.1	1.1
Of which:	Capital element		−2.9	0.0	−3.9	1.2
	Dividend stream		0.0	0.0	19.5	1.0
Prior claim			−0.4	−3.2	−0.5	0.1

5.8   CONCLUSION

Complex capital structures lead to difficulty in analysing the behaviour of the different securities issued by splits in response to changes in the value of the underlying investment portfolio. There are complex interactions between the investment portfolio value, its volatility, dividend yields, interest rates and the trust's financial structure which lead to value shifts between the different claims.

For ease of illustration, the prior claims that have been analysed in this chapter are pure discount securities, such as zero-dividend preference shares. However, there were often prior claims from bank debt as well and this further increased the risk of all lower ranking securities including any (geared) zero-dividend preference shares.

By introducing prior claims, the trust creates the opportunity to default on its obligations. The bear market that started in 2000 meant that a number of highly geared trusts were either wound up or forced to restructure as the consequences of their capital structures became manifest. There are costs attached to excessive gearing when trusts become financially distressed, and investors may be unsure as to whether the problem is due to bad luck or incompetent managers. The complicated non-linearity of the response to changes in underlying fundamentals, such as the level of the market, volatility, interest rates and dividend yields, further muddies the waters.

The financial structure of splits matters as it creates different types of securities whose expected return and risk is hard to understand *ex ante* without considerable analysis. Many of the more complex structures are difficult to evaluate, even for the expert, and the effect on their share classes and debt in response to changes in the performance of the investment portfolio is a trap for the unwary. Only the most sophisticated investors are equipped to understand fully the contingent nature of many of the securities issued by splits.

Were the complications of cross-holdings and financial engineering, coupled to gearing, a step too far for splits? The global bear market cruelly exposed the design weaknesses in some splits. In addition, as discussed elsewhere in this book, inadequate stress-testing contributed to the crisis. The sad fact is that the crisis and reputational damage to the sector have meant that some of the good features inherent in gearing and split capital structures have, like the baby, been thrown out with the dirty bath water.

5.9   REFERENCES

Brealey, R. and Myers, S.C. (2003) *Principles of Corporate Finance* (7th edn). McGraw-Hill/ Irwin, Burr Ridge, IL.

Cox, J., Ross, S. and Rubinstein, M. (1979) Option pricing, a simplified approach. *Journal of Financial Economics*, **7**, October, 229–264.

6

The Risks

JAMES CLUNIE

Is there any such thing as a safe investment? Is there any investment that is not a speculation?

Max Gunther

6.1 INTRODUCTION

Any observer of the splits market over the past few years will no doubt have read newspaper headlines such as "Splits probe widens in move to restore confidence" or "Demands for payouts over splits collapse". Quite probably, they will have formed their own idea of the risks involved in splits and arrived at the view that splits are indeed "risky" structures. But the reality is not so straightforward. This chapter will describe some of the risks that arise with splits, will explore some of the causes of these risks and will seek means of describing and measuring these risks. But, first, it is worth reviewing what is meant by risk. In his book *Against the Gods – the Remarkable Story of Risk*, Bernstein (1996) shows that risk can arise in many different forms in life as well as in financial markets. Taking account of this, I will attempt to consider split capital investment trust risks from as broad a perspective as possible, although the focus will be on investment risk. The possible financial gain or loss for shareholders in splits is important, but risk is borne by many other interested parties: the lenders of capital, the managers and directors of splits, regulators, politicians and financial intermediaries.

"Investment risk" is perhaps the most obvious risk that arises when considering splits, or indeed any investment product. It is the risk borne by investors in the product: the possibility of not achieving their expected outcomes. This risk can manifest itself in straightforward ways. For example, a zero-dividend preference share may not receive its full redemption value at wind-up, dashing the expectations of those investors who believed that the full amount would be paid. An investor might be disappointed at the cancellation or cutting of the dividend on an income share and experience one aspect of investment risk. Risk may be considered to work on the upside as well as the downside: the owner of the capital shares of a split may receive a surprisingly large windfall on wind-up, following strong performance of the underlying portfolio. A shareholder's expectations may be met exactly, but this does not, of course, mean that the shareholder bore no risk – there was always the *possibility* that those expectations would not be met. To think about risk only after an adverse outcome is to misunderstand risk. Implicit in each of the above descriptions is an understanding of the expectations of each shareholder. Shareholder expectations tend to develop from experience, through education and through receipt of corporate and media communications. Chapter 14 discusses in greater detail some of the ways in which expectations among shareholders developed and became established.

Banks experience investment risk on their loans to splits. Lenders have priority over shareholders with respect to income payments and the apportionment of assets on wind-up. So, loans have lower investment risk than shares in the same split, in exchange for lower expected return. Bank loans are also generally protected by covenants, which set rules on the ratio of assets to liabilities that must be maintained. These covenants allow the lender to foreclose or force restructuring of the split, if the ratio falls below a certain level (e.g., below 1.75 : 1). Despite this protection, bank loans to splits still bear investment risk. Although public information is not available, banks that lent to splits whose shares have been suspended or liquidated may not have achieved their expected outcomes. As an illustration, following the suspension of listing and appointment of receivers to Quarterly High Income Trust in August 2003, it was reported that "the banks will take a very substantial loss" on their loans (Cazenove & Co., 2003). In some academic studies, such as Gemmill (2002), bank loans are assumed to be "risk-free". But this is an assumption to simplify the mathematics of pricing, not a full reflection of reality.

6.2 MAJOR INFLUENCES ON RISK: ASSET ALLOCATION AND CAPITAL STRUCTURE

To understand investment risk for shareholders in splits, two factors are particularly important: first, the nature of the underlying portfolio of assets and, second, the capital structure of the split.

The portfolio of assets will have its own characteristics and its own risks. It is likely to be actively managed and thus changing over time. Shareholders will generally not know the full nature of the portfolio, but should have an approximate idea based on annual and interim reports produced by the company.[1] The success or otherwise of the underlying portfolio will strongly influence the ability of the split to meet income distribution targets over its life and its ability to return capital to shareholders at wind-up. The universe of split capital investment trusts displays huge variety in asset allocation and capital structure. In terms of asset allocation, for example, investors can choose splits comprising: a global balanced portfolio (e.g., Murray Global Return); UK corporate bonds and equity (e.g., Jove); or US private equity (e.g., JZ Equity Partners). Each asset category bears a different set of risks, and the behaviour of the assets of different splits will be quite different at times. All else being equal, a well-diversified set of investments will have a lower volatility of returns than a poorly diversified set. Of course, a specialised portfolio of European technology companies might have higher volatility than a

---

[1] The new Listing Rules which came into force on 1 November 2003 require listed investment companies to disclose on a monthly basis their holdings in other listed companies which do not have a stated investment policy of investing no more than 15% of their assets in other listed investment companies. They also require disclosure on a quarterly basis of at least the ten largest investments plus other investments greater than 5% of their investment portfolio. See Chapter 9 for further details of these rules.

split containing, say, a portfolio of global equities. But the former may play a valuable role as part of an investor's overall, diversified portfolio. Adding a portfolio with high volatility but low correlation to a client's existing portfolio might serve to reduce the volatility of the overall portfolio.

In studying the diversification impact of a split on an existing portfolio, the class of share under consideration is of vital importance. If one simultaneously buys all the share classes of a split in the appropriate proportion, or buys "package units" if they exist, the behaviour of the split investment will resemble that of the split's underlying net assets. But zeros or capital shares, say, in a split will have very different characteristics from the underlying asset portfolio. So, the effect of adding to an existing portfolio needs to be studied separately for each particular class of share.

The capital structure of the split determines the allocation of assets at wind-up. Capital structure also influences the income generation required from the underlying assets to service loans or pay dividends to income-bearing shares during the life of the trust. A higher proportion of bank debt or loan stock in a split, other things equal, always leads to greater gearing in a class of shares to the returns produced by the portfolio of assets. This increased "financial risk" manifests itself in the greater volatility of the net asset value (NAV) of each class of share. The presence of zeros in the capital structure creates capital gearing for the other lower ranked classes of share – zeros have a maximum redemption value and increase the gearing of capital shares or income & residual capital shares. The complexity of some capital structures can make it difficult for investors to evaluate the risks inherent in each class of share.

A risk-averse investor would generally seek to invest in a split with a high-quality, diversified portfolio of assets and low gearing. A risk-seeking investor would seek a more concentrated or volatile portfolio of assets, and greater gearing. The variety of asset portfolios and capital structures ensures that a wide range of choices exists for investors. The suggestion that "all splits are risky" is a myth. Splits and their securities may be low risk or high risk, depending on the underlying asset portfolio, capital structure and the class of share being examined.

Covenants on bank loans represent another important factor for shareholders to consider. By offering a degree of protection to the lender, covenants impose an additional risk to shareholders. If, after a fall in the ratio of assets to liabilities, a loan covenant is breached and the lender requires the sale of assets to repay or partly repay the loan, the lender's risk is reduced. But certain classes of shareholder are disadvantaged as a result. Capital shareholders, relying on the possibility of large capital gains from the portfolio of assets to generate value for their class of shares, normally lose upside potential when assets are sold to reduce borrowings. The mere existence of restrictive loan covenants creates the possibility of an adverse set of circumstances for capital shareholders. The more restrictive the loan covenant, the greater the risk to capital shareholders. At times of severe stress for a split (say, a collapse in the value of the underlying assets) the exercise by lenders of the rights contained in loan covenants can create "knock-out" events, such as the complete sale of assets. Capital shares might never recover from this type of event.

Cross-shareholdings, whereby splits invest part of their assets in each other's shares in a network of cross-ownership, are difficult to interpret with respect to risk. Does the existence of cross-shareholdings raise or lower risk, or leave it unaffected? By studying simplified models of universes containing just two splits and applying a "Value at

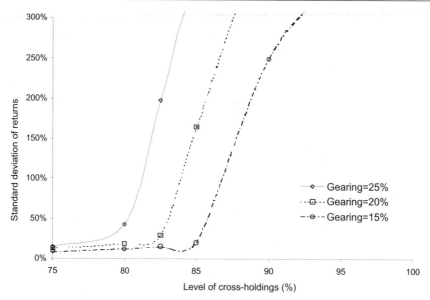

Figure 6.1   Portfolio volatility at different levels of gearing and cross-holdings.

Risk"-type analysis, one can show that high levels of cross-holdings generally raise the value at risk of a split. They also reduce the transparency and ease of understanding of risks within a split. The interaction of debt and cross-holdings has a particularly striking effect on the volatility of returns. For a given structure, increasing gearing and cross-holdings beyond certain levels can produce massive increases in volatility. Figure 6.1 is based on a model (Clunie and Lindemann, 2004) that considers a universe of just two investment trusts, each invested partly in the other. The proportion of cross-ownership is equal in both trusts and is shown on the horizontal axis. Both trusts are equally geared with bank debt. Three different gearing levels[2] have been chosen – each level being shown by a separate graph line, according to the legend. The vertical axis records the standard deviation of returns for the trust, based on Monte Carlo simulation (see Section 6.10) over a period of one year. It can be seen that up to some level of cross-holdings, there is relatively stable behaviour in that the standard deviation of returns is small; but, increasing the level of cross-holdings beyond a certain point results in a sharp increase in the standard deviation of returns. This level of cross-holdings can be thought of as a "tipping point".

Does the structure of expenses have a role to play in the risk assessment of splits? Expenses, which include interest costs, administration and management costs, directors' fees and any professional fees incurred by the split can be either proportional to gross assets, or partially fixed. They will be charged to the revenue account or the capital account according to a ratio set out in the listing particulars.[3] After periods when

---

[2] Gearing is defined as the ratio of gross assets to the assets attributable to shareholders.

[3] The Statement of Recommended Practice governing allocation of expenses sets out the principle that management and interest expenses should be allocated to the revenue account or to the capital account according to the proportion of expected return arising from capital gains or income. For example, if 60% of total return is expected to arise from capital gains (and thus 40% is expected to arise from dividends and interest), 60% of management and interest expenses should be allocated to the capital account and 40% allocated to the revenue account. Other (non-management) expenses are charged in most cases to the revenue account.

portfolio assets have fallen significantly, expenses that are expressed as a percentage of gross assets can become excessive relative to net assets and can therefore impose a significant burden on certain classes of share. Thus, the expense structure must also be considered in the risk assessment of splits.

Splits are also exposed to many of the risks to which traditional investment products are exposed. The degree of general economic confidence and the stability of global political structures are relevant risk factors. The level of inflation, interest rates and economic growth, and investors' expectations of them, also influence splits, but their influences are modified according to the capital structure of the split.

6.3   RISK FOR DIFFERENT SHARE CLASSES

Interest-rate changes can have a profound influence on the value of investment port-folios, be they bonds, equities, property or alternatives. For splits, changes in interest rates will not only influence the value of the asset portfolio, they will influence each of the different classes of share in a different way. Falling interest rates normally have a positive effect on the value of any zeros in a split. This is because the gross redemption yield on a zero would look more attractive as interest rates fall (all else being equal), leading investors to bid up the price of the zero until it reflected the new interest-rate environment. Other classes would be influenced according to their characteristics and will reflect interaction between falling interest rates, the value and volatility of the asset portfolio and its ability to generate income over the life of the fund.

Unexpected inflation (or deflation) will also influence each class of share in a different manner. Unexpected inflation will erode the real value of the final redemption payment for a zero. Conversely, unexpected deflation would, in theory, boost the real value of the redemption payment. However, deflation could hurt the value of the underlying portfolio, if invested in equities, and so could increase the risk of the redemption payment not being met in full. For capital shares, unexpected inflation might boost their nominal value if the underlying portfolio is invested in assets generating a real return. For income shares, unexpected inflation will influence the portfolio in two contrasting ways: it might lead to higher dividend payments, but the real value of any fixed redemption payment would be eroded.

Agency risk arises in investment products for which investment management com-panies provide services to investors in exchange for a fee. The investment management company is contracted to work on the clients' behalf and in the clients' best interests. However, a desire to maximise the management companies' revenues or profitability can conflict with this duty. This agency risk exists for splits, as for other investment products. But, in addition, the existence of more than one class of share in a split can introduce different objectives for each class of shareholder. The owners of any capital shares would seek an aggressive approach to the management of the asset portfolio, whereas the owners of zeros would generally prefer a more temperate investment approach – each is seeking to maximise their own utility. The directors must follow the approach and rules described to shareholders in the listing particulars and those set out in the Articles of Association. Generally, the Board is performing a "juggling act" between the classes – seeking fair treatment for all classes, while perhaps being mindful of the agency risks that arise in any traditional investment product managed on behalf of clients.

Different classes of share have different claims on the assets of a split. The "hierarchy" of claims provides vital information on the risks of each class. Bank loans or other loan capital have first claim on the assets at wind-up, giving them a higher probability of being repaid than is the case for any class of share in the same split. Additionally, the interest charge on loans has priority over distributions to holders of income-bearing shares in the split.

Holders of zeros receive no income during the life of the trust, but at wind-up they receive a sum of money up to the final redemption value of the zero, if assets are available after repaying prior ranking capital. As they receive no income during the life of the split, holders of zeros face no reinvestment risk.[4] However, the "duration"[5] of the zero is higher than would be the case for an instrument paying out income to shareholders. Greater duration means greater sensitivity to changes in interest rates.

Income shares expect to receive a large proportion of the income generated by the asset portfolio (after a proportion of management costs and interest payments have been taken to the revenue account). In receiving income, shareholders face the opposite situation to the one affecting zeros: duration is shortened but reinvestment risk increased. They face the possibility of cuts (or increases) to their income stream, and they have a lower priority than zeros to the assets at wind-up if there is a terminal asset value to be paid.

Capital shareholders have no rights to income and have the lowest priority to the assets of the split on wind-up. They are also geared to changes in the gross assets of the trust. Most capital shares could be described as "speculative".

Income & residual capital shares combine the features of income shares and capital shares described above.

6.4   INCREASING RISKS AND THE ONSET OF THE SPLITS CRISIS

How did the various investment risks come together for shareholders in splits, so as to cause a crisis in the sector? Was the sharp fall in global equity markets the sole cause of the collapse of those splits that invested in equities?

As interest rates fell significantly over the second half of the 1990s, the "search for yield" among private investors provided an opportunity for financial services companies to issue innovative income products (see Adams, 2003). In satisfying this demand for yield, however, the product providers used various devices that led to the creation of complicated, unstable trust structures. These devices included substantial levels of bank debt financing and investment in the income-bearing shares of other splits. As was shown in Figure 6.1, bank debt and cross-holdings can have a surprising interaction effect under certain conditions. During difficult market conditions, such as

---

[4] Reinvestment risk arises when the investor must reinvest any income received, and so faces the risk that interest rates may have changed since purchasing the original investment.

[5] "Duration" is the weighted average of times to the cash flows from the security, where the weights are equal to the present values of the cash flows.

during 2000–02, these unstable structures behaved in a highly volatile fashion. The inability to de-gear as markets fell, because of fixed term bank debt and illiquid assets, exaggerated the fall. The Financial Services Authority (FSA), in its Consultation Paper 164, concluded that a combination of gearing and cross-holdings caused more extreme losses for investors in splits during falling markets than for most other investment products.

6.5 LIQUIDITY RISK

As equity markets continued to fall in 2001 and 2002, a number of investment managers of splits sought to reduce their holdings in the income shares of other splits. Also, in some cases, lenders required the sale of assets to meet loan covenants, leading to further selling pressure on income shares. However, liquidity proved ephemeral, and many shares in splits became difficult to sell in size. During the crisis, it was common for some shares to experience no trading whatsoever over several days. For example, Exeter Equity Growth & Income Fund's ordinary shares experienced no trading on 51 days out of 66 during the fourth quarter of 2001, as its share price fell from 65 pence to 52.5 pence (source: Datastream). In fact, for some stocks there was no trading for several months. For example, Technology & Income Trust Ltd 9% Convertible Unsecured Loan Stock 31/07/09 experienced no trading for several months in early to mid-2002, even as its fair value declined considerably. This liquidity problem may well have been compounded by the difficulty in understanding the risks of those splits with high levels of cross-holdings. If an asset has just fallen sharply in value, might it fall further in future? Why buy such an asset, when it is difficult to understand the true risks? The growing media attention to the splits crisis in 2002 also made it difficult for investment committees to purchase shares in splits. How could one justify buying shares in such a "tainted" sector?

The Faculty and Institute of Actuaries (FIA, 2003), in their response to Consultation Paper 164, argued that the primary cause of the splits crisis was the poor liquidity that existed in splits, combined with a falling market. The prolonged fall in the equity market led to breaches in some loan covenants, which in turn often led to the forced selling of splits. In the absence of sufficient liquidity, this led to the collapse of more splits. Some disagree with this view, however, arguing that the absence of liquidity was because the quoted prices on some splits were artificially high. If more realistic prices had been quoted, some loan covenants would have been breached earlier, at a time when other assets could have been sold at higher prices.

6.6 REPUTATIONAL RISK

Even more risks became apparent as the crisis unfurled. The providers of some of the more aggressive splits had created contingent liabilities in establishing such products: the reputation of many of the product providers suffered and some investors were demanding compensation. The Treasury Select Committee investigation compounded the damage to hard-earned corporate reputations. The personal reputations of some managers and directors of splits, and the reputation of the splits sector, the wider investment trust sector, the UK financial services sector and the FSA were all questioned at various stages by commentators (including the press), analysts and market participants.

Damage to a brand is difficult to measure. The decline in the share prices of quoted firms involved in the splits business provides some idea of the extent of the brand damage, but the general fall in equity markets during 2000–03 also strongly affected share prices. Staff retention at the most affected firms might also have been influenced by fear of reputational risk. Chapter 13 discusses reputational risk in greater detail.

6.7 TRADITIONAL RISK ASSESSMENT MEASURES

A number of specialised risk assessment statistics, tailored to each class of share, can be used in analysing splits. Consider four classes of shares that are commonly found in splits: zeros, income & residual capital shares, income shares and capital shares. For each of these classes, the statistics below are produced routinely by stockbrokers and other financial practitioners. One of the most comprehensive and timely sources of such data is the "Splitsonline" site (*www.splitsonline.co.uk*) from Fundamental Data Ltd, which provides daily analysis of split capital investment trusts.

For zeros, the main statistics used by practitioners to assess risk are asset cover, hurdle rate and gross redemption yield. *Asset cover* (also known as *final asset cover* or just *cover*) is the ratio of gross assets less any prior ranking capital, to the assets required to pay the predetermined redemption amount of the zeros at the redemption date. If there are no cross-holdings and no prior ranking capital it gives a rough indication of the risk of the zero shareholders not receiving their full entitlement at redemption but does not take the term to redemption into account. It can be defined in several ways. Some analysts, for example, deduct future annual costs charged to capital (management fees, interest charges) in arriving at the total assets figure.

Hurdle rate (also known as *fulcrum point*, *growth to cover* or *final value hurdle rate*) is the required annual growth rate of gross assets to pay the full redemption amount of zeros. A negative hurdle rate indicates that gross assets could fall each year by the rate indicated and still be sufficient to repay the zeros in full. Hurdle rates generally take future annual costs charged to capital into account. A variation on hurdle rate is *wipe-out rate* which measures the annualised rate of decrease in gross assets that would just lead to no capital payment (or "wipe-out") on wind-up. This provides a more useful guide to downside risk. *Current price hurdle rate* and *initial price hurdle rate* are other such variations.

Gross redemption yield (GRY) of a zero is the internal rate of return, before any tax, based on the assumption that it is held to redemption and redeemed in full. The GRY can be compared with that of a British government bond ("gilt") of similar duration. Thus, *points over gilt GRY* gives a measure of the risk premium priced into a zero.[6] *GRY no growth* measures the GRY of a zero on the assumption that the capital value of the underlying gross assets remains unchanged between the present time and wind-up.

---

[6] There is a slight tax element as well as a risk premium in the yield differential. The majority of investors in zeros are, directly or indirectly, private investors who receive tax-free returns from zeros, because the returns are treated as capital gains that can be offset against the investor's annual CGT exemption allowance. The majority of gilts are held by institutions and taxed on a different basis, so the yield differential understates the perceived risk of zeros.

Plots of GRY or GRY no growth against cover or hurdle rate attempt to compare possible returns for zeros against some measure of risk.

Key statistics for income shares are asset cover, hurdle rate, yield on the portfolio and sources of income. The asset cover calculation is based on an income share's full redemption value. Wipe-out rate is also commonly used for income shares. *Net redemption yield* (NRY), often used in conjunction with various assumed annual rates of growth of dividends paid to the income shares and growth of gross assets, measures the annualised return to income shareholders net of income tax. The range of NRYs for different assumed rates of growth can be useful in risk assessment.

Hurdle rate, wipe-out rate and NRY are also used for income & residual capital shares. Additionally, gearing is used as a risk measure. It may be defined as the ratio of gross assets to the assets attributable to income & residual capital shareholders.

Hurdle rate, wipe-out rate and gearing are used as risk measures for capital shares, as with income & residual capital shares. Discount to NAV is a popular statistic for capital shares. However, if there are zeros in issue, the normal practice of "stepping up" the zeros by a predetermined periodic amount, instead of taking the full redemption value, complicates measurement of the net asset value of capital shares. As a result, Newlands (2000) describes quoted discount to NAV figures for capital shares as virtually meaningless.

Standard deviation has not proved a popular risk statistic for shares within splits. As described in Chapter 5, each class of share within a split has some form of contingent claim. This gives each class an asymmetric distribution of possible returns. The use of symmetric statistics (such as standard deviation) to describe such behaviour is generally inappropriate.

6.8   TRADITIONAL RISK ASSESSMENT MEASURES BECAME MISLEADING

Traditional risk assessment measures for more complicated splits, such as the aggressively structured splits issued in the late 1990s and beyond, must not be used in isolation. Other factors, such as the quality of the underlying portfolio of assets, capital structure, sources of income, expense structure, portfolio volatility and, critically, the amount of bank debt and details of bank covenants, must be considered, if such information is available or can be obtained.

Hurdle rates for shares in the aggressively structured splits appeared deceptively easy to achieve, for the following reasons:

- Hurdle rates are based on growth of the whole underlying portfolio, ignoring the fact that a substantial part of the portfolio may not be held in growth assets and thus could not possibly be expected to grow at anything like the projected rate of growth of the growth assets.

- Investors' expectations of returns from equities had been derived from the bull market of the previous quarter of a century.

- Many investors were unaware that the expected nominal return on equities will be low in an environment of low inflation and low interest rates. If there were holdings

Table 6.1 Characteristics of two hypothetical splits

	Ungeared trust	Geared trust
Total assets	100	100
Debt	0	50
Final zero repayment	80	30
Cover*	1.25	1.67
Hurdle rate (%)	−10.56	−10.56
Wipe-out rate (%)	−100.00	−29.29

*Cover is here defined as total assets minus debt, all divided by final zero repayment.

in the high-yielding shares of other splits, with dividend yield exceeding expected total return, it was in fact reasonable to expect erosion in their capital value.

- Any holdings in high-yielding bonds could suffer defaults and capital loss.

The last two reasons also make the asset cover statistic misleading. This statistic is even more misleading if the split's costs (both interest and fees) up to maturity are not deducted from gross assets.

It is possible to find two zeros with similar hurdle rates and cover but with very different risk profiles. Table 6.1 and the corresponding Figure 6.2 present the hypothetical case of a geared zero with equal hurdle rate and superior cover to an ungeared zero, but with greater sensitivity to large falls in the underlying asset portfolio.

Table 6.1 is based on the comparison of the zeros of a hypothetical geared trust with a hypothetical ungeared trust. Assume that both zeros have two years until redemption, and that interest and management fees are charged to the revenue account. The underlying portfolios of investments are identical.

Both zeros have the same hurdle rate, and the geared trust has a higher cover.

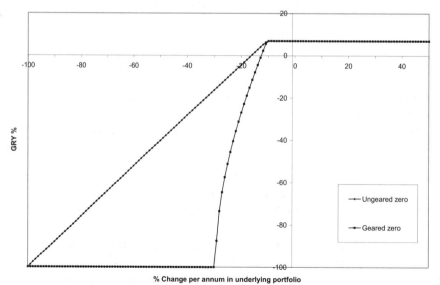

Figure 6.2 Sensitivity of a geared and an ungeared zero to changes in the underlying portfolio.

However, this does not mean that the geared zero is less risky than the ungeared zero. The geared zero has greater sensitivity to large falls in the underlying portfolio. Assuming both zeros trade on a gross redemption yield of 7%, Figure 6.2 shows how sensitive each zero is to changes in the underlying portfolio.

6.9 IMPROVEMENTS TO TRADITIONAL STATISTICS

Traditional risk measures can sometimes be dangerously misleading. However, there are ways in which they can be made more useful.

Total return to cover could be used instead of hurdle rate. It represents the total return (i.e., capital gain plus dividend yield) required on the underlying portfolio of assets for the zero to reach a cover of 1. The total return to cover can be compared with the expected return on the total underlying portfolio, to gauge whether or not the full redemption payment of the zero or the income share is realistic. Another variation on hurdle rate would be to measure the hurdle rate (or total return to cover) based only on that part of the underlying portfolio invested in growth assets. This would present a more realistic picture of the growth required on the growth assets if a significant proportion of the underlying assets is held to generate income.

As cross-holdings in other splits can increase risk, classifications of trusts by percentage of gross assets held in splits and high-yield funds have been launched. Further refinements include rating systems based on both cross-holdings and proportion of gross assets represented by debt (e.g., ABN Amro rating system). These systems are generally crude and could be improved by analysing the quality of the underlying securities held, rather than treating all investments in splits and high-yield funds as equally risky. These ratings also refer to splits in their entirety rather than classes of shares within a split.

A more developed approach (Merrill Lynch, 1999) to describing risk for a zero is to assign "credit ratings" to zeros, as with bonds. This involves estimating the probability of default and the returns expected on default. Comparing these numbers with the historical experience of a range of bonds with different credit ratings, a credit rating can be assigned to the zeros. Finally, an appropriate credit spread can be determined for each rating by reference to the bond market.[7] The anticipated spread is then compared with the "points over gilt GRY" (Section 6.7) to see if risk is appropriately priced. This approach takes account of the probability of default, so is generally more useful than traditional risk assessment statistics. It can also be used to explain the zero market's behaviour at times when bond market credit spreads widen. An example of this was the widening of zeros' credit spreads during the 1998 Russian bond default/Long Term Capital Management crisis.

Sensitivity analysis is a risk assessment technique which, when applied to splits, studies the impact of changes to one variable (such as annual expenses) on the outcome for each class of shareholder. Greater use of sensitivity analysis, showing GRY or NRY for various negative and positive total return scenarios for the underlying portfolio of assets (e.g., −10% p.a., −5% p.a., ..., +15% return, +20% p.a.) would aid understanding of the risks involved for a particular class of share. It is

---

[7] The tax element in the yield differential should also be taken into account.

important that a number of negative market scenarios are included in any such analysis. A plot of GRY (% p.a.) against percentage change (p.a.) in the underlying portfolio, as shown in Figure 6.2, would also aid in the assessment of risk for a class of share. There are, however, severe limitations to the use of sensitivity analysis for splits. Any covenant breach might lead to a forced portfolio restructuring. Thus, the use of steady changes in assets in risk models fails to take account of path dependence[8] in the life of the split. Alternative risk analysis techniques must be used to cope with this problem; this is addressed in Section 6.10.

6.10 USING MONTE CARLO SIMULATION OUTCOMES TO ILLUSTRATE RISK

Monte Carlo simulation is a technique that can be applied to splits to gain a better understanding of the risks involved for shareholders and, by implication, for product providers and financial advisers (Barrie & Hibbert Ltd, 2003). This technique entails running computer simulations of what might happen to the underlying assets in the future, while taking account of interest payments, dividend distributions and loan covenants. Thousands of simulations are generally performed. Assuming a knowledge of the portfolio of assets and the capital structure of the split, Monte Carlo simulation requires the creation of a set of rules for generating asset returns and paying liabilities over the various time periods to be modelled. A stochastic model[9] for equity returns, interest rates and credit transitions is used to derive the distribution of returns on each of the trust's asset classes. Expenses, interest charges, dividends and taxes are taken into account, and banking covenants are checked at the end of each time period (and if breached, the portfolio is reallocated according to a specified covenant breach rule). On wind-up of the trust, capital distributions are made to each class of share according to predetermined rules. Section 7.5 discusses Monte Carlo simulation further.

Given a series of simulations, it is possible to construct a cumulative probability distribution curve for gross assets at the wind-up date. A chart could also be constructed to show the mean path and, say, the 5th and 95th percentile of paths for gross assets at each stage in the simulation process. To understand better the risks associated with each class of share, separate "payoff cumulative probability charts" can be created for each class of share. Figure 6.3 shows one such chart for a zero, using an asset-generating model and the capital structure of a theoretical split. The horizontal axis shows the payoff (in £) for the shares at wind-up. The vertical axis shows the cumulative probability of such a payoff. Based on the outcomes from a series of simulations, the chart thus shows the probability that the payoff is equal to or less than any given value on the horizontal axis.

"Return probability histograms", such as that shown in Figure 6.4 for the income share of a theoretical split, can illustrate the risk/return profiles for a class of shares. The annualised returns up to the wind-up date for a class of share are based on the

---

[8] "Path dependence" refers to the fact that certain events may be contingent on previous events or "paths". For example, a drop in the ratio of assets to liabilities in a portfolio might cause a loan covenant to be breached, leading directly to a portfolio restructuring.
[9] A stochastic process is any price or rate series that varies over time in an unpredictable way.

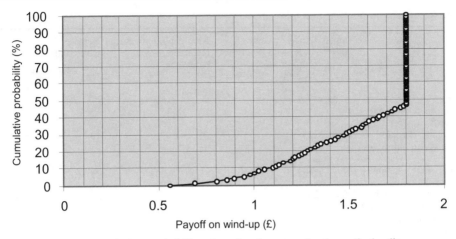

Figure 6.3 Payoff cumulative probability chart for the zero of a theoretical split.

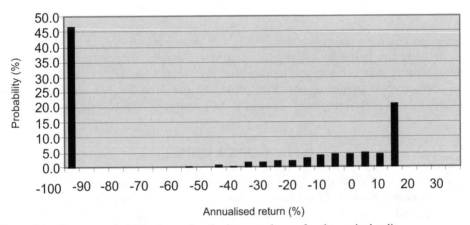

Figure 6.4 Return probability figure for the income share of a theoretical split.

outcome of a series of simulations. The probability associated with each range of returns is calculated as the proportion of simulation returns that fell within that range.

It is possible to study the sensitivity of the output to different assumptions in the asset return-generating model or to changes in the trust's structure. This helps in understanding the risks involved in the securities of existing splits and may be useful in the design of new splits. Scenario analysis, in which changes to more than one variable at a time are considered, can also be applied. Table 6.2 illustrates some of the ways in which scenario analysis can be applied using Monte Carlo simulation techniques for the theoretical split used in the above analysis. Note that if we were considering a "fund of funds" the analysis would be far more difficult.

The technique used in Table 6.2 could be useful in creating a suitable capital structure at launch, or in setting asset allocation at any stage in the split's life. For example, the probability of the zero paying out its full redemption value could be set at a certain value (e.g., 95%), or the probability of capital shareholders receiving nothing at

Table 6.2   Scenario analysis example

	Initial state	Replace income shares with bonds; set equity portfolio dividend yield to 4% from 3.5%	Alter capital structure; replace zeros with bank loan	Replace £10m of equities with bonds
Capital share wipe-out probability (%)	80	83	77	85
Probability of capital gain on capital shares (%)	17	15	20	13
Income share wipe-out probability (%)	47	44	41	44
Probability of capital gain on income shares from current share price (%)	30	28	33	25
Probability that zero pays out full redemption value (%)	53	56	58	55

redemption could be set at less than 50%. The investment risk associated with each class of share can be set by the product provider, directors or portfolio manager. By communicating such information to potential investors, while explaining the assumptions used in their modelling, product providers and financial advisers can help to manage client expectations and thus reduce the possibility of future disappointment.

6.11   CONCLUSION

The key features of splits that determine risk are the nature of the underlying portfolio and the capital structure. Other features, such as cross holdings, loan covenants and expense structure, also play an important role. However, the complex interaction of these features makes risk assessment for splits difficult. Traditional risk statistics for splits, such as cover and hurdle rates, are often inadequate in assessing the risks. A number of improvements can be made to traditional statistics and, when combined with sensitivity analysis, these provide a better description of risk. However, Monte Carlo simulation, which can take account of all the features of a split simultaneously, with the possible exception of cross-holdings, provides a superior tool. The use of simple histograms or cumulative probability charts to show the probability of certain events can be used to display the output from such simulations. Scenario analysis can be combined with Monte Carlo simulation as a technique to assist in designing new splits and describing risk to investors.

6.12   REFERENCES

Adams, A.T. (2003) *The Split Capital Investment Trust Crisis: Underlying Reasons and Historical Developments* (Third report of session 2002–03, volume II, appendix 3, Ev. 239–247). House of Commons Treasury Committee, London.

Barrie & Hibbert Ltd (2003) *Split Capital Investment Trust Monte Carlo Simulation Model.* Barrie & Hibbert, Edinburgh.

Bernstein, P.L. (1996) *Against the Gods – the Remarkable Story of Risk.* John Wiley & Sons, Chichester, UK.

Cazenove & Co. (2003) *Daily Report* (6 August). Cazenove & Co., London.

Clunie, J. and Lindemann, J. (2004) *Modelling Split Capital Trust Cross-holdings* (Working Paper 04.01). Centre for Financial Markets Research, University of Edinburgh.

Gemmill, G. (2002) *Testing Merton's Model for Credit Spreads on Zero-Coupon Bonds.* Cass Business School, London.

FIA (2003) *Response to CP 164.* Faculty & Institute of Actuaries, London.

FSA (2003) *Consultation Paper 164* (January). Financial Services Authority, London.

Merrill Lynch (1999) *Zero Dividend Preference Shares – What Are They Worth?* Merrill Lynch, London.

Newlands, J. (2000) *Split Capital and Highly Geared Investment Trusts.* Williams de Broë, London.

7

Valuing the Shares

JAMES CLUNIE

A commodity is only worth what another man will give for it.

Len Deighton

7.1 INTRODUCTION

The listing particulars for Real Estate Opportunities Limited state that: "An investment in the Company is suitable only for financially sophisticated investors who are capable of evaluating the risks and merits of such investment. . . ." This statement is also made in the listing particulars of a number of other splits. In Chapter 6 we considered some of the risks associated with splits. In this chapter we look at the techniques available for evaluating whether or not a share price is merited on fundamental grounds.

As explained in Chapter 5, shares in a split have "option-like" behaviour and so, in general, an option valuation model should be used to value them. There are three main approaches. Chapter 5 introduced the binomial model (sometimes known as the tree or lattice approach). In this chapter, I first discuss a second technique, closed-form option pricing. I then show how Monte Carlo simulation, a third technique, can be used to cope with some of the problems that limit the effectiveness of the closed-form option-pricing model. I also show how complexity in both the capital structure and the asset portfolio, combined with special features, such as loan covenants and cross-holdings, can complicate the valuation process considerably.

7.2 BACKGROUND TO VALUING SPLITS USING CLOSED-FORM OPTION PRICING

Investment vehicles similar to splits have existed from time to time in other countries. In the USA for example, "Dual-Purpose Funds" (first created in 1967) and "Primes and Scores" (first created in 1983) resemble traditional splits. In both cases, however, changes to the US tax code precipitated the demise of the product over time. Academic research relating to these two product types provides a useful starting point in valuing each class of share in a split. Although the capital structures of many splits are more complicated than those of Dual-Purpose Funds, or of Primes and Scores, the principles applied in valuing them remain valid.

In a Dual-Purpose Fund, there are two classes of share with claims on the same underlying portfolio. First, there are income shares, which have the right to any income that the fund may earn, subject to a minimum cumulative dividend, and are redeemable at a set price at the maturity of the fund. Second, there are capital shares, which pay no dividends and are redeemable at the residual value of the fund at maturity, after redemption of the income shares. Dual-Purpose Funds are thus similar to UK "traditional splits".

In a study of US Dual-Purpose Funds, Ingersoll (1976) creates a framework that can be used for pricing the components of UK split capital investment trusts. To derive an appropriate option-pricing model, he makes a number of assumptions. He assumes that capital markets are perfect. Thus, there are no differential taxes or transaction costs; assets are perfectly divisible; investors act as price takers; there is unlimited borrowing or lending at the risk-free rate of interest; there are no restrictions on short selling; and trading takes place continuously in time. These assumptions might appear unrealistic to a practitioner, but they are needed to simplify the mathematics of valuation, allowing the analyst to get started with a basic valuation technique. Ingersoll then applies research by Merton (1973, 1974) to derive pricing functions for both the capital shares and the income shares. Income shares are considered to consist of two separable claims: one on the dividend stream, the other on the final redemption payout. Capital shares are akin to call options on the underlying assets of the fund.

Drawing on this research, Gemmill (2002) shows that a zero-dividend preference share (zero) within a UK split may be considered equal in value to the present value of a zero-coupon risk-free bond less the value of a put option on the trust's gross assets. The bond has a maturity price equal to the final redemption value of the zero. The exercise price of the put equals the sum of the payments due at maturity on prior charges (such as bank debt) plus the final redemption value of the zero. Prior charges are assumed to be risk-free – this is an extreme assumption, as shown in Chapter 6, but one that simplifies the process. It is possible to change this assumption and undertake a more detailed analysis at a later stage. The payoff chart for a zero is shown in Figure 7.1.

To determine the price at which the zero should trade, the price of the put option must be calculated. A traditional means of doing this is to apply the Black–Scholes (1973) model. In using the model, six separate inputs must either be calculated,

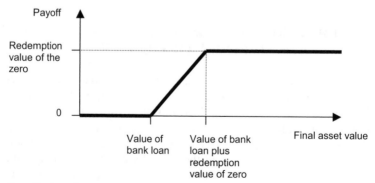

Figure 7.1 Payoff chart for a zero.

observed or estimated. Three of these are straightforward: time to redemption, redemption value of the zero and the risk-free interest rate. Three further inputs, however, present a problem. The value, volatility and income yield of the underlying gross assets are generally unknown. The value of the underlying gross assets could be estimated by taking the published net asset value (NAV) figure and adjusting for prior charges and estimated charges/management fees taken to the capital account over the remaining life of the split. The volatility of the underlying gross assets can either be estimated from historical norms, forecast either intuitively or via some form of time-series analysis, or derived from a history of the level of gross assets, if available. The income yield can be estimated as total investment income received in the last year, adjusted for expected income growth, all divided by estimated gross assets. The use of the Black–Scholes model to derive the price of an option is an example of the closed-form option pricing technique, which is an alternative technique to the tree/lattice approach described in Chapter 5. The aim in both cases is the same: to evaluate the price at which an option would trade in a market that meets the assumptions of the model.

The closed-form option-pricing model can be applied to other classes of share beyond zeros. In the remainder of this section we will confine our attention to splits with a bank loan, zeros, income shares and capital shares. Traditional splits and quasi-splits (as defined in Chapter 1) represent special cases of this type of structure. In the case of a traditional split, there are no zeros in issue; in the case of a quasi-split, the income shares and capital shares are combined as a single class of share (known as income & residual capital shares or ordinary income shares).

Capital shareholders are entitled to the residual assets once all prior ranking capital has been paid. The payoff for the capital shares is obtained by calculating the final gross assets of the split less the sum of prior charges and the final redemption values of the zeros and the income shares. If this calculated figure is greater than zero, it becomes the payoff for the capital shares. If less than zero, the payoff for the capital shares is zero. Thus, the theoretical price of a capital share is given by the price of a call option on the gross assets of the split, with an exercise price equal to the prior charges plus the final redemption values of the zeros and the income shares. The payoff chart for a capital share is shown in Figure 7.2.

Income shareholders are entitled to all the dividends paid out by the trust, plus a final redemption value on wind-up if sufficient assets are available. Dividends are generally set or targeted in advance, but boards have the right to increase or cut dividends as circumstances change, within the rules of Section 842 of the Companies Act.

The theoretical price of an income share is thus the discounted value of all expected future dividends, plus the discounted value of the final redemption value of the income shares, plus the value of the option "sold" by the zero shareholders, less the value of the option "sold" to capital shareholders. The payoff chart for an income share is shown in Figure 7.3.

The Black–Scholes model can be used to value each of these options, thus revealing the theoretical price at which each class of share in a split should trade.

Poor liquidity and wide market maker spreads in some of the underlying assets can make evaluation of the asset value of a split an unreliable science. If a split owns, say, income shares in another split and liquidity is poor, spreads are large or the market price is different from a calculated fair value, it may be difficult to have confidence in the quoted mid-market price of those income shares. Confidence in any estimate of the

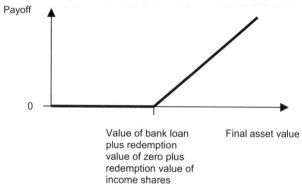

Figure 7.2   Payoff chart for a capital share.

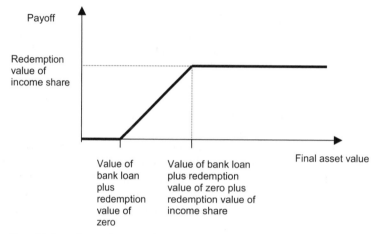

Figure 7.3   Payoff chart for an income share.

gross asset value of a split will, consequently, be low. One practitioner approach to this problem has been to write down the value of holdings in certain splits or high-yielding securities by some percentage – much as one might do with unlisted securities – to take account of poor marketability. Another alternative is to use estimated fair values rather than market prices for cross-held investments. These approaches would give a "fairer" estimate of gross assets, assuming that liquidity and spreads were unlikely to improve.

Complex capital structures, along with poor confidence in the valuation of the asset portfolio, can make valuing the shares a difficult task. Further examples of how certain facets of the asset portfolio or capital structure complicate valuation are given in Section 7.3.

7.3   PROBLEMS WITH CLOSED-FORM OPTION PRICING

Existing option-pricing models for splits make a number of simplifying assumptions. Several factors may reduce the effectiveness of such models:

- Gross asset volatility[1] must be estimated. The net asset value of a split is published regularly, but it is the volatility of the gross assets (i.e., net assets plus debt, including bank loans) that is the required input for the model. Gross asset volatility may vary over time, due to either changing market conditions or adjustments to portfolio holdings by the investment manager. Stochastic modelling techniques for gross asset volatility have been developed and these can help with this problem (e.g., Scott, 1997).

- Future management and administration fees may vary from current levels (e.g., some trusts have negotiated reductions in fee levels in recent years). Also, policy on the allocation of expenses between the revenue account and the capital account could be changed, affecting the value of different share classes.

- The possibility of changes to income share distributions and the impact of this on other share classes. Such changes may be due to the Board's discretion over distributions. The Companies Act imposes restrictions on dividend distributions for UK trusts.[2] To forecast future dividends, it is helpful to observe historical income share distributions and to understand how distribution changes are decided by the Board, although there is a major problem with funds of funds. Understanding can be assisted through knowledge of the trust's articles of association, the Board's method of achieving fairness between the different share classes, the revenue reserves and the income yield on the underlying asset portfolio. An algorithm could then be created to model the Board's behaviour, and this could form the basis of a modelling approach to the problem.

- Cross-holdings. Several splits own the income-bearing shares of other splits or high-yielding investment companies as a source of higher dividend income. However, the dividends from these holdings may be raised, cut or cancelled, and extreme capital losses are possible as a result. A fall or indeed a rise in the value of income-bearing shares in one split may have a resonant impact on other splits due to cross-holdings.

- Banking covenants and possible breaches of those covenants. If a covenant is breached, the lender may require the trust to sell assets to raise cash, thereby restoring the asset to debt ratio to some acceptable level and reducing the risk to the lender. This can create a path dependency problem that makes the use of simple closed-form or lattice methods for valuing options ineffective. Selling assets to raise cash will also lower the volatility of the underlying asset portfolio, which will have a negative impact on the value of any capital shares, particularly if they are out-of-the-money.[3] Note that banking covenants may be renegotiated during the life of the trust, further complicating the analysis. The Chairman's Statement in the Annual Report of Danae Investment Trust PLC (14 February 2003) gives one such example. Cazenove & Co. (2001) discuss how the interaction of covenant breaches and cross-holdings can lead to a systemic collapse among "barbell" investment trusts.

- Share buy-back programmes. The manager can enhance NAV per share and possibly smooth movements in the discount to NAV (Adams et al., 2002) by buying shares at

---

[1] "Gross asset volatility" may be defined as the annualised standard deviation of returns on the gross assets.
[2] The Companies Act 1985 disallows payment of dividends when the net assets of an investment company are less than the aggregate of its called up share capital and undistributable reserves (Section 264) or less than 50% of liabilities (Section 265).
[3] A capital share is "out-of-the-money" if the total assets of the split are less than the sum of the prior charges and the claims of all other classes of share in that split.

a discount and cancelling them. A buy-back may also change two of the inputs to the option model: gross assets and the volatility of gross assets.[4] Each class of share will be influenced in a particular way by the change in volatility. For example, capital shares will clearly benefit from any increase in volatility. It is necessary to maintain records of the number of shares remaining in each class after the buy-back, to allow for accurate calculation of the fair value of each share. Note that the Companies Act, which provides a net asset test, may restrict share buy-backs.[5]

- Credit spreads are not an explicit input to the option-pricing model for zeros, yet certain market events (e.g., sudden large-scale aversion to credit risk) may lead to wholesale changes in credit spreads. A study by Merrill Lynch (1999) showed that a snapshot comparison of a Black–Scholes pricing model to a credit spread pricing model gave a close relationship (R-squared close to 1). This suggests that both methods offer a valid means of valuing zeros. However, there may be times when a credit spread model provides a better explanation of share price movements than an option model and vice versa.

Merrill Lynch (1999), Gemmill (2001) and Cazenove & Co. (2002) studied the differences between market prices and option model values for both zeros and income & residual capital shares. Their studies revealed a mixed picture. An alternative approach to valuing shares is to calculate the implied volatility of each class of share using observed prices and a closed-form option-pricing model. Implied volatility can then be compared with the implied volatilities found in similar trusts, or to forecast volatilities. "Unreasonable" implied volatility would suggest mispricing.

In practice, option-pricing models for splits often allow for the "marked to market" pricing of debt and the writing off of certain high-risk cross-shareholdings. This approach is combined with an appraisal of the investment manager's performance history and visual interpretation of charts showing annual returns for each class of share for varying levels of growth of dividends or total assets, to gauge the attractiveness of a particular security.

7.4   A WORKED EXAMPLE USING CLOSED-FORM OPTION PRICING

In this section, I apply a closed-form option-pricing model to a specific split capital trust. I will highlight some of the problems associated with such modelling and seek to interpret the results. The split that I have chosen is Murray Global Return Trust PLC ("Murray Global"), one of the larger splits with total assets of approximately £162m at 31/5/2003 (its latest accounting year-end, at the time of writing). The primary aim of Murray Global is to achieve both capital and income growth from a portfolio of listed global equities, higher yielding securities and fixed income securities.

---

[4] Many managers will sell the "marginally least attractive" or most liquid assets in the portfolio to finance a buy-back; others may use cash holdings within the portfolio at the time of the buy-back. The volatility of gross assets will be influenced by the action taken.

[5] There has been at least one breach of the Companies Act in this respect. The Chairman's Statement in the Annual Report for Danae Investment Trust PLC (14 February 2003) stated: "On 12 December the Board announced that the purchase for cancellation of 14.9% of the Company's zero dividend preference shares had been ruled an unlawful transaction because on the date of the purchase the company was unable to satisfy Section 264 of the Companies Act."

It is first necessary to describe the capital structure. For Murray Global, the capital structure includes two classes of share: zeros and ordinary (otherwise known as income & residual capital) shares. There also exist package "units", each unit comprising one zero and one ordinary share. The existence of such package units does not change the methodology for calculating the fair value of each of the component classes. The fair value of the package unit is, in this case, simply the sum of its two component fair values. At 31/5/2003, there were 105,429,363 zeros and 107,402,735 ordinary shares (*Annual Report and Accounts 2003*). One problem encountered in assessing the capital structure is that the number of shares between reporting periods may change. In Murray Global's case, the company has been buying back zeros. Such buy-backs are announced to the market through the Regulatory News Service, and records of buy-backs are kept by some brokerage firms (e.g., Cazenove & Co.). When evaluating the fair value of the shares between reporting periods, this information is required.

Murray Global does not have a formal wind-up date, but the redemption date for the zeros is 19/3/2005. The ordinary shares need not be wound up on this date, so long as the zero holders' redemption claim is met in full. Murray Global also has a long-term debenture loan, providing gearing to the fund. This loan was made a number of years ago at a time of high interest rates and is unusual in that its maturity date of 20/2/2016 lies beyond the redemption date for the zeros. If the loan is repaid early, a significant premium is payable as interest rates have fallen since the loan was originated.

Having looked at the capital structure of the split, I now consider the underlying portfolio of assets. I need an estimate of the volatility of the gross assets for the Black–Scholes pricing model. I also need an idea of the "quality" and liquidity of the underlying portfolio – two factors that do not come into the fair value calculation, but which are still an important part of the valuation process. At 31/5/2003, Murray Global was invested in a diversified portfolio of global equities and sovereign bonds, with a heavy weighting toward emerging markets, such as Brazil and Mexico. With the exception of a small proportion invested in the shares of other splits, liquidity in the underlying portfolio is not a problem. In July 2003, Cazenove & Co. described the manager, Bruce Stout, as a successful stock picker with little regard for index tracking. Total assets less current liabilities (effectively gross assets) are given in the report and accounts as £162.3m.

The volatility of the gross assets is now estimated. A diversified equity portfolio generally has a volatility of gross assets between 15% p.a. and 20% p.a. Murray Global is well diversified, with bonds adding greater diversification to the portfolio, but with an emerging markets' exposure (equity and bonds) of approximately 38% adding to volatility. I therefore estimate volatility at 18% but undertake sensitivity analysis to understand the impact on the theoretical value of the shares when different volatility estimates are used. A suitable estimate for the risk-neutral interest rate on the calculation date can be obtained using the swap rate[6] of the appropriate term, and is taken here as 4.3% p.a. Expenses amounting to 70% of 0.75% of gross assets are charged to the revenue account. In conjunction with an estimated income yield for gross assets of 5.35%, this leads to a "leakage" of just under 5.9% from gross assets

---

[6] In an interest-rate swap, one party exchanges fixed interest payments for variable interest payments from another party for a specified period. The "swap rate" may be defined here as the fixed rate paid on an interest-rate swap (against the six-month London inter-bank offered rate) where the term is the time remaining until redemption of the zero.

per annum. Armed with this information, it is now possible to estimate the fair value of each of the two component classes.

For the zeros, the fair value at 31/5/03 would normally be calculated as the present value of a risk-free bond less the value of a put option on the trust's gross assets. The present value of a risk-free bond with a redemption price of 158.69p and 21 months and 19 days until expiry is 147.1p. To calculate the value of a put option on the gross assets of the trust, note that the gross assets should be adjusted downward to take account of the interest charge to the capital account over the remaining life of the zeros. Note also that the exercise price should take account of the cost of redeeming the high-yield loan: if the loan is repaid early, there would be an additional liability of approximately £3.1m,[7] in excess of the loan's book value of £19.4m. Incorporating these factors, the fair value of the put option equates to 34p. Thus, the fair value of the zero may be calculated as 113.1p.[8]

In valuing the income shares, we need an estimate of the dividends to be distributed over the remaining life of the trust. The ten-year record of dividend distributions is given in the *Annual Report and Accounts 2003* (p. 52), and further details are given on p. 39 in Note 7 to the Financial Statements. These show that the last three (quarterly) dividend payments have been 1.625p per ordinary share, having been cut from 2.125p per ordinary share previously. From the Statement of Total Return, it can be seen that £1.786m was transferred from revenue reserves to meet the dividend payments in the year to 31/5/2003. Examination of the revenue reserve alongside estimated dividend payments provides valuable information. In Murray Global's case, the revenue reserve of £12.296m (taken from the Balance Sheet) compares with total dividend payments of £7.495m in the current year. As the underlying portfolio generates an income very close to the target distributions, the generous revenue reserve suggests that dividend payments are sustainable if the directors so choose. From 31/5/2003 to the redemption date for the zeros, there are seven further dividend payments due. Taking the historical distribution rate of 1.625p over 7 periods, with the next ex-dividend date set at 4/7/03 and discounting at the rate of 4.3%, gives a figure of 11.0p for the present value of all future dividends. The option value attributable to the ordinary shares is the value of a call option on the gross assets with an exercise price equal to 158.69p, the redemption value for the zeros. From the Black–Scholes model, this is equal to 4.2p. Thus, the fair value of the ordinary shares is 15.2p.

The market price of Murray Global zeros at 31/5/2003 was 103.5p, somewhat below the theoretical price of 113.1p calculated above. The market price of the ordinary shares was 12.5p, also below their theoretical price of 15.2p. The package units traded at 114p, compared with the combined components price of 116p. Overall, the package units traded at a discount of 15.8% to the NAV of 135.4p. At first glance, it would appear that the zeros are undervalued. However, several special factors need to be taken into account. First, the investments in the shares of other splits may be less liquid than traditional securities, and the quoted mid-market prices may be unrealistic estimates of the realisable value of these holdings. A downward adjustment to the total assets may be required. Second, I have not incorporated any wind-up costs as the fund need not be

---

[7] This figure is taken from the Chairman's Statement in the *Annual Report and Accounts 2003*.

[8] Note that the zeros are "stepped" (i.e., the asset value attributable to the zero if the split were wound up increases in steps over time until it meets the redemption price of the zero). However, if we assume that the zero is held until redemption, this factor need not be introduced into the valuation methodology.

wound up on the date of redemption of the zeros. Including, say, a 1% wind-up cost would lower the theoretical zero price slightly. Third, there is ambiguity over how the revenue reserve should be apportioned at the redemption date of the zeros, if the zeros are not fully covered on this date. Generally, zeros would have first claim on all assets at wind-up to meet the redemption value. However, revenue reserves are generally considered the preserve of the income-bearing shares in a split. The prospectus is ambiguous as to how the revenue reserves should be apportioned in this circumstance, and this creates a valuation problem. Only by buying the package "units" would an investor become indifferent to this problem.

7.5 MONTE CARLO SIMULATION

With the complexities of many splits' structures undermining the effectiveness of closed-form option-pricing approaches, the use of Monte Carlo simulation represents a suitable alternative (Boyle, 1977; Barrie & Hibbert Ltd, 2003). Simulations can deal with many of the problems described above. Potential distributions of dividends and capital payments to each class of shareholder over the lifetime of the trust can then be estimated.

The starting point is to ascertain the structure of the investment portfolio, including percentages held in various asset classes (e.g., equity, possibly broken down by region or sector; bonds, described by coupon, maturity, rating and seniority; income-bearing shares in other splits, etc.). The trust's liabilities are then ascertained, including proportional and fixed fees and their allocation to revenue and capital accounts; loan interest and allocation; corporation tax; loan covenants and rules to be followed if these covenants are breached. The trust's share capital structure is also a required input to the model.

Some of the key features of the model are as follows:

- The model incorporates a set of rules for generating asset returns and paying liabilities over each time period.

- Using a stochastic model for equity returns, interest rates and bond credit transitions (e.g., from a credit rating of BBB to a credit rating of BBB+), the returns on each of the trust's asset classes are derived. Both capital returns and income returns are calculated, with income included in the trust's revenue account.

- Fixed expenses and expenses proportional to the underlying gross (or net) assets are charged to the capital and revenue accounts using the specified allocation rule.

- Interest is charged to the capital and revenue accounts using the specified allocation rule.

- Dividends paid by the trust are charged to the revenue account.

- Corporation tax rates are applied to unfranked income, after offsetting the trust's expenses and interest payments.

- Banking covenants are checked and, if breached, portfolio reallocation is carried out according to a specified covenant breach rule.

- Situations, such as a loan extending beyond the life of a split, cause complications and would need to be "custom"-programmed into the model.

- If the test in Section 265 of the Companies Act 1985 rule is not met, dividends that would otherwise have been paid are held in a revenue reserve account for payment if compliance is achieved later. If compliance is not achieved later, this reserve would be distributed as capital (but only after prior ranking parties have been paid in full).

- On wind-up of the trust, capital distributions are made to each class of share according to predetermined rules.

Modelling cross-holdings in a split is a considerable challenge. One approach is simply to treat income-bearing shares as high-beta equities. A more sophisticated approach would be possible if the portfolio holdings data for all trusts in the splits universe could be obtained. It would then be possible to "drill down" to the effective underlying holdings for each trust. This approach would present a better picture of the underlying portfolio for each trust, but would be time-consuming, even if the required data could be obtained easily. Additionally, a holding in an individual class of shares in another split represents a contingent claim on the underlying assets, rather than indirect ownership of those assets.

A fair value for each share can be estimated from knowledge of the mean redemption values and all dividend payments across the simulations (calculated under the risk-neutral measure). The market price of a share may differ from its estimated fair value. There are several possible reasons for this. First, the model may be mis-specified in some way. Second, there could be poor liquidity in the splits market and difficulties in undertaking arbitrage (due to poor fund transparency and difficulties in short selling). Finally, there could be an investor sentiment effect. For example, investors might shun a segment of the stock market that has been under regulatory scrutiny, leading to seemingly irrational market pricing. We will compare market prices with estimated fair values in the next section.

7.6 PRICING DURING THE SPLITS CRISIS

It is possible to study the market prices of the components of a split and compare them with fair value estimates of each component produced using one of the above valuation techniques. Research by Gemmill (2001) suggested that ordinary shares were overpriced relative to fair value at the date of analysis (5/7/2000). Reasons cited include a clientele effect for debt.[9]

Researchers at the University of Edinburgh's Centre for Financial Markets Research have compared share prices with fair value estimates obtained using Monte Carlo simulation for each class within the entire splits universe at various times. The aim was to identify patterns or changes in market behaviour at various dates. Before the splits crisis, it was observed that capital shares were generally overvalued, but income shares and zeros were generally fairly valued. As the splits crisis began to take effect, in late 2001 to 2002, capital shares remained overvalued and other shares remained fairly valued. But, toward the end of the splits crisis, zeros in particular became heavily undervalued. In late 2002, some zeros appeared to be as much as 40% undervalued. Even as

---

[9] It may be more costly for retail investors to borrow money than it is for splits. As such, retail investors may be attracted to splits that have bank debt, as this allows them effectively to borrow money at a lower cost.

markets recovered in 2003, several splits were suspended or liquidated as they became overwhelmed by their debts. However, a number of splits recovered strongly, and extraordinary gains accrued to the zeros. For example, the zeros of Murray Global Return rose by 57.2% between March and December. Although it is difficult to find an entirely suitable benchmark for Murray Global return zeros, the above rise in price is more than double the rise in the FTSE All-World Index (a widely-used global equity index) over the same period.

7.7 PRICING OF SPLITS COMPARED WITH CONVENTIONAL INVESTMENT TRUSTS

Gemmill (2001) collected data from 76 of the 82 splits that existed on 5/7/2000. Using cross-sectional regression, he attempted to explain how the capital structure of a split influenced the discount to NAV on the entire split trust. He also sought to identify the sources of any added value arising in a split relative to a conventional trust with a similar underlying portfolio. His study concluded that the average split had a discount that was approximately 11% less than that found in a conventional trust with a similar underlying portfolio. He attributed this to the existence of a wind-up date and to leverage within the split (which lead to a tax benefit and a clientele effect for debt). Gemmill's study, however, only used one date in the analysis. By extending such research and analysing the impact of capital structure on several dates, it would be possible to understand better how the market perceives capital structure and to study how this influences the prices of shares in a split. Before the splits crisis was widely acknowledged, the presence of zeros and high-yielding income shares in the structure of a split can be shown to have added value. However, once the crisis was widely recognised, this situation reversed and these factors had a negative influence, while the presence of capital shares became beneficial. Perhaps bullish investors saw capital shares as a means of gaining geared exposure to a stock market recovery. Alternatively, mid-market prices might not have been a fair reflection of dealing prices. As global stock markets fell, the presence of bank debt in the capital structure of a split tended to increase the discount, and trusts with more distant wind-up dates became more fully valued than shares with near wind-up dates. Clearly, the impact of capital structure varies through time and depends on both market conditions and the prevailing expectations of investors.

7.8 CONCLUSION

Because of the option-like behaviour of each class of share in a split, valuing the shares requires an option-pricing approach. Three techniques are available: lattice/tree methods, closed-form option pricing and Monte Carlo simulation. With the aid of a worked example, it has been possible to identify some of the problems that may arise in valuing the shares. These problems can include poor liquidity in some of the underlying investments, difficulty in estimating volatility and ambiguity in the rules for apportioning assets at wind-up. Comparing fair value estimates of shares in a split with market prices reveals some differences, and these differences vary over time. Such differences may be due to the difficulties in estimating fair value, poor liquidity or, possibly, irrational market pricing. Comparing the prices of splits with conventional investment trusts with similar underlying portfolios shows that splits tend to trade at smaller discounts than conventional trusts. However, these differences in discount also vary over time and may be attributed to different causes depending on market circumstances.

7.9 REFERENCES

Adams, A.T., Macpherson, R. and Moretta, B. (2002) Assessing the effects of buybacks on investment trust discounts. *Proceedings of the 8th Joint Institute & Faculty of Actuaries Finance and Investment Conference* (13 pp.).

Barrie & Hibbert Ltd (2003) *Split Capital Investment Trust Monte Carlo Simulation Model.* Barrie & Hibbert, London.

Black, F. and Scholes, M. (1973) The pricing of options and corporate liabilities. *Journal of Political Economy*, **81**(3), 637–654.

Boyle, P. (1977) Options: A Monte Carlo approach. *Journal of Financial Economics*, May, 323–338.

Cazenove & Co. (2001) *Barbells Unbalanced.* Cazenove & Co., London.

Cazenove & Co. (2002) *Zeros as Options.* Cazenove & Co., London.

Gemmill, G. (2001) *Capital Structure and Firm Value: A Study of Split-capital Closed-end Funds in the UK.* City University Business School, London.

Gemmill, G. (2002) *Testing Merton's Model for Credit Spreads on Zero-coupon Bonds.* City University Business School, London.

Ingersoll, J.E. (1976) A theoretical and empirical investigation of the dual purpose funds. *Journal of Financial Economics*, **3**, 83–123.

Merrill Lynch (1999) *Zero Dividend Preference Shares – What Are They Worth?* Merrill Lynch, London.

Merton, R.C. (1973) The theory of rational option pricing. *Bell Journal of Economics and Management Science*, **4**, 141–183.

Merton, R.C (1974) On the pricing of corporate debt: The risk structure of interest rates. *Journal of Finance*, **29**, 449–470.

Scott, L.O. (1997) Pricing stock options in a jump-diffusion model with stochastic volatility and interest rates: Applications of Fourier inversion methods. *Mathematical Finance*, **7**, 413–424.

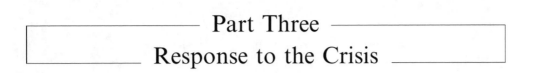

Part Three
Response to the Crisis

8

The Media Response

ANDREW ADAMS

> *The printing press is either the greatest blessing or the greatest curse of modern times, one sometimes forgets which.*
>
> (Sir J.M. Barrie, 1860–1937, author of *Peter Pan*)

8.1 INTRODUCTION

There was considerable press coverage of the splits crisis, particularly during the time of the House of Commons Treasury Select Committee enquiry. The fact that colourful personalities from the splits industry, such as Chris Fishwick and David Thomas, were called to give evidence before the committee added to the media interest.

This chapter provides an overview of the media's reporting of the splits crisis up to the end of 2002, starting with discussion of the generally positive articles on splits and zeros while the aggressive structures built up in the sector, through to the generally negative articles when it became widely understood that there was a problem. Particular attention is given to the handful of articles warning of the potential dangers of the new splits before the summer of 2001.

There were two main types of coverage – news items and feature pieces, the latter generally to be found in the weekend personal finance pages. There were also several supplements devoted to splits.

8.2 FAVOURABLE VIEW

The favourable view of splits and the attractions of zeros as low-risk investments were reinforced by much of the relevant press coverage up to the spring of 2001, although the volume of coverage was generally low, certainly compared with the media interest after the crisis broke. Journalists often relied on information from product providers and other "experts" who had vested interests in portraying a rosy picture. There was some criticism of new splits launches but most articles missed the point that the bulk of splits floated since 1998 had aggressive structures, very different from those that went before. The high yields offered on income-bearing shares in an environment of falling interest rates and the fact that no zero had failed to pay out its predetermined maturity value were often mentioned.

The following quotes are examples of the kind of comment found in articles about splits, up to the spring of 2001:

> *While some investors will have the knowledge, time and experience to invest directly into shares of splits, most of the investment community will not. However, this should not exclude people from accessing the benefits of splits. A few fund management groups run pooled investment plans, investment trusts or unit trusts which invest in splits, allowing investors to capitalise on the expertise of specialist split capital investment trust managers.'*

(Fund of funds: Using the knowledge of experts when buying split caps. *Investment Adviser*, 11 December 2000)

> *Zero dividend preference shares are well worth considering for people looking for less volatility and more certainty of returns. . . . Where zeros are concerned, there is the danger that the assets of the trust will fail to grow sufficiently during its lifetime to repay the maturity value. To date, this has never happened. But in view of recent stock market falls, it's wise to check the "hurdle rate" before buying. This shows how much further the shares can fall without risk to your capital. As zeros produce predictable returns and are less volatile than conventional shares, they are an alternative to other fixed-interest products, and attractive to low-risk investors, who can sleep at night knowing there is a predetermined redemption price at the end of the trust.*

(Go for a zero, not a hero. *Sunday Telegraph*, 25 March 2001)

In neither of the above quotes is there any serious hint of possible problems ahead either for "funds of funds" or for zeros. The second quote advises that in view of stock market falls it's wise to check the "hurdle rate" but this is not clearly defined and, in any case, as shown in Chapter 6, is an inadequate measure of risk.

8.3   THE EARLY WARNINGS

It is often said that there were no warnings in the press about the problems building up in the splits sector before 2001. This is not true. There were a number of such warnings from the end of 1998, although they rarely mentioned the dangers of geared zeros. Some of the more significant warnings in the press are briefly discussed below, each concentrating on a different aspect of concern. Many other warnings from published sources can be found in an independent report produced by Newlands and Griffin (2003).

There were two highly critical articles in the *Financial Times* as early as 28 November 1998, both written by Jean Eaglesham. The first entitled "Too close for comfort?" raised concern about a "pack of cards" effect and included the following:

> *The concern centres on a small "magic circle" of split cap managers who hold stakes in each other's apparently rival funds. The biggest three split cap managers – Aberdeen, Exeter and BFS Investments – are at the centre of the circle. The diagram [in the FT] shows the position for just two of these managers, but the web of cross-holdings stretches across the sector. Each member appears keen to help the others. Indeed, just under half the £40m raised recently by Exeter for its Enhanced trust came from the other two groups.*[1]

---

[1] In Section 12.7, Andrew McCosh states: "The allegation that there was a 'magic circle' of companies, who assisted each other by buying shares in each other's offerings, is consistently repudiated by all the companies whose comments I have seen."

The second article on splits headed "A trade-off between risk and reward" concentrated on the dangers of high yields and high gearing and included the following:

> *Anyone who is impressed with the recent performance of the specialised splits should bear in mind that gearing can have a dramatic effect when markets are going down as well as up.*

An article by Lawrence Lever in *Sunday Business* (11 April 1999) asked the question: "Are split cap funds a house of cards?" He argued that certain splits with cross-held shares were in danger of collapse, saying:

> *One particular danger is those split capital trusts whose portfolios are full of the income or ordinary income shares of other trusts. What this effectively adds up to is gearing on gearing.*

He did not say that there was anything wrong with splits, just that the characteristics of their securities varied widely. He set out four cardinal rules when considering investing in splits: do not invest in anything which you do not understand; always look at the underlying portfolio of the trusts; get yourself some reliable performance statistics; and find a broker with expertise in split capital trusts.

A generally positive article on splits in *Investment Adviser* by Rupert Walker, an associate director of AIB Govett Asset Management, on 26 July 1999 included the following warning:

> *However, there is a danger the market for split caps is close to saturation, which might worsen an already heavy reliance on income share cross-holdings to achieve the desired yield ... The problem with cross-holdings (or funds of funds) lies in the hidden costs of layers of charges and the danger of a spiral of dividend cuts in the future that might cause an income implosion.*

These were prophetic words given that the splits boom had only just begun. As we saw in Chapter 4, there was indeed a spiral of dividend cuts in the months following the European Technology & Income dividend suspension, almost exactly two years later. Soon after that, in August 2001, Rupert Walker became even more outspoken and lost his job as a result (see Section 8.5).

The Jupiter Dividend & Growth launch in November 1999 attracted much press controversy regarding the promotion of the headline yield of 9% on its ordinary income shares. An article in *The Independent* (20 November 1999) headed "Investing for income: the risk's in the small print; don't trust those dazzling adverts that promise high income returns" quoted Jason Hollands of BEST Investment as warning: "If something seems to be paying considerably higher levels of income than prevailing interest rates, it may be taking higher risks with the underlying investments. Or maybe they're doing something odd with the charges." Another article in *The Times* (27 November 1999) reported the same analyst as saying: "In the case of Jupiter Dividend & Growth ordinary income shares, the assets of the trust will need to grow by 5.5 per cent per annum over the next six years – just to pay back their capital. If the assets of the trust don't grow, then investors will lose 84 per cent of their capital."

The March 2000 edition of *Money Observer* included the article "Signs of a setback ahead for splits", by Fiona Hamilton. In this article she pointed out that the ordinary income shares of some of the recently launched trusts had very demanding hurdle rates of 10% or more which were unlikely to be achieved. These aggressively structured trusts, she said, could prove an embarrassment to the investment trust industry. She also suggested that other trust experts were just as concerned as her but had not spoken out because "investment houses do not like to be seen throwing stones at each other."

There were at least two significant press articles after the European Technology & Income restructuring in November 2000. An article in the *Daily Telegraph* on 29 November 2000 included the following:

> *Split-capital investment trusts such as this one sometimes attract criticism because of the tendency of the same circle of investors to buy into each other's funds. One analyst, who did not want to be named said: "All the people that have suffered want to keep it under wraps because they are part of the magic circle in split-level trusts. They didn't have any way of rebalancing if the market bombed-out."[2]*

An article in the *Financial Times* on 9 December 2000 included both warnings and reassuring sentiments. It argued that breaches of covenants should be of concern to investors and that selling part of a portfolio to pay off bank debt could mean that investors lose out on any market upturn.

8.4   STRONGER WARNINGS

From the spring of 2001, stronger warnings were appearing about barbells, bank debt and the "magic circle". The article "For whom the barbell tolls ..." (Adams and Angus, 2001) has already been discussed in Chapter 4. Newspaper headlines included: "Tech trust sparks fears of collapse" (*Financial Times*, 31 March 2001); "Investment trusts geared up for a fall" (*The Observer*, 1 April 2001); "When the splits start to show" (*Money Observer*, April 2001); "Gurus' warning over risks of barbells" (*Sunday Herald*, 1 April 2001); "Technology falls may mark death of bank debt for split trusts" (*Financial Times*, 4 April 2001); and "Barbell trusts may shatter confidence" (*Money Marketing*, 5 April 2001). The collapse of Framlington NetNet.Inc in March 2001 was a major story in the news. There was still generally little concern about zeros, although the *Money Observer* article, which was devoted specifically to zeros, argued that not all zeros were low risk, quoting John Newlands, then of Williams de Broë, as saying that "an above average gross redemption yield is a warning sign."

The Cazenove report "Barbells unbalanced" dated 25 July 2001 (see Section 4.9) received a great deal of attention in the national and financial press. Many of the articles repeated warnings from the report about the dangers of "barbell" trusts. There was generally little mention of zeros in the press but an article in the *Sunday Telegraph* with the headline "Split-cap trusts risk collapse" on 29 July 2001 specifically mentioned the risk to zero shareholders, stating:

> *Holders of capital shares are most at risk, but even those with zero-dividend shares in the riskier trusts may lose out ... Zeros have so far never failed to deliver, but there are real fears that the first default could be soon.*

Fund Strategy (20 August 2001) highlighted the Cazenove report and argued that the

---

[2] This allegation has not been established.

Financial Service Authority (FSA) did not seem to be viewing things that seriously. An FSA spokesperson was reported as saying that the regulator saw its role primarily as one of ensuring that investors were fully aware of the risks but an investigation into cross-holdings was not on the cards. The article urged the FSA to get to grips with the implications of the cross-holdings problem instead of getting bogged down in the minutiae of adverts for zeros.

A rather sensationalist article "Caz warns of 'systemic' City failure" was published somewhat belatedly in *The Observer* on 26 August 2001. It said that Cazenove had "warned of a 'systemic collapse' of a large swath of the investment trust market."

8.5   RUPERT WALKER STEPS OUT OF LINE

Not long after the Cazenove report, Rupert Walker (see Section 8.3) voiced concerns to the *Financial Times* about a network of investment trusts that invested in each other. He did this apparently without permission from his employer. He was then quoted in an article by Kate Burgess in the *Financial Times* on Saturday 11 August 2001 under the heading "Split capital trusts come under fire" as saying:

> *Management companies and their broker advisers issue new split capital trusts with scant regard for market conditions. It seems to be a scheme for investment management houses and their advisers to earn fees through a cosy relationship of quid pro quo ... Unfortunately private investors are persuaded to buy shares ... attracted by the headline yields they see in the adverts.*

His employer wasted no time in responding. The following Monday, Rupert Walker was suspended by the Chief Executive of Govett Investments and told to leave the building. A letter from H.J. de Sausmarez, Managing Director of Investment Trusts at Govett Investment Management, to the editor of the *Financial Times* was then published on Saturday 18 August. In the letter, he said:

> *Rupert Walker's comments reflect his own views rather than those of Govett or the industry ... The fact that other investment management groups are the biggest buyers of this type of investment has more to do with a general need for higher yield products than it does a "cosy" relationship ... As always, it is market demand that will determine the extent of split capital investment trust issues and not the business ambitions of investment management groups.*

Rupert Walker was then "summarily dismissed" by the Chief Executive of Govett Investments in early September 2001 as his employer regarded his actions resulting in the *Financial Times* article to be "gross misconduct". Govett argued that Mr Walker had been suspended for talking to the press but Allied Irish Bank, which owned Govett, overturned this decision on appeal. He was offered an alternative job within the firm, but not as a bond fund manager, and he resigned from Govett.

Rupert Walker was one of the first fund managers from within the splits industry to voice concern publicly. However, probably the main significance of the episode was that, thereafter, the *Financial Times* and journalist Kate Burgess in particular, seemed to take a much keener interest in splits – as we will see later.

8.6 INCREASING CONCERN OVER ZEROS

Investors who still treated zeros as a single low-risk asset category had a rude awakening on reading the *Weekend FT* on 6/7 October 2001. The article titled "Merrill says zero-dividend shares are high-risk" started with the words:

> Thousands of private client investors who bought zero-dividend preference shares as low-risk investments, were sold high-risk instruments, Merrill Lynch, the investment bank has said.

The article reported Merrill Lynch as saying that: zeros had hidden risks that the market does not understand; zeros were as exposed to the split capital trust sector's woes as the higher risk ordinary shares; most zeros were overpriced; and to price the shares efficiently, managers needed to disclose more information about the portfolios underlying the trusts with zeros in their capital structure.

Money Marketing (October 2001) then published an article "'Flawed and risky' zeros are slated in Merrill report" which quoted Merrill Lynch equity market director David Curry as saying:

> It is inevitable that there is a massive mispricing in the zero sector because of the lack of transparency at portfolio level. Some are safe but some are very risky. It is crucial that IFAs back a manager that understands the sector.

However, the article also quoted Exeter Asset Management fund manager Nick Brind as saying:

> The Merrill Lynch study is intellectually interesting but I disagree with their overall assessment. Pricing zeros using derivatives is very theoretical. At the end of the day, you have to use common sense.

Other articles followed, offering different views of zeros, including three in the *Financial Times*: "Big bargains to be had" (20 October 2001); "Safe haven split wide by bank debt" (27 October 2001); and "'Low-risk' investments require close scrutiny" (17 November 2001).

8.7 THE FSA STEPS IN

The regulatory authorities had made pronouncements on the way splits' products were being sold to private investors in March 2001 and again in August 2001, even before the FSA assumed the role of "super-regulator" for the City on 1 December 2001. But the press took a much keener interest in FSA action or inaction on splits after its managing director, John Tiner, voiced concerns about highly geared splits that invest in each other at a Treasury Select Committee meeting in October 2001.

The *Financial Times* (17 October 2001) reported that John Tiner had told MPs: "At a stock market level of 4,500 we would have concerns about systemic risk ... But at the moment our general posture is a watching brief." The FTSE 100 closed at 5,082 the previous evening but had fallen below 4,500 about a month earlier on 21 September. It was also reported that the FSA had demanded details of cross-shareholdings and bank debt from about 120 trusts, and that the FSA was processing the results. An article in the *Sunday Times* (21 October 2001) headed "FSA may force 'magic circle' to come clean" said the FSA was considering putting its weight behind calls for investment trusts to disclose details of their holdings on a monthly basis.

The *Financial Times* (12 December 2001) said that the FSA was to propose changes to the Listing Rules for splits to force them to disclose investments in rival firms. But there was generally little comment in the press concerning the FSA's Discussion Paper 10 (DP10), issued in December 2001. This was perhaps surprising because in my view DP10 had revealed that the FSA's understanding of the real issues facing the splits sector was rather limited.

Even before the deadline of 15 February 2002 for responses to the FSA's DP10, Kate Burgess reported in the *Financial Times* (6 February 2002) that the FSA was to launch a probe into splits. This was the first public investigation that the FSA had launched since taking on its new powers. Then the following day, the same reporter revealed in a significant article "Split trusts face fierce examination" that: "Teams of FSA regulators will this month start visiting managers, directors, investment advisers and brokers. The FSA is looking for evidence that managers bought each other's shares to prop up the prices. If so, managers may have breached new FSA rules on market abuse and may face fines. Some may even be barred from the industry."

8.8 MORE BAD NEWS

Things then went from bad to worse. Articles were appearing in the press with headlines such as: "Why split trust plunge has sparked a crisis" (*The Scotsman*, 12 March 2002); "Scandal of the 'safe' shares that crashed" (*Daily Mail*, 20 March 2002); "When 'low risk' becomes 'lose your shirt'" (*Daily Telegraph*, 23 March 2002); "Split-caps head for zero" (*Sunday Telegraph*, 31 March 2002) and "Split without a difference" (*The Guardian*, 13 April 2002).

Even *The Sun* was taking an interest in splits. Its article on 30 April 2002 headed "Punters get £4m free ride" concentrated, for some reason, on the chief investment officer of Aberdeen Asset Management (AAM), Katherine Garrett-Cox. This was strange, as she had no responsibility for splits within AAM. The article pointed out that AAM had waived around £4.5m in customers' fees in splits but went on to say: "Some funds have come close to collapse. And the issue is threatening to become the next big City scandal."

Further announcements by the FSA ensured that the negative press comment on splits continued. The FSA's policy statement published on 16 May 2002 gave rise to headlines such as: "Magic circle's castles in the air come crashing to the ground" (*Business Scotsman*, 17 May 2002); "The inspector uncovers a rather nasty pong" (*Financial Times*, 18 May 2002); and "FSA to act on split-cap collusion" (*Sunday Telegraph*, 19 May 2002). Reaction in the press to the FSA's announcement on 9 October 2002 that it was to carry out a formal investigation into alleged collusion concentrated very much on AAM although other fund management firms were thought to be involved.

The *Financial Times* also had an item in its Observer column on 10 October 2002 that focused on Enhanced Zero Trust, launched in February 1999 by AAM. The investment policy of this trust was "to take advantage of opportunities of predictable capital growth offered by zero dividend preference shares and to enhance capital returns by utilising gearing in the form of bank borrowings." Observer commented under the headline "Zero tolerance":

> *Aberdeen Asset Management, the embattled fund manager, can boast one piece of good news amid the prevailing doom and gloom. One of its investment trusts has the rare distinction of trading at a premium to its net asset value. The downside is that the net assets of the Enhanced Zero Trust are, er, zero.*

8.9   THE MEN WHO WIPED OUT BILLIONS

The BBC's Money Programme special on 16 October 2002 entitled "The men who wiped out billions" was devoted to the splits crisis and was broadcast on TV at a prime time slot. The programme explained that, while the nature of many newer zeros was very different from conventional zeros, the low-risk marketing message of zeros had remained unchanged. Case studies involving real human financial tragedies were included, leaving viewers with the impression that ordinary trusting private investors had been ripped off by unscrupulous City sharks. Unfortunately, although he tried, the reporter, Michael Robinson, didn't manage to interview the three City figures featured in the programme, Chris Fishwick, Tony Reid and David Thomas, and instead showed large photographs of them. There was a strong view expressed in the programme that private investors deserved compensation if they had been sold zeros as low-risk investments and the zeros had subsequently collapsed in value.

Mr Fishwick left AAM two days before the TV programme was shown, the reason given being that he had become "increasingly unhappy in recent weeks". But he received a year's salary, worth more than £350,000, together with £1.4m in deferred bonuses. Martin Dixon of the *Financial Times* tried to get to the bottom of the story and in an article "The curious case of Mr Fishwick's resignation" (16 October 2002) concluded that Mr Fishwick had not in fact handed in his notice. Apparently, Martin Dixon was told by the chairman of AAM's compensation committee that the Board had decided that it was in the best interests of the company that Mr Fishwick stood down.

It was stated later in evidence before the Treasury Select Committee (29 October 2002) that Mr Fishwick proposed that he should resign and a mutual decision was reached between Mr Fishwick and Mr Gilbert that it was in the interests of both AAM and Mr Fishwick that he should resign (HCTC, 2003).

8.10   THE TREASURY SELECT COMMITTEE HEARINGS

The first Treasury Select Committee hearing on split capital investment trusts on 11 July 2002 had caused some interest in the press. For example, an article by Kate Burgess in the *Financial Times* (13 July 2002) with the headline "Trust bosses wilt under fierce grilling from MPs" described how the committee had been angered by the non-appearance of Mr Fishwick and reported that Mr Godfrey, Director General of the Association of Investment Trust Companies, "had seen evidence of a 'magic circle' of managers working together to buy each other's shares and prop up prices. This in turn propped up assets under management and therefore fees."

But the press interest in the first hearing was nothing compared with the media frenzy at the time of the hearings in October and November 2002, which became quite personal. Even before the hearings started, an article in the *Financial Mail on Sunday* (20 October 2002) headed "Drinking like a Fishwick with £1.4m" reported that four days before his departure from AAM, Mr Fishwick "was doing a brilliant job of hiding his despair ... in the bar of the swanky Mandarin Oriental Hotel overlooking London's Hyde Park."

Much of the press comment on the Treasury Select Committee hearing of 22 October 2002 concerned the allegation by Stephen Alexander of Class Law that the FSA had ignored a warning from the Guernsey regulator (HCTC, 2003). The *Financial Times* (23 October 2002) reported Tory MP David Ruffley as accusing John Tiner of ignoring a "smoking gun" and saying "the Guernsey regulator put you on notice and you should have done something about it." *Business AM* (23 October 2002) reported the story under the headline "FSA 'ignored split cap warning from fellow regulator'" whereas *The Scotsman* (23 October 2002) quoted a spokesperson at the FSA as saying later: "the suggestion that we were tipped off and failed to act is inaccurate, absolutely categorically. He (Alexander) did not produce a smoking gun, more a water pistol."

Press reports of the Treasury Select Committee hearing on 29 October 2002 often included photographs of Chris Fishwick, his house or his car. Most articles on the day after the hearing quoted his comments, including: "this is the way the City has always been run" (*Financial Times*); "I have invested in every single product we have launched and I have kept every single share" (*Business AM*); "I don't believe I am the unacceptable face of the City" (*The Scotsman*); "... heavily criticised for trying to save trusts, and we wonder why we bothered" (*Daily Telegraph*); and "I do not look after the public. I look after the trust" (*Business AM*). *The Scotsman* reported that David Thomas, head of the investment trust team at Brewin Dolphin, was given a particular roasting by MPs who said he was the obvious "brains" behind the architecture of the split caps. The *Daily Telegraph* reported that David Thomas admitted that he "in common with everyone" who designed splits, failed to realise that increasing the gearing increased the risk.[3] The *Financial Times* said that Andrew Tyrie, Conservative MP, compared Mr Thomas to Professor Branestawm "sitting in his lab twiddling the dials and blowing us all up."

A thoughtful article in *The Independent* (2 November 2002) with the headline "We relearn the bitter lessons of risk" argued that the prime suspects in the split capital investment trust *débâcle* did little to inspire confidence when they appeared before the Treasury Select Committee, saying:

> The reality is that split-capital trusts are examples of financial engineering that in a number of cases have run foul of two things: (1) the over-egging of a good, original idea; and (2) a set of outcomes that were against the odds, but still well within the range of possibilities. The managers and promoters of the worst-offending trusts are compounding their original error in creating a product more complex and risky than they pretended it was by going into denial about their responsibility for not allowing for the worst-case scenario.

---

[3] At the Treasury Select Committee hearing on 29 October 2002, Mr Fishwick stated in an answer to Dr Palmer MP: "If you borrow money and assets go down, you start to get in trouble. It is straightforward mathematics. Anyone who thinks any different must be crazy." (HCTC II, Ev. 159).

Sir Howard Davies and John Tiner faced tough questioning before the Treasury Select Committee on 14 November 2002. London's *Evening Standard* reported the same evening that Sir Howard battled to keep his cool during the $2\frac{1}{2}$-hour mauling by the committee. The article reported David Ruffley MP as saying that Guernsey's chief financial regulator, Peter Moffatt, had warned the FSA of the dangers posed by split trusts in discussions held in January 2001 and repeated his concerns in a letter to the FSA three months later. The article continued:

> *Ruffley, a former City executive, said it seemed to him that the FSA had failed to regulate the split trust industry. "You were just giving regulatory approval to pyramid selling," he suggested. But Davies replied "that is an extraordinary definition of my responsibilities." Ruffley said the "poor, old, little Guernsey regulator had proved lighter and more nimble than the FSA." However, Sir Howard said he refused to discuss other regulators. Conservative MP Michael Fallon told Davies: "You were asleep on the job." The watchdog replied: "I don't think so."*

The article also said that John Tiner was accused at the meeting of misleading the committee the previous month when he denied Mr Moffatt had ever written such a letter to the FSA, but Mr Tiner said he was not aware of the letter's existence at the time.

Headlines in the press the following day (15 November 2002) included: "Sir Howard denies FSA was 'asleep on the job'" (*The Scotsman*); "FSA chief hauled over coals by MPs in split cap inquiry" (*Business AM*); "Davies suffers in FSA grilling" (*The Express*); "Watchdog that did not bark" (*Daily Mail*).

Criticism of the FSA and Howard Davies over splits and other *débâcles* continued during the subsequent weeks. Even *Private Eye* ("HP sauce", 29 November 2002) took an interest, reporting that Sir Howard Davies and John Tiner had received a "terrible mauling" from MPs David Ruffley and Michael Fallon but that these Tory members "should be careful about prowling too deeply into the problems of split capital investment trusts." This was because "A director of two companies in the Jupiter combine – Jupiter Dividend Trust and the Investment Trust of Investment Trusts – is none other than Lord Lamont, former Tory chancellor of the exchequer.

On 13 December 2002, many newspapers reported the surprise decision by Howard Davies to quit early as executive chairman of the FSA and become director of the London School of Economics. Comment ranged from discussion of the criticism he had recently suffered to his achievement at bringing together many different regulatory bodies.

8.11   BUST-UP IN THE TRUST INDUSTRY?

The Treasury Select Committee hearings were a stressful time for all concerned, and the press reported what it saw as tensions between the "established" part of the investment trust industry and sections of the splits industry.

An article in the *Sunday Telegraph* (10 November 2002) reported that Martin Gilbert, chief executive of AAM, wrote to the Association of Investment Trust Companies (AITC) asking for an explanation for evidence presented by its Director General, Daniel Godfrey, to the Treasury Select Committee in what was described as an effort to pressure him to resign. However, Mr Godfrey had insisted that he had no plans to stand down and was quoted as saying "I am happy and my board is happy that our approach is one that has had integrity." The *Sunday Times* on the same day quoted a person close to the AITC as saying that Mr Godfrey was facing a "fight to the death with Aberdeen".

The Independent (11 November 2002) reported Mr Gilbert as saying it was "complete and utter rubbish" that Aberdeen wanted to oust Mr Godfrey. Nevertheless, press interest in the disagreement continued. The *Financial Times* (12 November 2002) reported Jeremy Tigue, manager of Foreign & Colonial investment trust, as saying of Mr Godfrey: "Since most of the members in the association have nothing to do with splits, I think he is right to be open about their problems." But another trust manager was quoted in the same article as saying, "He should be supporting his members and the trusts until they are proved guilty. He is a quisling, and he is going in the interests of the FSA, or of Daniel Godfrey, but not its members."

An article in *Professional Adviser* on 14 November 2002 headed "Fighting helps nobody" argued that "many intermediaries believe in-fighting is making matters worse for the battered splits sector ... The problem with the whole sorry affair is that in the mind of the investing public every provider is potentially tarred with the same dirty brush."

Finally, an article by Daniel Godfrey in *Scotland on Sunday* on 17 November 2002 included both conciliatory and defiant comments. He argued that "despite the inevitable disagreements that have accrued between us from time to time, no manager has been more proactive than Aberdeen in working with us to improve transparency and disclosure" but also that "The AITC will continue to stand up for shareholders and investment trust companies even if we have to step on more toes along the way."

8.12 ADVERSE SENTIMENT GOES TOO FAR

Before the splits crisis unfolded, the vast majority of press comment on investment trusts had been favourable. But according to Metrica, an independent media evaluation agency, over the quarter October–December 2002, only 55% of 2,133 investment trust press mentions were positive, with splits accounting for 90% of the unfavourable coverage. For example, the *Sunday Telegraph* (10 November 2002) said: "There are signs that traditional investment trust investors are now switching into unit trusts ...". *Bloomberg Money* (31 December 2002) talked of "... the rapid decline of the split-cap sector, with negative sentiment even hurting the share price of splits uninvolved in the circle and widening discounts on conventional investment trusts." *The Express* (20 November 2002) talked of the "virtual collapse of the split-capital investment trust sector."

Professional Adviser has a weekly section called "Sound blasts" in which independent financial advisers (IFAs) say what they think on current topics. On 14 November 2002, the topic was: "What impact, if any, has the split cap scandal had on your view of investment trusts?" Five responses to the question were published, all negative. Two of them follow:

To be honest I think it has put people completely off the asset class as a whole. I think they're staying away from conventional trusts too, even though they're not really affected, because the whole concept of an investment trust makes them nervous.

(Meera Patel, senior investment adviser at Hargreaves Landsdown)

There has been so much negative publicity surrounding the split cap débâcle it has under- standably made clients nervous. This comes at a time when clients are already wary of the stock market, having received successive lower valuation statements. It may well be some time before the industry is able to regain the confidence of investors.

(Juliet Schooling, head of research at Chelsea Financial Services)

8.13   COMPARISON WITH OTHER MIS-SELLING DISASTERS

Given the relatively small amount of money lost in comparison with, say, the pensions or Equitable Life mis-selling disasters, the splits crisis took up a lot of column inches in the press. This may have partly reflected the identifiable figures, such as Chris Fishwick and David Thomas at the centre of the crisis, and the FSA investigation into allegations of collusion. But some journalists may have pursued the issues surrounding splits vigorously because the same journalists had hyped up splits and zeros in the boom years and now felt guilty about it. They may also have felt let down by the investment trust industry.

All zeros tended to be lumped together in press comments and were generally treated as simple products up to at least the summer of 2001, despite the fact that zeros of bank geared and/or cross-invested splits were complex instruments. Journalists generally didn't succeed in understanding the new zeros even though sufficient information could be obtained by a diligent investigator to suggest that some might indeed be risky. Whether it is reasonable to expect the majority of journalists to understand such a technical issue and seek the relevant information is debatable. Nevertheless, in my view obtaining information was easier than with the endowment and pensions disasters in which it can be argued that there was insufficient information available to investigative journalists at an early stage.

The press promoted split cap products over many years. But, just as with endowment mortgages and Equitable Life policies, when things went wrong, journalists swung completely in the opposite direction, perhaps too far on occasions.

8.14   IMPLICATIONS FOR THE MEDIA'S PERSONAL FINANCE COLUMNS

It is perhaps not surprising that there was little criticism in the personal finance columns of the role of the financial press in the splits boom. However, an article "Bananas splits" in *Private Eye* (29 November 2002) pulled no punches. It strongly criticised the fund managers, stockbrokers and IFAs involved but argued that there was another guilty group: "the very same financial sections which are now castigating the City suits and regulators." The article went on to say that throughout the splits boom "business pages were regularly splattered with impressive advertisements at premium prices and editorial 'puffs' led by managers such as Aberdeen, BFS, Exeter, LeggMason and Framlington."

Readers of personal finance columns might expect articles to be written by experts. But the splits crisis demonstrated that this is not generally the case. Why is this? With some notable exceptions, financial journalists typically have no relevant practical experience on the matters they are commenting on. Some have gone straight into journalism from university. Others have moved on from trade journals to national newspapers where they are expected to comment on the more technical aspects of City matters.

There are no specific controls on financial journalists. Cases of misreporting are soon forgotten with no adverse consequences for the journalist concerned in most instances. The lesson to be learned for investors is not to read comments in the press uncritically and to be aware that some journalists are higher quality than others.

Journalists need to take a more cynical view of what they are told by product providers. This would involve investigating the risks and costs of complicated products and explaining to their readers that if something seems too good to be true, it probably is.

8.15   CONCLUSION

The press had a generally positive attitude toward splits up to the spring of 2001 but the volume of media coverage of splits was generally low before the summer of 2001. Media interest built up in the second half of 2001 and into the first half of 2002, fuelled by events such as the Cazenove report, the Rupert Walker saga, growing FSA involvement and the collapse of confidence in splits.

The reporting of events at the time of the Treasury Select Committee hearings increased to a wider reporting base and tended to be sensationalist. The media constituency of the political arena is by its nature different from that of the investment trust sector, particularly on social issues. To me, featuring the sad cases of ordinary prudent savers suffering hardship in the media was fully justified. However, the exaggerated negative stories, which put investors off the entire splits sector and even investment trusts as an asset class, were not.

The *Financial Times* deserves much credit for the articles warning of the potential problems at an early stage and for pursuing the real issues as the crisis unfolded. But the general standard of reporting in the press varied enormously. Much of it was poor. Journalists naturally concentrate on reporting events rather than issues and there was a general lack of understanding of the products involved. In particular, zeros were normally treated as a single-asset category, with little differentiation between low risk and risky products. Rarely did financial journalists distinguish between geared and ungeared zeros after the latter had started to become more numerous at the end of the 1990s. Journalists rarely carried out detailed investigative work themselves, often relying on industry "experts" who may have had a vested interest in the success of the splits market. While there may have been growing concern among investment trust specialists as bank debt and cross-holdings increased, little of this concern translated into press articles.

An informed financial press is clearly in the investing public's interests. But real progress toward achieving this goal will require a significant increase in the level of practical experience and expertise among financial journalists. The introduction of a qualification devoted to financial journalism would help, based on examinations covering a range of financial topics. Alternatively, journalists could be encouraged to take relevant examinations such as the Financial Adviser exams or even the Investment Management Certificate of the UK Society of Investment Professionals. Journalists would take such financial qualifications more seriously if they felt accountable for what they wrote.

It would be helpful if there were some kind of publicly available "league table" for financial journalists to encourage greater learning and higher standards in a commercial world dependent on short-term results. City surveys would help here, perhaps along the lines of the Extel rating of investment analysts which encouragingly has recently been reintroduced to the investment trust sector.

Above all, an aim for higher standards, widely debated in the financial services arena, would benefit from recognition of standards. This would lead to far more articles built on a conceptual grasp of the issues and risks surrounding the investment product in question, with more emphasis on genuine investigative journalism. Articles simply churning out messages from product providers or others with vested interests do not give readers a balanced view. If there is a financial incentive for newspapers and magazines to write positive articles about a financial product, they should be required to disclose that interest. Otherwise, until such time as the investing public becomes financially literate, which will be decades away, the financial crises and scandals to which we have become accustomed are bound to recur.

8.16   REFERENCES

Adams, A.T. and Angus, R.J. (2001) For whom the barbell tolls ... *Professional Investor*, **11**(3), April, 14–17 [see Appendix A of current book].

HCTC (2003) *Split Capital Investment Trusts* (Third report of session 2002–03, volume II: Minutes of evidence and appendices). House of Commons Treasury Committee.

Newlands, J. and Griffin, P. (2003) Split capital investment trusts: The warning signs. *Newlands Funds Research*, November.

Robinson, M. (2002) The men who wiped out billions. *BBC TV Money Programme Special*, 16 October.

The Regulatory Response

PETER GARDNER and GEOFFREY WOOD

> *This is not the end. It is not even the beginning of the end. But it is, perhaps, the end of the beginning.*
>
> (Winston Churchill, speech given at the Lord Mayor's Luncheon, Mansion House, London, 10 November, 1942)

9.1 INTRODUCTION

This chapter focuses on what the financial regulators did in response to the splits crisis, why they acted as they did and what might have been done differently. The chapter starts by describing the regulatory and market background to what went wrong, turns to the pressures for a quick response and then describes and comments on the response itself. It concludes with some conjectures about future regulatory and governance developments.

9.2 THE FINANCIAL SERVICES AUTHORITY

The Financial Services Authority (FSA) is responsible for the regulation of deposit taking, insurance and investment business. It is also responsible for promoting public understanding of the financial system, reducing financial crime and policing market abuse. On 1 December 2001, the FSA assumed its powers and responsibilities under the Financial Services and Markets Act 2000 (FSMA). In so doing, it replaced a number of regulatory organisations including the Investment Management Regulatory Organisation (IMRO), the Personal Investment Authority (PIA), the Bank of England's Banking Supervision Department (BoE) and the Securities and Futures Authority (SFA). Currently, the FSA employs over 2,500 people.

The FSA aims to regulate participants in the financial markets so as to maintain a well-run and creditable UK financial services industry, while at the same time attempting to protect UK investors from any form of financial exploitation. It currently regulates over 11,000 firms.[1] This includes more than 9,000 investment firms, 670 banks (including e-money issuers), 800 insurance companies and friendly societies,

---

[1] This number of firms will increase to over 30,000 once the FSA assumes responsibility for mortgage regulation and general insurance.

and 670 credit unions. It also regulates the Lloyd's insurance market and 148,000 approved individuals (FSA, 2003b).

The FSA also regulates all individuals within the financial services sector who carry out a function within their organisation that the FSA deems sufficiently important to warrant that person's possessing and maintaining a thorough and up-to-date working knowledge of the position they hold and the sections of the *FSA Handbook* that cover such activity.

The four statutory objectives of the FSA are:

1 *Market confidence*: maintaining confidence in the financial system.
2 *Public awareness*: promoting public understanding of the financial system.
3 *Consumer protection*: securing the appropriate degree of protection for consumers.
4 *Reduction in financial crime*: reducing the extent to which it is possible for business carried on by a regulated person to be used for a purpose connected with financial crime.

It is worth differentiating between the responsibilities of the Financial Ombudsman Service (FOS) and those of the FSA. The FOS is responsible for investigating individual disputes between consumers and regulated firms whereas the FSA is responsible for the regulatory system as a whole. (Part of that responsibility is to ensure that regulated firms deal with complaints properly.) In the execution of these responsibilities it would not be unusual for both organisations to be seeking similar information from the same regulated firm. In fact, the Treasury Select Committee requested the FSA and the FOS to prepare a joint statement on their duties and responsibilities regarding the split capital trust investigation in order to clarify their roles and prevent any confusion. The joint statement, known as the *Memorandum of Understanding*, appeared in July 2002 (FSA/FOS, 2002).

9.3   THE FSA'S APPROACH TO REGULATION

In the publication *Introduction to the Financial Services Authority* (FSA, 2001b), the FSA states its aims as being to produce a regulatory regime which:

- Focuses on risks to its objectives arising from whatever source.
- Is built on a clear statement of the realistic aims and limits of regulation, in particular the fact that it does not aim to prevent all failure.
- Recognises the proper responsibilities of consumers themselves and of the firms' own management, and the impossibility and undesirability of removing all risk and failure from the financial system.
- Is founded on a risk-based approach to the regulation of all financial business, which integrates and simplifies the different approaches adopted by the previous regulators.
- Operates a transparent new framework for identifying and addressing the most important issues facing firms, markets and consumers.
- Uses the full range of tools, including consumer education, available to the FSA under the new legislation.
- Switches resources from reactive post-event action toward pre-emptive intervention.

- Creates incentives for the firms to manage their own risks better and thereby reduce the burden of compliance.

It is clear from the above points that the FSA acknowledges that it cannot prevent all failures, that it recognises the responsibilities of both consumers and investment firms, and that it will seek to be proactive in its actions. These are certainly worthwhile goals. They do, however, place the FSA in the position of a teacher/mentor to the participants within the financial services industry, an ombudsman to all, a policeman and a judge. This multiplicity of roles will surely lead to difficulty within the decision-making processes of the FSA. When should they teach, or mediate, and when should they police and perhaps punish? It may also lead to some confusion within the industry and among the investing public as to which role the FSA is likely to adopt, when it will change and how it will inform all parties concerned of its revised position.

Following the FSA's adoption of its new responsibilities, a handbook was published, which superseded all the other UK regulatory handbooks. The handbook was published in stages; it took effect from November 2001. This brought together in one document a handbook for the majority of the participants within the financial services sector. The FSA has since issued almost on a monthly basis a series of consultation and discussion papers, seeking to engage with the industry in order to gain the industry's input into the development of the handbook. The FSA also monitors firms through regular reporting by the firms to it, periodic visits, telephone interviews and thematic enquiries.

It is through these methods that the FSA assesses each firm's level of compliance with its handbook and whether the firm is likely to go against any of the FSA's objectives. Once assessed, a firm is assigned to a department of the FSA in which the level of monitoring is thought appropriate to the level of risk that firm is seen to present to the FSA's objectives. A firm may be assigned to different departments as its risk profile changes.

9.4   THE REGULATIONS

The *FSA Handbook* is a comprehensive set of rules and procedures covering all the activities of a UK regulated firm. The regulations form very much a top-down approach and are specifically designed to be descriptive rather than prescriptive. This places the onus on the managements of firms to operate in such a manner that they can demonstrate their compliance with all the FSA's requirements. Compliance includes the management of information and promotional literature (written, verbal and electronic) to the UK public, the financial stability of the firm, risk management, and the training and competence of all employees, in particular the employees individually regulated by the FSA.

The FSA expects firms actively to manage risks. In the ongoing episode of alleged mis-selling of endowment mortgages, some individuals accused the firms involved of not informing them of the risks at the time of purchase. The FSA has an expectation that all regulated firms should have in place appropriate systems and procedures to establish that the advice given to individuals is appropriate for the individual and that the risks associated with the decision are explained to and understood by the individual receiving the advice. (N.B. "Understood by" is hard to test after the event, particularly if there is a complaint.)

It is important to stress that investment trusts are only partially regulated by the FSA (or its predecessor UK regulatory bodies). Investment trusts are not regulated products and so do not require specific approval by the FSA. However, they are subject to the Listing Rules, and managers of investment trusts and those who advise consumers to invest in them are subject to FSA Conduct of Business rules.

9.5   THE TASKS AND IMPACT OF THE FSA

The FSA has a difficult job. It has to write new rules and regulations, train staff and maintain credibility in the UK and in the global financial marketplace. This is an enormous task. The UK has a sophisticated and well-developed market, far more so than the market in Japan and most continental European countries. The only country that has a comparable financial services industry is the USA. That country has several regulators. Some are nationwide and some confined to individual states, but its best-known regulator, and the one most relevant in the present context, is the Securities and Exchanges Commission (SEC). The SEC was established in the 1930s following the traumas in the US stock market in the run-up to and immediately after the crash of 1929 (Chapter 2).

It is difficult to compare the FSA and the SEC given that the FSA is still in its early stages of development. Even though the SEC has been in existence for over 70 years, events such as the collapse of Enron and WorldCom, and the recent mutual fund scandals, continue to occur. This emphasises the old adage that you can only effectively discipline those who wish to be disciplined.

It may be useful to consider the impact on the business world of another recent substantial governmental body. Up until the early 1970s, HM Customs & Excise was a relatively small UK organisation dealing with the normal taxing of international trade, alcohol and petrol. Then, as part of convergence with Europe, not to mention another method of raising tax revenue, Value Added Tax (VAT) was introduced. That catapulted HM Custom & Excise into every business in the UK. VAT inspectors were hurriedly recruited from every government department, given the handbook and told to go forth and collect revenue from organisations with less knowledge of VAT than themselves. Of course, there were teething troubles but VAT is now an integral part of business life. A probably unintended consequence of its introduction is that many more businesses now maintain up-to-date books and records. Analogous to this, it is to be expected that the creation of the FSA will have an increasingly important role in influencing how financial services businesses conduct their affairs.

9.6   FINANCIAL MARKET BACKGROUND

Before examining the regulatory issues affecting the FSA in the splits crisis, it may be helpful to set this episode against the backdrop of the financial markets in the run-up to the collapse of some of the split capital trusts.

The UK stock market had witnessed a remarkable bull market that lasted for almost ten years, starting in the early 1990s. The FTSE All-Share Index stood at 960 in October 1990. By September 2000 it had reached 3,266, an increase of some 240%. Financial services companies raced to offer the public new products, some even purporting to guarantee the level of growth or income, and in some cases both. It was a new era. Technology had changed the world. The old ways were no longer appropriate, so out went value investing. Assets and cash flows were old hat. Sales and market share were all that mattered. Some companies even reinvented themselves so as to appear to be technology companies, and their shares were re-rated as a result.

What about the people who were creating all of this supposed wealth, the management, executives and employees of the companies? Surely they should also benefit. Many decided to introduce remuneration packages that were linked to the share price of their company. This introduced another element to the spiralling process. Management who were previously focused on delivering to shareholders sustainable high-quality earnings focused instead on strategies aimed at boosting shares prices in the short term, thus increasing their remuneration and the value of shareholders' funds.

Many shareholders came to believe that markets could only move up. Then, the bull market ended. The magnitude and longevity of the subsequent fall took most by surprise. Thousands of people who had lost money on their savings, pensions and endowment policies looked to find ways of making good their losses. It was often asserted that they were either not told of the risks involved or they did not understand the risk when explained to them. Many said that their advisers should have warned them of the risks involved. Unfortunately, in many cases the advisers themselves may have misunderstood the risks or may not have retained adequate records to prove whether they did or not.

Allegations of mis-selling became the most important issue facing both the FSA and the investment management industry. The mis-selling of endowment and pension products is well documented and has similarities with the possible mis-selling of splits products. But, in the case of splits, some products were sold as low risk. There were also allegations that a small number of people had deliberately orchestrated a situation whereby, through a series of cross-holdings, share prices of some trusts had been artificially maintained.

Before turning to the response of the regulators, it is useful to set out a timetable of relevant events (Table 9.1).

9.7 THE FSA'S INITIAL RESPONSE

Following the FSA's internal investigations, comments from independent analysts and increasing interest in the developing crisis in the financial press, the FSA decided to gather information on 113 split capital closed-end funds at the end of September 2001. The FSA then issued a discussion paper in December 2001 and a policy statement in May 2002.

During the second half of 2002, the Treasury Select Committee was taking evidence and shareholder action groups were being formed to seek legal redress. In addition, communication between the Guernsey Financial Services Commission and the FSA on the possible mis-selling of split trust products in Guernsey led the Guernsey authority to issue a press release in October 2002 clarifying the extent to which communication

Table 9.1 Timetable of events

Bull market	1990–1999
Technology bubble	1998–2000
Major expansion of splits	1998–2001
Bear market starts	2000
Concerns mounting	2001
FSA *Discussion Paper 10*	December 2001
Treasury Committee agrees to talk to the FSA	April 2002
FSA *Update Report*	May 2002
Shareholder complaints	May 2002
Treasury Committee takes oral evidence	July/October 2002
Guernsey Financial Services Commission letter	October 2002
FSA *Consultation Paper 164*	January 2003
Treasury Select Committee Report	February 2003
Responses to *Consultation Paper 164*	April 2003
FSA Guidelines published	October 2003

between the two authorities had covered the selling of split trust products in Guernsey (GFSC, 2002). The FSA therefore became increasingly aware that it would be involved in an investigation into the possible mis-selling of split trust products.

Following discussions with a number of investment trust practitioners, the FSA produced *Consultation Paper 164* in January 2003, in which it laid out what it saw as the main causes of the problems within the new split capital investment trust sector. These included:

- Gearing.
- Cross-holdings.
- Ineffectual boards.
- Dominant investment managers.
- Financial promotions.
- Consumer understanding of risk.

The investigation into the split trust crisis has been the largest investigation so far undertaken by the FSA, employing up to 60 members of its enforcement team. Of necessity, however, *Consultation Paper 164* had to be produced speedily as a reaction to the crisis and (inevitably, given the circumstances) it contained proposals for reform which many in the industry thought too sweeping. As a result, it evoked a response unprecedented in terms of both the number of responses and the intensity of the scrutiny of some of the proposed changes.

While the sellers of the investment trust products are subject to FSA regulation, the actual trusts, as companies governed by company law, are not. However, the FSA was now in charge of the UK Listing Rules. It saw this as the only way of introducing regulation to the UK-quoted investment trust sector without the government's having to redefine the shares of investment trusts as collective investment products and thus be subject to FSA regulation. (This latter course would have placed investment trusts on a par with unit trusts and would have taken much longer to effect.)

9.8   THE FSA PROPOSALS AND QUESTIONS

In its *Consultation Paper 164*, the FSA proposed:

- A limit of 10% on the amount of a listed investment company's gross assets that can be invested in other investment companies whose investment policies allow investing in other investment companies.

- Mandating the inclusion of risk warnings in the listing documents for investment companies and identifying some of the specific issues with which they should deal.

- Monthly disclosure of any investment that exceeds 0.5% of the value of the portfolio of an investment company, together with 100% disclosure of all funds in other investment entities.

- Enhancements to the FSA Conduct of Business risk warnings provided to those investors proposing to acquire holdings in geared investment companies.

- Changes to the relationship between the investment company and its manager.

- A requirement for all material changes to the company's investment policy to receive prior shareholder approval.

As well as the above proposals, the FSA requested responses from the industry on a number of questions. These questions are reproduced in Appendix B of this book in the response by the Centre for Financial Markets Research (University of Edinburgh) to *Consultation Paper 164*.

9.9   OBJECTIONS FROM THE INVESTMENT TRUST SECTOR

All investment trusts were, in varying degrees, affected by some or all of the proposed changes and responded accordingly. Some of the major issues of concern were as follows. Preventing investment trusts from investing in other investment trusts could, far from reducing the risk to shareholders, actually increase the risk; a means of risk diversification would no longer be available to the investing trust. The disclosure threshold of 0.5% would benefit arbitrageurs, market makers, analysts, hedge funds and professional investors rather than retail investors; having to compile the data monthly would also be onerous. Proposed changes to the eligibility of certain directors to remain on the board and the total exclusion of a representative from the investment manager being a director were regarded by some as inconsistent with the European Convention on Human Rights and could lead to a reduction of industry-experienced directors being available.

9.10   THE FSA'S POWERS AND INVESTIGATIONS

The FSA's powers are conferred on it by FSMA 2000. The Act prohibits a person from carrying on a regulated activity in the UK or purporting to do so, unless authorised or exempt. This is known as the general prohibition and any infringement of it is a criminal offence. In order for a person to carry out a regulated activity they require FSA authority to do so. In addition, FSMA 2000 provides the FSA with extensive powers of investigation, enforcement and intervention. Further details are contained within the FSA's *Enforcement Manual* and *Decision Making Manual*.

The FSA has the power to obtain information and documents from a firm irrespective of whether there has been a breach of the regulation or whether there is a formal investigation into the firm. As regards its investigative powers, the FSA can initiate a formal investigation by appointing an investigator who has extensive powers to obtain information and documents not only from the persons under investigation but also from various third parties.

Under section 165 of the Act, the FSA can, by notice in writing, require an authorised person or a connected person to provide specific information or documents, or information or documents of a specified description.

The FSA has the power to fine or censure publicly both firms and approved persons. The FSA's powers are unique in the UK. But they will not prevent all future problems. The SEC has had these powers for a number of years in the USA. Despite this, scandals still emerge. This suggests that co-operation as well as coercion have a role to play.

In addition to raising the questions in *Consultation Paper 164*, the FSA followed on from the Treasury Select Committee's work and investigated the areas in which the participants in the collapse of part of the split trust sector may have breached one or more of its statutory objectives. The investigation into the mis-selling of the products was comparatively straightforward as historic marketing documents were available and the individuals who had lost money, and their legal representatives, were very happy to share their information with the FSA.

The second aspect of the investigation, which has proved to be significantly more difficult, was the search for possible examples of market abuse. (Note that preventing such abuse was a responsibility that the FSA had been given under FSMA 2000.)

In some respects the FSA is very powerful. It can close a business down, fine companies and individuals, and, probably more important to the individuals under investigation, it can stop them from ever working again in the financial services industry. It is therefore not surprising that the firms and individuals involved are taking these investigations very seriously and are employing legal resources that would be appropriate in a serious criminal investigation. The result has been a protracted and highly legalistic approach to what the FSA had hoped would have been a series of discussions.

We have even seen the FSA agreeing terms with the City of London Police (COLP) for the arrest of individuals who refuse to attend a voluntary interview with the FSA. The resulting Memorandum of Understanding (COLP/FSA, 2003) records the agreed best practice for co-operation between the COLP and the FSA with regard to the arrest and questioning of suspects when the FSA seeks the assistance of the COLP.

9.11   THE FSA'S RESPONSE

In October 2003, the FSA finalised new rules for investment companies, including investment trusts, designed to increase the information and protection available to investors in such companies.

Michael Foot, FSA Managing Director, said:

These new rules aim to reduce still further the risk that retail investors will buy shares in an investment company without understanding the main risks of that investment. The changes will ensure clearer warnings for investors about the nature of these products and associated key risks and will also place limits on the investment practices that accelerated the collapse of some splits.

We have also considered carefully the issues surrounding the governance of investment companies and will be making changes to our rules that enhance the independence of the investment company from its manager. The provision of relevant information to shareholders will place them in a position from which they should be better placed to protect their interests.

He continued:

The responses we received to CP164 were largely supportive of the measures we proposed. However, having listened to the views expressed by our respondents, we have modified three of our initial proposals that relate to investment company cross-holdings, portfolio disclosure and the independence of the board.

The key safeguards that were introduced into the Listing Rules according to the FSA Press Release on 2 October 2003 (FSA, 2003c) were:

- *Limit on cross-holdings – Under our new rules listed investment companies may not invest more than 10% of their gross assets in fellow UK listed investment companies unless those companies have a stated policy that allows them to invest no more than 15% of their assets in other UK listed investment companies. This will allow the continued operation of main line 'funds of funds' while curbing the cross-holdings that facilitated a downward spiral in the prices of some investment companies during the bear market;*
- *Risk factors in all listing documents – Listed investment companies will be required to include an explanation in the prospectus of the risk factors specific to the issuer, its industry, its investment policy and securities it proposes to issue;*
- *Increased portfolio disclosure – Listed investment companies must disclose on a monthly basis their holdings in other listed investment companies which do not have a stated policy of investing no more than 15% of their assets in other listed investment companies. They are also required to disclose on a quarterly basis at least the top 10 investments plus other investments greater than 5% in their investment portfolio;*
- *New Conduct of Business risk warnings – There will be a requirement to include risk warnings to investors proposing to invest in listed investment companies that are highly geared or companies who propose to invest in other highly geared investment companies;*
- *Increased board independence – Rules will be introduced defining an independent director as one who is a director of only one other company with the same investment manager. These rules will also limit to one the number of investment manager associates who can be appointed to an investment company's board, subject to annual re-election by shareholders. This will ensure the independence of the investment company's board from the investment manager;*
- *Changes to investment policy – We are introducing changes to require prior shareholder approval of any material change to the stated investment policy of an investment company at any time during its life.*

There was concern that the new Conduct of Business risk warnings were so vague that they would be applied to all investment trusts. As a result, the Association of Investment Trust Companies (AITC) issued guidance in February 2004 in an attempt to clarify the situation, as follows:

Whilst it is impossible to say precisely where the dividing line between a geared trust and a highly geared trust lies, the AITC believes that the typical conventional investment trust with no underlying or structural gearing, and with effective financial gearing in place below 30%, should not be treated as being subject to the new rules.

(AITC, 2004)

9.12   CONCLUSION

The response by the FSA to the splits crisis might have been different had the FSA been in existence for a number of years before the market fall. By then, the FSA's ability to monitor and react would have been more developed. In particular, it could have reminded directors of investment trusts of their responsibility to ensure that the risks of gearing were fully understood by the managers and explained to the shareholders (who then would have the choice of selling or not applying for their shares if they were unhappy with the increased risk). All the existing regulatory responsibilities of directors clearly imply that they should have ensured that their organisations practised good governance and that they exercised their own fiduciary duties properly.

As it was, not only were investment trusts never wholly under the control of the FSA or its predecessor regulatory bodies but also the FSA, through no fault of its own, came to the situation late in the day and had to react to the problems rather than prevent them. Moreover, it was expected to react rapidly, while also dealing with many other issues. To date it has stressed that mis-selling did occur and that it is determined that those affected will be compensated. Its investigation into market abuse continues and it looks as if this will develop into a formal legal process with the concomitant expenditure by both sides of considerable amounts of time and money. Whatever else may be its outcome, we can at least be sure that there will be an increased awareness in the investment management world that every action taken should be well-documented and risk-assessed both for the investor and the company.

There are several areas of commonality between investment trusts and unit trusts. In particular, investment trusts are marketed so as to suggest that private investors in them can gain exposure to a large portfolio of investments in return for a modest transactional cost. That is certainly no different from the main benefit of a unit trust. There are, of course, some differences between the vehicles. Investment trusts can gear, while units in a unit trust are always purchased and sold at prices based on asset value. Nevertheless, there is a strong similarity in the underlying *rationale* of the two types of investment, and it is still possible, though unlikely, that the Treasury will decide they should face a similar regulatory regime.

But we conclude on a more optimistic note. Better corporate governance, brought about by simply paying heed to existing best practice, could have prevented many of the problems of the splits sector. The shock of these events may well ensure such improved governance for many years to come.

REFERENCES

AITC (2004) *AITC Guidance* (17 February). Association of Investment Trust Companies, London.

COLP/FSA (2003) *Memorandum of Understanding* (July) City of London Police and Financial Services Authority, London.

FSA (2001a) *Discussion Paper 10* (December). Financial Services Authority, London.

FSA (2001b) *Introduction to the Financial Services Authority* (December). Financial Services Authority, London.

FSA (2002) *Policy Statement Newsletter* (May). Financial Services Authority, London.

FSA/FOS (2002) *Memorandum of Understanding* (July). Financial Services Authority and Financial Ombudsman, London.

FSA (2003a) *Consultation Paper 164* (January). Financial Services Authority, London.

FSA (2003b) *FSA Annual Report 2002/03*. Financial Services Authority, London.

FSA (2003c) *Press Release* (2 October).

FSA (2003d) *Policy Statement on Investment Companies* (*Including Investment Trusts*) (October). Financial Services Authority, London.

GFSC (2002) *Press Release* (23 October). Guernsey Financial Services Commission.

10

The Political Response

JOHN McFALL MP[1]

> *At length corruption, like a general flood,*
> *Did deluge all; and avarice creeping on,*
> *Spread, like a low-born mist, and hid the sun.*
>
> (Alexander Pope on the South Sea Bubble of 1720)

10.1 INTRODUCTION

In the 2002 post-Enron debate in Congress, one financially sophisticated Senator, Joseph S. Corzine, a former head of Goldman Sachs, commented that any momentum to legislate for reform of financial markets depended on how much stocks went down. Otherwise, he asserted, "these can become issues that are hard for people like my mom to understand."

So there we have it – from one of the masters of the financial universe intimately involved with the esoteric world of high finance. The money makers ask for our money, he seems to imply, but only in the event of a major market crash will there be pressure to do anything to explain what went wrong.

There were many people like Senator Corzine's mom who wrote to me in my capacity as Chairman of the House of Commons Treasury Committee complaining that their investment in split capital funds had almost sunk without trace. In many cases they were talking about almost 100% loss within a year or two of the original investment.

At first, the letters arrived in a trickle, but as the media focus increased they were piled thick and high on my desk.

They came from a wide range of individuals, from those with substantial resources offshore who could suffer considerable financial loss without their lifestyles being put at risk, to those with the proverbial widow's mite on a low pension who were rendered almost penniless as a result of their investment wipe-out. How, one asked, could the value of their investment have fallen by almost 80% when over the same period the FTSE 100 Index had decreased by only 15%?

One letter, from a shareholder of a high-income fund, described how his investment of £6,100 had fallen to £25 in less than a year. This individual, who was retired, referred to himself as a fairly seasoned investor who could afford the loss, but added "my

[1] Mr McFall has arranged for the fee to be paid for his chapter to be donated to the hardship fund for splits investors established by the Association of Investment Trust Companies (AITC).

feelings are for the elderly less well off, who were depending on the income from this trust. I think something must be done." He went on: "I was absolutely amazed at the performance of the broker to whom I entrusted my investments. All I can say is that over the years all he did was to accept an extortionate commission and a fee to boot. ... [A] double-glazing salesman would have more ethics. I really think the whole investment industry wants looking at."

The mountain of correspondence received on the subject gave rise to the Treasury Committee enquiry.

10.2   THE COMMITTEE'S ENQUIRY

To date, the Committee's traditional work had focused principally on macroeconomic or public sector issues. Not until the mid-1990s did it begin to look more at the financial regulatory system by investigating BCCI and financial regulatory issues (Treasury and CSC, 1991–93, 1993–99). But, with the introduction of the Financial Services and Markets Act 2000 (FSMA, 2000) and the Committee oversight of the Financial Services Authority (FSA), there was now a clearer responsibility for investigating financial services.

Although it was a very relevant and topical enquiry, the Committee's traditional strengths lay in other areas, such as macroeconomics. So, the question confronting us was: How could we go about gaining an understanding of such an impenetrable subject? Given that our advisers' expertise lay elsewhere, who could we enlist to guide us in this tour of the City labyrinths?

I reflected on the outcome of the 1720 South Sea Bubble scheme. In that case wild speculation was followed by a massive collapse in the same year. Three hundred years later, did the same reckless and speculative spirit play a part in the splits scandal?

With such thoughts occupying my mind, the subject was discussed in committee in April 2002.

The following month I wrote to the FSA Chairman, Sir Howard Davies, on behalf of the Committee. I informed him that the Treasury Committee had been observing with mounting concern the difficulties being experienced by some splits. We noted the comments in the FSA's report into the splits market (FSA, 2002) that "the investment trust sector as a whole does not pose particular risks or problems at the present time. It is still an efficient investment vehicle for retail investors who wish to gain equity market exposure and who understand and accept the associated risks." In relation to splits, it stated that the values of many "have fallen during the past two years due to the decline in underlying stock markets, rather than any unusual or inappropriate investing or financing arrangements." However, the scale of the decline in share prices, as quoted in the update report, for splits with cross-holdings in other splits – numerically over 60% of the splits sub-sector and just over half in terms of market capitalisation – was of great concern and had had a severe effect on many investors. It seems likely that the impact of this on market sentiment toward the splits sub-sector as a whole may also have contributed to the significant underperformance, compared with the FTSE 100 and the FTSE All-Share Indices, of splits without cross-holdings.

It was the splits sub-sector that the Committee was investigating, and I informed the

FSA on 17 May 2002 that the Committee might invite the Authority and others to give oral evidence on the difficulties facing the sub-sector.

We were clear from the outset that it was the splits sub-sector which captured our attention. We were aware that the investment trust movement had a long and successful history stretching back 100 years or so, but it was events within the split sub-sector which was earning the rest of the industry a bad name.

That it was causing the entire industry to be brought into disrepute was not in doubt. But how could we as a parliamentary select committee hope to be able to discriminate between the "guilty" and the "innocent" parts of the splits industry? This seemed a task too far for me at that time.

On a visit to the BBC for an appearance on *The Business Programme*, I happened to bump into Daniel Godfrey, the Director General of the Association of Investment Trust Companies (AITC). He expressed his concerns to me about the adverse publicity generated by the splits *débâcle*. As a result he was keen to be of help to me on this subject. Coming from an insider this proved enormously helpful in appreciating the scale and parameters of the problem. In pinpointing the problem area, Daniel was keen to separate the rest of the investment trust world from those parts of the splits sector characterised by bank gearing and cross-investment in other trusts. This background information was vital in attempting to assess the mindset of those involved in this sub-sector of the splits industry.

Another point hugely relevant to this debate was the bull market environment in which the participants were operating. Like the USA, stocks in the UK rose inexorably through the 1980s to the late 1990s. The bull market is reckoned to have started in 1982 and – with a slight blip for the October 1987 crash – accelerated through to 1999. The flip side of this coin, the bear market (defined by one observer as "when it hurts to look at the stocks in the newspapers in the morning"), came about in 2000 and continued until very recently. In the space of three years from the end of 1999, the FTSE 100 dropped from around 6,900 to around 3,800, wiping over £650bn from share values.

Many commentators believe that markets suffer from a "herd mentality" and that once a direction is discerned a stampede effect occurs. Certainly, this phenomenon seemed to be present in the splits market where investors were enticed with what were often described as low-risk investment opportunities and even quasi-guaranteed annual growth; levels of 8% and more featured in the literature. In this world everyone was reckoned to be a winner – that is, until the bear market began to appear, disaster struck and, as a consequence, the letters of complaint began to flood into the companies, the Financial Ombudsman Service (FOS), the FSA and the Treasury Committee.

Our central objective was simple: we were determined to gain an understanding of what had really gone on in the sector and identify those in the investment industry who were culpable. We recognised that the stock market had fallen by some 30% in the past year or two. But why did many investments drop by almost 100%, with all the consequent pain and misery for many thousands of investors? The proffered explanation that this was simply a market phenomenon and could not have been prevented was not satisfactory. We had to dig deeper and deeper in order to identify whether or not any individuals or firms were at fault, and whether or not any investors deserved compensation. We felt that such an investigation would enable us to make recommendations to ensure that such a scandal would never happen again.

The last point was very important to the Committee as we are strongly supportive of the investment trust industry as a whole. We were concerned that the potential fallout from this localised disaster could have a profound and highly damaging long-term impact on the entire sector. When the Government is encouraging people to save for their retirement and when a £27bn annual shortfall in savings has been identified by industry experts (ABI, 2001) this is not a time for a major collapse in confidence in the investment industry.

10.3   MISLEADING IMPRESSIONS

In pinpointing the problem areas, the Committee was adamant that shareholders of the cross-invested and high-bank-debt splits were at best extremely badly served by the fund managers and sponsoring brokers. We believe there is no doubt that there is a case to be answered that clients were recklessly misled. We also believe that it would be possible to draw that conclusion without even considering whether or not there was rule breaking, collusion or worse.

In my view, any buyer of a zero who has lost substantial sums of money has a strong moral case to claim that they were misled, and evidence for this lies within the prospectus itself. Of course, the prospectus does state that it is possible to lose money, but the warning tends to be buried in the document with no real effort made to ensure that it is brought to the attention of the investor.

But consider this: the description of income or capital shares would regularly include a wipe-out hurdle rate. Anyone reading this would immediately have recognised the circumstances under which the shares would lose all their value and could take a view as to how likely they thought such an outcome would be.

Turn next to the section in the prospectus on zeros and often the only hurdle rate we find is one that will return the full final entitlement, and that doesn't look too demanding. So what impression is a lay person going to take from that? They will think that there is no way that they could lose all their money. But, as we now know, many did.

When you combine the misleading impression created by the prospectus with some of the quoted comments of representatives of the fund managers and sponsoring brokers in the press and some of the headline advertising slogans, an overall impression that you could not lose a great deal of money was well and truly rammed home.

Of course, the manufacturers did not believe that the zero investors could lose all their money either. It is almost certainly the case that the impression of invulnerability was given in good faith given the prevalent bull market mentality. But this excuse does not absolve manufacturers in any other line of business from responsibility for their products going wrong, and nor should it do so in this case.

I know that this has not been tested in a court of law, but it is my strong view that the quite reasonable inference of zero investors that they were swapping a cap on their upside for low risk gives ground for a case for restitution. These were not, in my view, greedy people, chasing the latest high-risk, high-return investment fad and cannot be accused of ignoring risks that should have been self-evident. They cannot be accused of ignoring the dictum "you can't get something for nothing" or "if it seems too good to be true, it probably is."

And it is just not good enough for the fund managers and sponsoring brokers and their professional advisers to say, as they did to our Committee, that the zero buyers were indeed buying a low or lower risk product, and that they can prove that they were entitled to describe zeros as such at the time. Some (broadly speaking the traditional zero largely issued before 1999, ungeared by significant bank debt and without much exposure to other splits) have proved to be low risk, but they are not the ones we are talking about.[2]

I do not accept the view that it was legitimate and correct to describe the zeros that subsequently collapsed as lower risk because there was such a slim chance of the market conditions arising that could undo them. This is disingenuous. The customers did not interpret descriptions of risk in this way. They thought "low" or "lower" risk meant that they almost certainly could not lose money and if they did, it wouldn't be very much. When you look at the statements and assertions being made in the larger type-face copy of the ads and brochures, rather than the small print, it is evident they were very much being allowed to persist with this incorrect interpretation of the words.

To claim now that investors had misunderstood the meaning of "low" or "lower risk" and that the manufacturers and their professional advisers therefore have no liability to zero holders is wrong. I strongly believe that if this argument were ever brought before the courts, the investor would quite likely win. The manufacturers and lawyers have been complacent in the belief that their prospectuses and other documents and all the small print therein mean that they have a watertight case. Far from it.

Income shareholders, of all varieties, have a somewhat different case. At least these shares were described as having a higher risk profile and anyone who bought them without reading this should have stopped to think that you can't get a high income without paying for it in some way – whether through risk that the suggested income might not materialise or through risk that capital may be eroded. It is depressingly clear, however, that many elderly investors, needing income at a time of falling interest rates, walked into income shares with their eyes tight shut, imagining that they were getting a high income and the security of a building society.

So, some income shareholders do not have the strength of claim of the zero holders. However, they may still have a strong claim – applying equally to capital shareholders – that however high the risks were painted as being, they turned out to be higher.

This is because the fatal cocktail of cross-holdings and bank debt was not understood and the manufacturers and their professional advisers clearly had given little thought to the devastating impact that the domino effect could bring.

10.4   RESPONSIBILITY WITHIN THE INDUSTRY

All this, of course, provides arguments for restitution to be paid even before any considerations of wrongdoing.

From the evidence we received, both oral and written, and subsequent private conversations with many practitioners in the industry, it is plain to me that the suspicion of significant levels of wrongdoing hung over the splits sector. But, sadly, it will be hard to obtain the required standard of proof of any wrongdoing. There is unlikely to be much

---

[2] Though the correlation with those trusts which had high gearing and/or cross-investments is, of course, far from exact.

of a paper trail, and all those who may have colluded with each other have the same interest in keeping silent.

There was undoubtedly a group of managers and advisers who launched splits in circumstances in which it is difficult to avoid the conclusion that they had to take each other's shares to keep the chain going and that this was a more important consideration than whether the shares had any intrinsic merit. This fuelled a long new issue cycle in the splits market in which many individuals in the fund management and broking industry made more money in a few years than ordinary working people will earn in a lifetime. It is easy to believe that in such circumstances corners might be cut and why professionals convinced themselves that it would all work out OK. The market would continue to rise, right?

Many people believe that when the whole thing started to unravel, some of the recapitalisation operations, in which shares in splits were swapped for new shares, compounded the problem. Some were a desperate measure taken to try to keep the plates spinning, but in the end all they succeeded in doing was to destroy yet more value for the zero holders.

The industry representatives from the AITC described some of these practices in their evidence to the Committee (HCTC, 2003):

CHAIRMAN: Last time you were here you told us you were keeping your eyes and ears open for evidence of breaches of regulations. Can you tell us if you have learned anything since your last appearance?

MR GODFREY: Yes, we have. We have continued to receive information which we have passed to the Financial Services Authority. I would say there are probably two key areas of new, dubious conduct that we have heard about since we were last here. One has been a practice whereby we have been told that a manager was selling shares in a split that had gone ex-dividend, from one split which they also owned, and immediately buying them back for another split they owned with something which is called a special cum dividend being applied by the market maker, thereby enabling them to effectively get two dividends for two different funds from the same share. Therefore, if the fund involved had a zero-dividend preference share which was under water at the time, it would have involved effectively taking money from the zero dividend preference shareholders and giving it to the income shareholders as income. ... The second thing we have heard which has caused us some concern has been an allegation ... that when they modelled these trusts, they had a model which the accountants looked at and the accountants signed off independently; but that model comes by way of a dummy portfolio and says, "These are the sort of shares we will invest in and this is how it will work." We have also been told there were instances towards the end of the launch glut where trusts were beginning to run into trouble and there was not so much cash available from the other funds to invest in new funds but when they went out to do the marketing, they were told, "We cannot give you cash but we can give you these shares in other splits as a swap for your new issue" ... and as a result of that the starting portfolio may have looked quite different to the model on which the sponsoring broker, the accountant and even the board had signed off ...

Some financial advisers also bear a heavy responsibility for letting down their clients.

Whether by their failure to diversify adequately, to understand what they were recommending or by simply making misleading descriptions of risk, they were committing mis-selling and will be liable to pay compensation to their clients. Indeed, some has already been paid.

That is not to say that all advisers who recommend splits that later failed are guilty of one of the above errors. Many will have acted in good faith and with reasonable skill on the basis of the information they were provided by the managers and their advisers. The compensation culture should not sweep them up in its wake.

10.5 COMPENSATION

I am well aware that both the FSA and FOS investigations and the law firms who are attempting to seek restitution on behalf of their clients are being met with defensive, delaying tactics. Even if they find that restitution is due, whether because of misleading prospectuses, rule breaking or fraud, it is going to be a long time in coming.

Of course, many of those who might be in line for compensation cannot afford to wait. That is why the Select Committee in the wake of this scandal is fully supportive of the Association of Investment Trust Companies' decision to launch a hardship fund for those in the most immediate need.

I understand the caution of firms and their anxiety that a financial contribution might be seen as an admission of liability. However, I have seen the criteria that the hardship fund is applying and it is self-evidently nothing to do with compensation by another name. No fair person would see any contribution in any way as being an admission of liability.

I very much hope that all the firms who were involved in the splits sector and who made money in the good times will now step forward to make a meaningful contribution to the hardship fund. It is vital for the good name of the firms and the sector that they help those who now find themselves in desperate need as a result of losses experienced in splits.

10.6 LOOKING TO THE FUTURE

So much for blame and restitution. But what of the future?

The Treasury Committee report called for consideration to be given to whether or not investment trusts should be fully regulated by the FSA to avoid any possibility of a regulatory gap in the future. If this is to happen, it will not be overnight, so we are encouraged by the steps that the regulator and industry are taking to strengthen controls, checks and balances in the meantime.

The FSA has brought forward proposed changes to the Listing Rules which provide necessary strengthening to the rules concerning the holdings of investment trusts by other investment trusts, and which ensures that we will never again see this catastrophic domino effect of an incestuous circle of funds investing in each other. The rules also introduce greater transparency of holdings by investment trusts, especially where they hold other trusts; this too should help to ensure that early warning signs will be spotted and help to avoid any future misjudgement. There will also be measures to strengthen the independence of boards from the potentially disproportionate influence of their managers if things start to go pear-shaped.

There is little doubt that the fact that shareholders of investment trust companies were not directly covered by the FOS in respect of the actions of the investment trust's manager has turned out to be a gap in the protection of consumers. The Committee would like to see this filled as quickly as possible.

Following a recommendation of the Select Committee, the Treasury is currently considering the options for future regulation of investment trusts and will be consulting in due course.[3] We await the results of this process with keen interest.

But, ultimately, it is for the investment trust industry itself to use the power in its own hands to embrace change and strengthen its own governance, and to show the world that it is ready, willing and able to make the best possible use of an exceptional structure for making money for shareholders over the longer term.

The AITC has recently published a corporate governance code. It is vital that investment trust companies embrace that code in the spirit in which it is so clearly intended. Investment trust Boards should not be cautious in their use of this code, nor of the new combined code developed by Derek Higgs. These codes provide Boards with a framework of issues which they must consider, and impose a requirement that they must disclose their conclusions.

The *Combined Code* and the *AITC Code* often suggest an approach to the issues, but it would be sad and wrong if Boards decided to do something they thought was not in the best interests of shareholders just to avoid the hassle of disclosing "non-compliance". If every answer could be found in a book, there would be no need for Boards! Boards should have the courage of their convictions, and I, for one, would applaud Boards who take a contrary view and are prepared to put themselves on the line to explain openly to their shareholders why they do so.

The Committee was astounded by some of the criticism aimed from within the industry at the actions of the AITC over the course of our hearings. We needed to understand what was going on so that we could come to measured and sensible conclusions. Had it not been for the frankness of the AITC's evidence and the co-operation of Director General, Daniel Godfrey, the industry would have found itself subjected to months of criticism on a far broader front than was the case in the end.

As the industry works to repair the damage of the scandal, Boards should play their part by supporting their trade association, by taking an active role in membership and by demonstrating support for the code of governance.

The splits *débâcle* has damaged the industry, but if the industry pulls together it can rebuild trust. Its reputation is not destroyed and most people understand very well that the problem was limited to a sub-sector of the industry. As markets recover, the investment trust industry can recover its position as a serious contender for long-term savings.

This is a role which the country needs investment trusts to fill, now more than ever. As individuals have to save more than ever before, what better way than in a low-cost, closed-end investment company with a strong and independent Board to look after their interests?

---

[3] House of Commons Debates, 21 October 2003, col. 482W.

10.7   CONCLUSION

It is clear that the lethal cocktail of increased gearing, aggressive accounting practices and extensive cross-holdings in other splits changed the nature of splits' products beyond recognition. A case can be made against the architects of these splits on the basis that they did not fully understand the product they had created and were marketing to others. Indeed, one of these architects conceded at one of our hearings that "the zero which is geared by a bank loan is now a very dangerous thing" (HCTC, 2003b). Given that over 20,000 investors have lost hefty amounts of money and that more than £6.5bn has been wiped from the value of split capital shares since launch, it is astonishing that the sponsoring brokers were unaware of the vulnerability of the structures of the trusts they created.

The Committee's report makes it clear that there are lessons to be learned for everyone in the industry. As the *Financial Times* leader (14 February 2003) stated when the report was published:

Nobody emerges with much credit from the scandal around split-capital investment trusts – except, perhaps, the Commons Treasury Committee whose report on the subject was published yesterday. Its forensic analysis highlights failures among the managers who ran splits, the stockbrokers who sponsored them and the independent financial advisers who sold them. It also says the Financial Services Authority was slow to spot the emerging scandal and deal with it.

As the report explains with admirable clarity, the losses in splits arose from a toxic combination of high gearing and investment in other split capital trusts ...

Some of those responsible for these losses are still in denial. They blame the exceptional bear market – one told the committee it was not unreasonable to expect some form of equity growth each year. Yet investors in the splits that were geared up and heavily invested in cross-holdings were certain to lose money even under less severe market conditions. It was, as the report says, little more than a sophisticated form of pyramid selling.

It beggars belief that the sponsoring brokers continue to claim not to have understood the fragility of the structures they created. Equally culpable are the independent financial advisers who recommended splits. They blame the sponsors for falsely reassuring them that one type – zeros – were low risk investments. They passed this judgement on to clients, who might have expected them to earn their fees by probing the prospectuses.

As for the Treasury Committee, it will continue to probe this and other issues on behalf of the consumer as long as some in the industry continue to give the impression that it is all about generating money for producers and retailers and little to do with consumer interest and protection.

In my two years on the Treasury Committee the biggest surprise for me has been the apathetic attitude of some in the industry to the interests of their customers. The financial services industry contains some of the best brains in society – indeed, it has a greater concentration of intellectual talent than any other industry. Yet it appears to the public that the industry mindset is reminiscent of Sherman McCoy – the fictional Wall Street bond trader with a salary like a telephone number – who thought of no one's interest other than his own. It would not be unreasonable for an observer to come to the conclusion that in this world, *caveat emptor* – buyer beware – was sometimes replaced by "let the buyer be fooled".

Whether we are talking about Equitable Life, split capital investment trusts, pension mis-selling or even store and credit cards, it would not be surprising if problems like these were to turn up in the future with depressing regularity.

I acknowledge that there are many thousands of individuals in the industry who exhibit the highest ethical standards. Unfortunately, their worthy contribution is often undermined by the actions of the McCoys. It is time the good guys cleared their throats and declared that six-digit salary figures are not the only things that motivate them. They could add that there is such a thing as society and that they are more than willing to play their part in ensuring a fairer one.

If the view of the good guys does not dominate, the FSA may have to step in and do it for them. Nobody wishes to see such an outcome. As the *Economist* (20 September 2003) stated:

> The light regulatory touch has had its problems. The wholesale sector – companies selling services to companies – has been tarnished by the Wall Street scandals; research in London was as tainted as (almost) anything that Wall Street churned out. But the retail sector – companies selling services to individuals – has seen the worst troubles. First came the mis-selling of private pensions, then problems with endowment mortgages, the disaster of Equitable Life, which had sold pension policies it was unable to honour, and split capital trusts, which apparently divided up the trusts' capital into different risks, but which lost investors a packet. Supervisors, it is now clear, were asleep on their watch.
>
> There is a good argument for regulating those who sell products to ordinary people more closely than those who sell to the Prudential, say: such a big financial firm, it is generally assumed, should know what it is up to. Heaping costly regulation on big City institutions will simply drive their business elsewhere. The fear is of a one-size-fits-all regulatory policy that won't actually fit.
>
> The danger is that the FSA reacts to all these pressures by becoming as prescriptive and rule-based as the SEC. That would drive up costs for the banks – their London legal teams would have to rise to the size of those in America – and thus discourage them from maintaining large London operations. It would also increase the cost of regulation. The FSA (which has 1,200 staff to cover all financial intermediaries, compared with the SEC's 3,100 to keep tabs on a much narrower range of instruments) would have to get far bigger.

So, how is the investment industry shaping up to the future? One leading figure who strikes a pessimistic note is Sir Howard Davies, recently departed head of the FSA, who, after six years in the post, stated, "The biggest disappointment of my time at the FSA has been the failure of firms, and particularly senior management, to learn the lessons of past mis-selling".[4]

That sounds a gold-plated warning to the industry that if they do not undertake the clean-up of their own affairs in a quick and efficient manner, then the regulator and the politicians will do it for them. Only the industry, by running a fair and transparent enterprise, can keep those wolves from the door. Let the industry beware.

10.8   REFERENCES

ABI (2001) *The future Regulation of UK Savings and Investment: Targeting the Savings Gap* (report by Oliver, Wyman & Co.). Association of British Insurers, London.

---

[4] Speech to FSA AGM, 17 July 2003.

FSA (2002) *Splits* (Update report on FSA's enquiry into the split capital investment trust market). Financial Services Authority, London.

HCTC (2003a) *Split Capital Investment Trusts* (Third report of session 2002–03, HC 418-II Ev. 201 (Q850)). House of Commons Treasury Committee.

HCTC (2003b) *Split Capital Investment Trusts* (Third report of session 2002–03, HC 418-II Ev. 185 (Q690)). House of Commons Treasury Committee.

Treasury and CSC (1991–93) *Banking Supervision and BCCI* (2nd and 4th reports of session 1991–92 and 2nd report of session 1992–93). Treasury and Civil Service Committee, London.

Treasury and CSC (1993–99) *Regulation of Financial Services in the UK* (4th report of session 1993–94; 2nd, 5th and 6th reports of session 1994–95; 4th report of session 1995–96; and 3rd report of session 1998–99. Treasury and Civil Service Committee, London).

Part Four
Management Issues

11

Corporate Governance

ROBIN ANGUS[1]

> On Friday, the 21st June, the Board of the South Central Pacific and Mexican Railway sat in its own room behind the Exchange, as was the Board's custom every Friday. On this occasion all the members were there, as it had been understood that the chairman was to make a special statement ... The Board always met at three, and had generally been dissolved at a quarter past three. Lord Alfred and Mr Cohenlupe sat at the chairman's right and left hand. Paul Montague generally sat immediately below, with Miles Grendall opposite to him, but on this occasion the young lord and the young baronet took the next places. It was a nice little family party, the great chairman with his two aspiring sons-in-law, his two particular friends, the social friend, Lord Alfred, and the commercial friend, Mr Cohenlupe, and Miles, who was Lord Alfred's son. It would have been complete in its friendliness, but for Paul Montague, who had lately made himself disagreeable to Mr Melmotte ...
>
> It was understood that Mr Melmotte was to make a statement. Lord Nidderdale and Sir Felix had conceived that this was to be done as it were out of the great man's heart, of his own wish, so that something of the condition of the company might be made known to the directors of the company. But this was not perhaps exactly the truth. Paul Montague had insisted on giving vent to certain doubts at the last meeting but one, and, having made himself very disagreeable indeed, had forced this trouble on the great chairman ... What nuisance can be so great to a man busied with immense affairs, as to have to explain or to attempt to explain small details to men incapable of understanding them? But Montague had stood to his guns. He had not intended, he said, to dispute the commercial success of the company. But he felt very strongly, and he thought that his brother directors should feel as strongly, that it was necessary that they should know more than they did know. Lord Alfred had declared that he did not in the least agree with his brother director. "If anybody don't understand, it's his own fault," said Mr Cohenlupe...
>
> (Anthony Trollope, The Way We Live Now, Chapter XXXVII, The Board-Room)

---

[1] Mr Angus has arranged for the fee to be paid for his chapter to be donated to the hardship fund for splits investors established by the Association of Investment Trust Companies (AITC).

11.1 INTRODUCTION

There you have it: from the corporate governance point of view, the board from hell. Even the most casual reader will be able to spot many things wrong with the conduct of the Board of the South Central Pacific and Mexican Railway. Although it did at least meet weekly (rather than quarterly, as seems increasingly to be the case with investment trust boards), it was not usual for all its members to attend (*"on this occasion all the members were there"*). The meetings were short, lasting generally for a quarter of an hour. Of the directors, two were close friends of the Chairman and two others were seeking the hand of his daughter in marriage. The Company Secretary (a singularly ineffective one, as Trollope later makes clear) was the son of one of the directors. Lord Nidderdale and Sir Felix Carbury, Miss Melmotte's two suitors, evidently knew little of the Company's affairs and were content to receive such morsels of information as might fall from the Chairman's lips. For his part, the Chairman was brusque, secretive and intimidating, while Paul Montague, the "rebel" director, obviously felt that his fellow directors were not as well informed as they should be. However, Lord Alfred (portrayed earlier in the novel as a financially embarrassed nonentity interested only in playing whist) did not agree, while Mr Cohenlupe (an MP, so no doubt used to voting as he was told and not asking questions) blamed Paul Montague himself, not the Chairman, for his lack of understanding.

Although *The Way We Live Now* was written more than 130 years ago, the account of the Board meeting has a familiar ring – which is why I have chosen it as my starting point. It highlights the importance, when legislating for corporate governance, of understanding human nature and working within the limits it imposes. Most of us in the business world have known company directors like Lord Nidderdale or Sir Felix, out of their depth and living off their own past reputations or (as in this case) the reputations of their forebears. We may also have encountered from time to time a *"Miles, who was Lord Alfred's son"* or a selfish and cynical Cohenlupe, while a few of us have perhaps known or encountered a Melmotte and may even have found ourselves, or seen others find themselves, in the painful position of a Paul Montague. Most of us, too, will recognise the temptations that beset the members of the Board of the South Central Pacific and Mexican Railway: temptations not to go out on a limb; not to betray one's ignorance; not to question success too closely; not to make a fuss; not to bother busy and important people, especially brusque ones; not to make life difficult for one's friends; and not to put at risk one's own prospects or the prospects of one's children. These are all subtle temptations, not dramatic ones. They are especially potent when one is in any case unsure of one's ground and is quite prepared to admit that one may be wrong. They are temptations which beset the weak rather than the wicked, and all of us have our weak spots. As temptations, in short, they are very human.

11.2 WHAT LEGISLATION CAN – AND CANNOT – DO

No amount of legislation can change human nature. The best we can hope for (but it is something well worth struggling to achieve) is a system of corporate governance that recognises and allows for the human factor – that helps us to avoid being led into temptation and does its best to deliver us from evil. How can our system of corporate governance be strengthened to achieve these ends? And what went wrong during the split capital trust boom that better corporate governance might have prevented?

I may as well put my cards on the table. I cannot see how a different *régime* of corporate governance could have averted the split capital crisis, although it might have lessened it to some degree and helped some of its worst excesses to be avoided. Indeed, it is ironic that perhaps the only type of Board that might have been able to predict the true nature and extent of the problem and so take steps to prevent it from happening[2] would have been a Board of a type deemed unacceptable nowadays in the investment trust sector for reasons of (allegedly) good corporate governance. By this I mean a Board containing one or two experienced fund managers active in the investment world themselves, or recently retired from it. In general, I am not an advocate of having fund managers on trust Boards, on the "too many cooks" principle. But while the fundamental flaws of the splits were to my mind simple (too much bank debt and too many cross-holdings),[3] their structures were nevertheless often complex and the *rationale* for those structures was highly technical – well outside the scope of intelligent non-specialists who knew a little about investment and thought they knew more.

This is one of the dilemmas that those legislating for corporate governance face: that those who are independent enough are usually not expert enough, while those who are expert enough are (at least as conventionally defined) usually not independent enough. *The Way We Live Now* demonstrates it on nearly every page. As those who have read it will know, Paul Montague (whom we today would call an executive, or non-independent, director) was able to tackle Melmotte only because he had specialised knowledge of the business of the railway. However, the "independent" directors, like Lord Nidderdale or Lord Alfred Grendall, were so ignorant of the business as to be useless, even had they been much stronger characters than they actually were.

11.3   THE SPLITS CRISIS REALLY *WAS* DIFFERENT

The split capital trust boom was, in the true sense of the word, an extraordinary event. It tested trust directors in a way that (except in the case of a few individual trusts) they had not been tested for at least a generation. It is notoriously difficult to legislate for the exceptional and the unforeseen, so it is little wonder that the trust industry, to say nothing of the compilers of the City's various recent codes and reports, did not succeed. Undoubtedly, there were failures on the part of the Boards of some of the splits. I am not convinced, however, that more stringent legislation or more restrictive definitions of so-called "best practice" could have done much about it. Umbrellas keep the rain off but are no use if lightning strikes.

Anyone can criticise; not everyone can deliver. Those inclined to condemn the directors of splits for having failed in their duties should consider the fate of Herbert Henry Asquith and Neville Chamberlain. Today they are seen as tragic figures because they were not successful war leaders. Yet, they were perfectly adequate (in the case of

---

[2] Apart, that is, from a Board of young children with enough innocent wisdom to exclaim, "*But the Emperor has no clothes!*"
[3] See Section 11.4, "How much could directors have been expected to foresee?"

Asquith, considerably more than adequate) as peacetime prime ministers, which is all they expected to be and is what they were elected to be. So it was with the Boards of split capital trusts. When an unforeseen crisis arose, demands were made of them which they can never have expected and about which very few can have warned them. Most of them will have been told to expect very much a part-time, "hands-off" position on the Board of a small investment trust company in return for a few thousands a year – a useful but modest and low-key role in exchange for useful but modest remuneration. When we think of the considerable experience, the high profile and the not ungenerous remuneration of Lord Simpson and John Mayo and then ponder the fate of Marconi, how harshly dare we judge the directors of split trusts?

Nor was it the case that the traditional system of Board recruitment and training within the trust industry failed the splits and their shareholders. The system was not, in itself, bad or weak. On the contrary, its intrinsic strength and flexibility have brought the industry great benefits over the years. Rather, the problem was that in this particular and unusual case the traditional system could not work.

Those joining the Board of an investment trust can usually "learn on the job" by serving alongside more experienced colleagues and drawing on their fellow-directors' memory bank of shared experience. This was, however, by definition impossible for those who made up the Boards of the newly launched splits. These were new trusts of a new type, and for the directors of a new trust of a new type there is no fund of shared experience and no chance of "learning on the job". All on the Board are novices together. True, there had been waves of new trusts before. These, however, had generally been straightforward in policy and simple in structure and so had presented many fewer problems for their directors, who were in general called upon to contribute to the Board's deliberations chiefly in their own areas of experience and expertise. The combination of newly launched trusts and new and untried structures which we saw in the split capital trust boom had not been seen for decades, and possibly not since the sector's earliest days.

11.4 HOW MUCH COULD DIRECTORS HAVE BEEN EXPECTED TO FORESEE?

So, the structures of the split capital trusts were new. What, exactly, was new about them? There were two things, at once conceptually simple but far-reaching and complicated in their effects: very high gearing, while it was to pose major problems later, was not new; but long-term bank borrowings on a substantial scale were new and completely changed the rules for splits. As Andrew Adams and I wrote in April 2001:

> The inclusion of bank debt in trusts' capital structures means that a major subscriber of capital to a trust now has the right to blow the whistle and demand either repayment or changes to the portfolio before the end of the game, regardless of the effect on the other subscribers of capital (the various classes of shareholder).

(Adams & Angus, 2001)

At the time of the launch of these trusts, no one envisaged assets falling sufficiently to breach the covenants. It seemed just a matter of theory and small print – of "theology", as it is commonly (if unfairly) called. Had any of the promoters of the splits envisaged that the banks' powers would actually be used, it is hard to imagine that the splits would ever have been floated. This is why it would have been useful for Boards to have been appointed earlier, as recommended in the *AITC Code* (AITC, 2003). They might then at least have been able to question the managers and the trusts' advisers at an earlier stage and test what later proved to have been the managers' overoptimistic assumptions.

The second new thing was the effect on the value of the splits' portfolios of their cross-holdings in the geared securities of other split capital trusts. There is nothing new in cross-holdings themselves, and nothing that is necessarily risky either.[4] What was new here was the risk of implosion of portfolio value brought about by the holdings of what proved to be highly risky securities in split trusts which themselves held the highly risky securities of other split trusts. Could the directors of such splits have foreseen this? Probably not, unless they were very seasoned investment managers who had lived through market cycles (as remarked before, not a type of investment trust director encouraged nowadays) or else were people of strikingly independent minds. Should they have asked questions about the possible effects of the splits' cross-holdings in the event of a severe market decline? Of course they should have – but it is easy to say, "*of course they should have*" after the event. When markets were rising, and when lots of similar trusts were being launched to general acclaim and the managers and one's own fellow-directors were beaming with confidence, those asking such questions would have looked distrustful or foolish. It takes huge courage to risk looking foolish, especially if one is a newcomer anxious to prove oneself or a veteran trying not to appear past one's prime.

Ours is a "culture of the expert", in which we regard ourselves as experts in our own professions and trust others to be experts in theirs. We guard ourselves against accusations of incompetence or malpractice not by thinking things through for ourselves (there is no legal protection in that) but by getting expert opinions to which we can refer our critics if need be. This means that as the financial world has become more consciously specialised, it has become ever more dependent on taking on trust the opinions of others. So, even if questions had arisen in the minds of the directors of the new splits about the long-term soundness of their structures in different sets of market conditions, I dare say that at the time it would have seemed much more prudent to "leave it to the experts".

"Leaving it to the experts", however, meant that Boards did not always fully understand the stresses to which the structures of their companies might be subjected, and the effect on the companies that the stresses might have. Everyone involved in the investment trust industry will know of directors of split capital trusts who were absolutely first rate in terms of intelligence and probity but who simply lacked the training, the experience and the information to see why such structures might come unstuck.[5] They trusted the promoters and managers of the new splits to know their own business, and we now know that they were *too* trusting. It is a judgement that is easy to make after the event.

---

[4] See Section 11.8, "Initial involvement and continuing information flow", where I return to this subject when discussing Principle No. 21 of the *AITC Code*.

[5] During my working life I have come across not a few professionals in related disciplines (finance, accountancy, the law) who are unclear about the meaning even of such basic concepts as "gearing".

11.5 THE NEW *AITC CODE OF CORPORATE GOVERNANCE*

The split capital crisis had, and still has, the capacity to do serious damage to the investment trust industry as a whole. The reputational risk has proved frighteningly high, and has been fourfold: to the manager and the management house; to independent financial advisers (IFAs); to trust directors themselves; and to the trust industry as a whole. I am not going to concern myself here with the managers and management houses, or with the IFAs. But it will already be evident that I have considerable sympathy for directors who feel they have let down their shareholders, and I am even sorrier that the industry as a whole (to which I have given my entire working life) now has a cloud over it and that the eyes of the regulators have become fixed on it. As Claudian sadly wrote of Rome at the end of the fourth century AD:

> *Ei mihi quo Latiæ vires urbisque potestas*
> *Decidit! In qualem paulatim fluximus umbram!*[6]

The industry, however, has not been idle in the face of trouble. As referred to earlier, the Association of Investment Trust Companies (AITC, 2003) has recently produced its own *Code of Corporate Governance* ("Code"). This is an important development within the investment trust sector and deserves careful and sympathetic scrutiny. I am glad to see that the AITC's approach seems to be practical and realistic. In his letter to directors accompanying the Code, Daniel Godfrey, Director General of the AITC (and one of the great unsung heroes of the trust industry in recent times), wrote:

> *The code is not intended to promote a box-ticking mentality. Rather, it is intended to ensure that Boards are in a position of strength from which they may consider all the key issues that lead to the delivery of shareholder satisfaction. The code will be a living document and will, in due course, be updated on our website with occasional re-prints made available to Directors to round up substantial changes over a period of time.*

This realism is further made apparent in the introduction to the Code:

> *The intention behind the AITC Code is to provide Boards of our Member Companies with a framework of best practice in respect of the governance of investment trusts and closed ended funds. Notwithstanding the existence of the Combined Code, which is soon to be revised to incorporate the findings of the Higgs review, there are a number of additional factors that apply to investment companies and others where the characteristics of investment companies suggest that alternative approaches to those set out in the Combined Code may be preferable. The AITC Code is intended to form a comprehensive guide to best practice in these areas and will therefore have some overlap with the Combined Code although the focus of attention is on the points of difference. The AITC Code is "principles" rather than "rules" based and the detailed recommendations recognise that most issues Boards will face may have different "right" approaches depending on the individual circumstances of the company. At the same time, to give greater transparency to investors, it should be best practice for AITC Members to state in their annual report whether they are adhering to the principles and following the recommendations in the Code and if not, to explain why and/or to detail the steps they intend to take to bring themselves into line in future.*

(AITC, 2003)

---

[6] Claudii Claudiani, *De Bello Gildonico*, Liber 1, lines 44–45. "Woe is me! Where is fled the might of Latium and the power of Rome? Into what a shadow of our former selves have we little by little declined?"

How might the Code help in avoiding further crises such as the splits *débâcle*?

It begins with a section entitled "Putting the Code in context", which comments briefly on the Code's relationship to the Listing Rules and the *Combined Code* and stresses the importance of recruiting and training directors. It then lists what, in the AITC's opinion, investment company shareholders want from the trust securities they hold, considers the role Boards can and should play in achieving these objectives and defines what are considered to be the fundamentals behind the Code. The second part of the Code, "The Principles", sets out a series of principles concerning the Board, Board meetings and the relationship with the manager and elaborates on each of these in what is described as an appendix but is, in fact, the longest and most detailed part of the document.

In "Putting the Code in context", the Code's analysis of what shareholders want is clear and, in the best sense, obvious:

- *The best possible share price return with an acceptable level of risk consistent with the objectives of the company.*
- *Clear objectives and transparent investment policies so that they can understand what they are buying and the risk/reward dynamics that apply.*
- *A low expense ratio consistent with proper incentivisation for outstanding performance and quality service.*
- *Good liquidity so that they can sell (or buy more) shares easily.*
- *Good communication from the board and portfolio managers.*

No one would argue with any of this. What is more relevant to our purpose is the Code's consideration of "*the role Boards play in delivering against these objectives*". While I am not sure how one can "*deliver against*" anything, the meaning is clear enough and so are the Code's statements. The first statement defines a Board's duty:

- *To bear the ultimate responsibility to shareholders at all times and over all issues notwith-standing any sub-contracts.*

It is good to see this spelt out so forcefully. Boards carry the ultimate responsibility for everything a trust does and it is important that not only the shareholders but also the directors themselves should be aware of it. Whatever happens within or to a trust, the buck stops with the Board. I first joined the Board of an investment trust in 1984. Before taking up the appointment, at the suggestion of a senior colleague I consulted a corporate lawyer for advice on the duties and responsibilities of a company director. After an hour with the lawyer I left shaken and pale, not exactly discouraged but considerably in awe of what I was about to undertake. And so I should have been. To take on a directorship of a public company is a very serious thing, and it is even more so in 2004 than it was in 1984.

The directors of a trust also hold the purse-strings on the shareholders' behalf. The Code affirms that a Board is responsible for:

- *Striking the right balance between cost control and incentivisation to retain as much value as possible for shareholders whilst providing appropriate encouragement to managers to deliver superior returns at acceptable levels of risk.*

This is always a topical subject; and in my experience it can show Boards both at their best and at their worst. I have known of cases where Boards have unhesitatingly – and rightly – vetoed what might have been over-generous incentivisation schemes for managers or management companies. I have also known of Boards who have been cheese-paring in the extreme as regards cost control, wasting large amounts of Board and management time and emotion over trifles. This, of course, is only to be expected. Board members, being all too human, like to leave a Board meeting feeling that they have "made a contribution". One obvious area to comment on for directors with nothing else to say is that of minor economies, on which everyone is an expert. The price one sometimes has to pay for having a Board which is vigilant over big things is that over small things it may be a thorough nuisance.

11.6 HOW CAN DIRECTORS PROVIDE AN "OBJECTIVE VIEW"?

With the Code's assertion that Boards should provide *"an objective view on the benefits and timing of gearing decisions"* we approach the heart of the splits crisis. How should Boards provide this objective view? Here it may be helpful to compare the role of the Board of an investment trust with that of a constitutional monarch in Bagehot's celebrated definition.[7] As Bagehot defined them,[8] the rights of a constitutional monarch are three in number: the right to be consulted; the right to encourage; the right to warn. And what he goes on to say of a constitutional monarch might also be true of a Board: that one of great sense and sagacity would want no other rights. In my experience, trust Boards are most useful not when they lay down the law but when they test managers' thinking and help them refine it, both by judicious questioning and by deliberately playing devil's advocate from time to time. This "testing and refining" role is as relevant to decisions about gearing as it is to the investment management process in general.

There are those who would argue that, during the time of the splits boom, trust Boards should have used their "right to warn" in a more pugnacious way. Perhaps they did and were ignored, or (more likely) were too easily blinded by science into letting their concerns drop. How can we know what happened behind closed doors at the Board meetings of splits? It may be, though, that trust Boards' "right to warn" is less important at present for the sector's well-being than their "right to encourage". There is a danger that in the wake of the splits crisis all gearing will be seen as bad. This could be compounded by the way in which some conventionally structured general trusts have seen their performance dragged down by gearing taken out in more optimistic times. To quote words from a recent Quarterly Report I wrote for the shareholders of Personal Assets Trust:

> *I find it infuriating when Managers' reports blame "gearing" for underperformance, as if their gearing were some sort of unlucky accident beyond their control. Who made them gear in the first place? To borrow a phrase used by Scots children as a lame excuse for their*

---

[7] Walter Bagehot, *The English Constitution*, 1867. By "English Constitution" he meant, of course, the constitution of the United Kingdom of Great Britain and Ireland.

[8] Bagehot in fact considerably – and in my view deliberately – underrated the active role played by Queen Victoria in politics and government in the 1860s, setting out what he wanted to be true rather than what he knew the reality to be; but that is another matter.

misdemeanours, there is today sometimes a sense of "a big boy geared up my trust and ran away" about Managers' reports. And why didn't they hedge the gearing later? Even if trusts do have a geared balance sheet, this does not mean they must at all times have a geared portfolio. One can neutralise gearing by holding gilts or other fixed interest securities, or by selling FTSE 100 Futures ... [D]on't fall into the trap of supposing that gearing is always a bad thing. Ten years ago, people fell into the opposite trap of thinking it was always a good thing. Neither is true. Gearing is an investment tool which it is appropriate to use at some times but not at others, and which can be a good servant but a bad master.

(Angus, 2003)

It would be unfortunate for the trust industry, and a dereliction of duty, if the experience of the splits were to frighten Boards into becoming wholly negative about gearing. It is, however, useless – indeed, worse than useless – for Boards either "to encourage" or "to warn" unless their encouragement or warning is rooted in knowledge and understanding. So, it is vital that Boards should know what gearing is and how it works, and what its effects might be in different sets of circumstances. This cannot be taken for granted; and it throws into even sharper relief the need for the education of directors in what might be called the basic grammar of investment. I am glad that this is alluded to in the Code and I hope, also, that the new agitation for directors to hold office for short, fixed terms will not work against directors with education and experience. I am glad that the Code does not fall into the trap of recommending a fixed term for directors, such as nine years, but instead contents itself with asking Boards to have a policy on tenure which is disclosed in the annual report.[9]

11.7 MONITORING MANAGERS, COMMUNICATING WITH SHAREHOLDERS

The remaining objectives set out for Boards by the Code fall into two main groups, one concerned with monitoring the managers and the other with looking outward to investor relations and the marketplace.

The objectives in the first group – *"regular review of the structure, objectives, target audiences, fund manager and existence of the company"*, *"maintaining proper internal controls"*, *"ensuring that the fund manager manages within the agreed parameters"* and *"objective monitoring of fund manager performance and willingness to press for remedial action if necessary"* – are all well-established and familiar parts of a Board's duties. Two of the Code's suggestions here, however, are worth singling out for special comment. The first is that a Board should from time to time review the existence of the company. My heart leapt up when I saw this. Just because a company exists is not a reason it should continue to exist. All those involved in the trust sector will have known companies which had lost any *raison d'être* but soldiered on from year to year without real

---

[9] Such a policy should in my opinion, be simply that it is a matter for the shareholders whether or not they want to re-elect individual directors and that they should regularly – say, every three years by rotation – be given the opportunity to do so. I shudder to think what state this country would be in today if over the last century or so it had been subject to the findings of recent reports on corporate governance. The Queen has done a superb job for 52 years. It would have been a pity had she been forced to abdicate in 1961, after nine years on the throne. But then there might not have been a throne at all had Churchill been compelled to retire at 65 in 1939, which history suggests would have been rather an inconvenient year for the country to lose his services.

purpose – or, worse, kept resorting to elaborate schemes and expedients just to give themselves the illusion of a purpose. As The Bible says, there is "*a time to be born, and a time to die; a time to plant, and a time to pluck up that which is planted*" (Ecclesiastes 3: 2). Boards can play a useful role sometimes in such plucking up.

The second suggestion that cheers my spirits is that Boards should keep under review the company's target audience. For whom is a trust run? Every Board should ask this question – and should keep asking it at frequent intervals. The two trusts of which I am a director have a very clear answer. They are run for private individuals. Of course, we cannot stop an institution from buying our shares; but we do not run the trusts with institutions' requirements in mind. While not every trust is designed specifically for private investors, it has nevertheless long been my conviction that the trust industry should see itself as being as much a service industry as an investment management industry. This accords well with the second set of objectives the Code sets out for trust Boards: "*ensuring that marketing, promotion and investor relations is conducted professionally, efficiently and cost effectively*", "*ensuring that effective shareholder communications are established*" and "*monitoring and responding to shareholder opinion*".

The last of these, "*monitoring and responding to shareholder opinion*" can be dangerous if (as sometimes seems to be the case) the Board interprets it as meaning that the views of a handful of institutional shareholders should dictate every major decision. I see this recommendation as a challenge to Boards to attempt something much broader, and in this there are many examples of good practice. Let me give three. Alliance Trust and Second Alliance Trust in Dundee have done a superb job in marketing, promotion and investor relations at minimal cost to the investor and at a profit to the trusts themselves. Since their investment plans were launched in 1987 the number of plans of various kinds outstanding has grown to over 36,000, with a total value of £1.2bn (Alliance Trust PLC, 2004). This proves that the two trusts know what their shareholders want and are successfully giving it to them. Second, I am a particular fan of the "Witan Wisdom" campaign, which seems to feature in the kind of magazine I read myself. It is witty, literate and stylish – all of them qualities I like to see associated with investment trusts. Third, the boards of the two trusts of which I am a director, Personal Assets Trust and Collective Assets Trust, have a policy of ensuring that the trusts' shares, unlike those of most other investment trusts, do not sell at other than a nominal discount to net asset value. This, our shareholders tell us, is what they want; and this is therefore what we make sure they get. We achieve it by issuing new shares at a small premium, or buying in shares for cancellation at a small discount, whenever necessary. (For both of these actions we obtain the necessary powers from shareholders at each AGM.) As a result, the shares of Personal Assets, the longer established of the two trusts, have not sold at a discount to net assets of more than a percentage point or two since 1995.

11.8   INITIAL INVOLVEMENT AND CONTINUING INFORMATION FLOW

Rounding up the section entitled "Putting the Code in context" (AITC, 2003, p. 10) comes a statement of what the AITC calls "fundamentals" behind the code of best practice in the corporate governance of investment companies:

- *Directors must put the interests of shareholders above all others.*
- *Directors must treat all shareholders fairly.*
- *Directors should be prepared to resign or take steps that could lead to a loss of office at any time in the interests of long-term shareholder value.*
- *Directors should ensure that they address all issues of relevance and that they disclose the outcomes of those deliberations in a way that non-financial shareholders can understand.*

The second of these – that directors must treat all shareholders fairly – is of special relevance to split capital trusts, which have different classes of share with different entitlements. These entitlements must be fully understood and must be honoured. It is important, too, that the directors should report to shareholders in a way that non-financial shareholders can understand. This applies also to the company's Report & Accounts, where – even if there are statutory or conventional ways of putting things – an effort should also be made to explain to shareholders what they actually mean.[10]

As noted earlier, the Code contains an appendix setting out 21 principles applying to investment trust corporate governance. It takes 16 pages to do so and it would be a simple matter to devote a further 16 pages to discussing them – and particularly to discussing the definitions of "independence" which so dominate thinking on corporate governance today. Some of the most independent trust directors I have ever known were ones who would never have qualified as "independent" under any set of rules I have ever seen. Independence is not a paper qualification but a cast of mind. Nor is there much merit in recruiting outsiders or the inexperienced just for the sake of it.[11] There is a revealing story of Arthur Ponsonby (1871–1946), son of Sir Henry Ponsonby, Private Secretary to Queen Victoria. Ponsonby was Labour MP for Sheffield Brightside. When he asked one of the selection committee there why he had been chosen as candidate rather than someone of more obviously working-class credentials, he was told that the constituency *"had had unfortunate experiences with working-class members, who when they returned from Westminster would say that the Tories weren't so bad after all, and that some of them were even very decent chaps. The Tories, of course, had made fools of them. 'Now you,' he said to Ponsonby, 'have known these people all your life. They won't be able to make a fool of you'."* (Cooper, 1953).

Two of the principles set out in the Code are, however, worthy of closer examination here because they are of special relevance to the split capital crisis. They are Principle No. 10 and Principle No. 21.

Principle No. 10: *The Chairman (and the Board) should be brought into the process of structuring a new launch at an early stage.*

Here the Code's recommendations – very sensible ones – are as follows:

---

[10] I once attended an AGM of an investment trust at which a shareholder queried why several million pounds in fees were being paid in the company's stockbrokers. They weren't. However, the accounts did show several million pounds as being "due to brokers". This referred to the payment due for shares bought before the year-end date but not due for settlement until after it. To an intelligent person without financial experience, however, the entry in the accounts looked as if it referred to a payment of fees for some unnamed purpose.

[11] To go back to my earlier example of Churchill, he was not less bold and independent-minded for being the "insider" Old Harrovian grandson of a Duke; and in the case of the Stephen Lawrence inquiry we saw a notably radical report from another "insider", Sir William Macpherson of Cluny, Bart, 27th Chief of the Clan Macpherson, whose length of lineage makes even the Churchills seem Johnny-Come-Latelys.

- *New companies naturally tend to be created by the manager or sponsor. No Board exists at the outset for the independent appointment of new Directors.*

- *The Chairman should be selected at the earliest practicable point in the process of launching a new company, and should be involved in the selection of the rest of the Board as soon as possible thereafter.*

- *The new Board should assume their responsibilities and be involved in the process at the earliest possible point. The new Board should satisfy itself that the proposed new company is fundamentally sound and has a raison d'être in the market place.*

- *The new Board should be able to seek independent advice paid for by the manager and sponsor, should it feel the need, in the process of its due diligence. Recently, turbulent markets have served as a sharp reminder that Directors can be personally liable for any errors, omissions or misleading statements in a prospectus.*

- *New companies applying for admission to membership of the AITC should be able to confirm that they have complied with this principle and disclose any deviation from the recommendations.*

The split capital trusts *débâcle* showed only too clearly the need for Principle No. 10. By the time the Chairman and other directors were appointed, the structure and investment policy of a new split were all too often *faits accomplis*. I referred earlier to the tendency to "leave it to the experts". In the case of the splits, this had unhappy results. The contribution which a Board could make to the planning and refining of new trusts is considerable, and those approached with a view to becoming directors of such trusts should be careful to ensure that they have power as well as responsibility.

Principle No. 21: *The Board should ensure that shareholders are provided with sufficient information for them to understand the risk : reward balance to which they are exposed by holding the shares.*

Information is the life-blood of good corporate governance: information to the directors, and information to the shareholders. It must, however, be the right information and in the right quantity. Information can be used to confuse and to obscure as well as to enlighten:

- *All holdings in other investment companies should be disclosed on a monthly basis and attention should be drawn explicitly to any material cross holdings.*

This recommendation obviously owes its place in the Code to the unfavourable comment there has been about cross-holdings among the splits. No one denies how harmful these were. However, across the sector as a whole the concern about holdings in other investment companies is in my opinion greatly overdone. What went wrong with the splits was not that they had holdings in other investment companies. Indeed, some of them might still be around today if they had put all their money into the likes of Foreign & Colonial, Alliance Trust or Scottish Mortgage and had held no other equities at all. The problem was that they had holdings in the riskier securities of other highly geared and cross-invested investment companies, the values of which collapsed.

The implication of this section of the Code, that investment companies are more risky than other companies, is unfortunate. They are not. They should be, on average, *less* risky. It is just that a relatively small number of newly launched investment companies of an unproven type turned out to be very risky indeed. This was a disaster for those who invested in them, but they were no more typical of investment companies than Marconi was typical of FTSE 100 stocks. For once, and to my own surprise, I here find myself agreeing with the Financial Services Authority (FSA) rather than the AITC, since the new Listing Rules about disclosure of holdings in other trusts are sensibly limited in their scope.[12]

I also find myself disagreeing with Principle 21's recommendation about portfolio disclosure:

- *Shareholders should normally know precisely in what securities their company is investing. There may, however, be circumstances when a Board decides that such disclosure would not be in the best interest of shareholders (e.g. Huntingdon Life Sciences or a programme of buying or selling an illiquid portfolio). The full portfolio list should be published at least once a year in the annual report.*

I wholly agree that shareholders should normally know precisely in what securities their company is investing, and as far as exceptions to this are concerned I will concede that the point about buying and selling an illiquid portfolio is a strong one. However, I should prefer to know if an investment trust in which I was an investor held shares in a controversial company like Huntingdon Life Sciences, about which I might hold strong views of my own. Not telling me is taking away my freedom to make a moral decision, which might in itself be held to be an immoral act on the part of the Board.

After this quibble, however, I am glad to be able to report that I have nothing but praise for a further set of recommendations under Principle No. 21 which are aimed specifically at split capital trusts and cover both the problem of high but semi-hidden expense ratios (Adams and Angus, 2001, 2002) and the difficulty of gauging the tensile strength of splits' structures. They include a sensitivity analysis showing: the effect on the asset backing of each share class of a matrix of possible returns; the calculation of wipe-out hurdle rates for all share classes except annuity shares; the impact of expense ratios and interest costs on capital erosion per class of share; and much more detailed disclosure of the terms of banking covenants and the various possible consequences were they to be breached.

These recommendations are greatly to be welcomed – indeed, to be applauded. Had they been in place before the splits boom began, much financial loss and bad publicity would have been avoided. Shutting the stable door? Perhaps, but the point is that there are still plenty of horses left in the stable and the AITC, like all others who value the trust sector, is keen to keep them there.

11.9 CHANGES TO THE LISTING RULES

Like other good things, the "fund of funds" is capable of misuse. As a director of one,[13] however, I am convinced of their value and of their rightful place in the range of options available to private investors. For this reason, I was very worried when in response to the split capital trust crisis the FSA indicated that severe restrictions

---

[12] See Section 11.9, "Changes to the Listing Rules".
[13] Collective Assets Trust PLC.

might be placed on trusts' ability to hold the shares of other trusts. However, the changes to the Listing Rules announced by the FSA in September 2003 were much less draconian than I and others had feared.[14] Indeed, were I not temperamentally averse to any such controls I might even have welcomed them! Beginning with the threatened change that worried me most (restrictions on the extent to which trusts could hold shares in other trusts), the new rules essentially mean that investment trusts will still be able to operate as "trusts of trusts" as long as they do not invest more than 10% of their assets in other trusts holding over 15% of *their* assets in other listed investment companies. In other words, one can have "trusts of trusts" but not "trusts of trusts of trusts". If one accepts the principle of regulation at all, this one makes sense.

Much as I dislike regulators and regulations, I have to admit that the other changes in the Listing Rules are also mostly common sense. Included in all listing documents from now on should be a prominent Risk Factors section setting out the risk factors specific to the company (including risk through its gearing), its industry, its investment policy and the securities it proposes to issue. Then there is to be increased portfolio disclosure, notably monthly disclosure of all investments in other trusts which may hold 15% of their assets or more in other trusts, enhanced COBS (FSA, 2001) risk warnings and a requirement for all material changes to the company's investment policy to receive prior shareholder approval.

11.10 CONCLUSION

I come back to Trollope's daunting question for the nervous but worried non-executive director:

What nuisance can be so great to a man busied with immense affairs, as to have to explain or to attempt to explain small details to men incapable of understanding them?

After all my thousands of well-meant words, what answer can I give? Perhaps the late (and much missed) Sir Denis Thatcher, an experienced company director who knew more than most about dealing with those "busied with immense affairs", can reply on my behalf:

I'm not very bright, you know. I just read the papers before the Board meeting, and the others usually don't. And I can add up.

11.11 REFERENCES

Adams, A.T. and Angus, R.J. (2001) For whom the barbell tolls ... *Professional Investor*, **11**(3), April 14–17 [see Appendix A of current book].
Adams, A.T. and Angus, R.J. (2002) From barbell to dumb-bell. *Professional Investor*, April, 13–16.

[14] For my views and those of my collaborator, Dr Andrew Adams, see Appendix B (p. 233).

AITC (2003) *The AITC Code of Corporate Governance: A Framework of Best Practice for Member Companies.* Association of Investment Trust Companies, London.

Alliance Trust PLC (2004) *Annual Report & Accounts for the Year Ended 31 January 2004.* Alliance Trust PLC, Dundee.

Angus, R.J. (2003) *Quarterly Report No. 27* (February). Personal Assets Trust PLC, Edinburgh.

Bagehot, W. ([1867], 1966) *The English Constitution* (edited by R.H.S. Crossman). Collins/ Fontana, London.

Claudii Claudiani ([398], 1922) *De Bello Gildonico.* Loeb Classical Library, Cambridge, MA.

Cooper, D. (1953) *Old Men Forget, The Autobiography of Duff Cooper (Viscount Norwich).* Rupert Hart-Davis, London.

FSA (2001) *Conduct of Business Sourcebook.* Financial Services Authority, London.

Trollope, A. ([1875], 1982) *The Way We Live Now* (edited by John Sutherland). Oxford University Press, Oxford, UK.

12

Some Ethical Considerations

ANDREW M. McCOSH

> *You must not curse the deaf, nor place a stumbling block in front of a blind man,
> instead you must behave justly and with righteousness.*
>
> (Leviticus 19: 14)

12.1 INTRODUCTION

An article in the *Financial Times* on 28 July 2003 reported an interview with Mr Andrew Proctor, enforcement officer of the Financial Services Authority (FSA). The report made him sound rather plaintive. The people they wanted to talk to about split capital investment trusts, or "splits", were not co-operating with the inquiry. Their lawyers were doing everything possible to slow the investigation down. The lawyers were treating the inquiry as though it was a full-scale litigation. A third of the personnel of the FSA enforcement team were allocated to the one subject. Phone calls equivalent to 13 years of talking would have to be listened to. Tons of paper would have to be read.

The behaviour of the lawyers was intriguing to a writer on financial ethics, or at least to this one. If a lawyer really believes that the best way to defend a client's interest is by non-co-operation with the appointed regulator, there must be something really interesting in there somewhere.

At the same time, it is clear that it will be a long time before we can expect anything definitive to come out the other end of the FSA exploration. I do not rely on that output. Instead, I intend to note a number of allegations that have been made during the split capital investment trust saga. Many of these are mentioned in the third report of the House of Commons Treasury Committee (HCTC, 2003a) or in the responses to it (HCTC, 2003b). I will then express an opinion concerning each group of alleged actions, saying whether the actions which comprised each allegation would be ethical or would be unethical. I am not making any claim that the alleged actions have actually occurred. That is for the FSA, the Financial Ombudsman Service (FOS), and other authorities to decide.

12.2 THE EXISTENCE OF SENIOR DEBT

The history of the splits saga has been rehearsed thoroughly in earlier chapters of this book. The early splits, launched in 1997 or earlier, were perfectly workable and did the job they were supposed to do. They rarely had debt, so any zero-dividend preference shares, "zeros", were the safest securities in their capital structure. They lived their lives of eight or so years, and the ending capital was distributed among the income shares, the capital shares and the zeros exactly according to plan. There were dozens of different capital structures among the splits, each of which produced its own unique result. I am not making any attempt to deal with the array of structures encyclopaedically.

Investors were told, by their independent financial advisers (IFAs), that the zeros were safe securities to buy. So they were, at that time. I do not see how any IFA who supplied a zero in a split which had no debt capital and which had significant amounts of ordinary income shares and capital shares could be criticised at that time for un-ethical behaviour, provided the underlying portfolio was broadly spread and did not have overly demanding yield requirements. These shares *were* safe, as safe as any investment with an equity aspect can be expected to get.

Unfortunately, this happy state of affairs was not to last. The reason, as usual, was the greed of the shareholders; in this instance, the greed of the shareholders (and perhaps some of the executives) of the investment management companies who spon-sored the splits. Perhaps also the greed of some of the shareholders of the new splits themselves. The publicly quoted investment management companies who were promot-ing splits were subject to the same pressures for "shareholder value" as most other quoted companies. The pressure for performance on the part of public companies has been building steadily for at least 20 years. The profits of last year should be improved on this year. Obviously, the build-up of pressure proved too great eventually. The "corner-cutting" to "make the numbers" that began in earnest during the slump of 1991 led eventually to the huge problems in Enron, WorldCom and other firms. I predicted serious corner-cutting, and some of the consequences, in a book which first appeared in 1995, and was published officially four years later (McCosh, 1999). Unfortunately, I did not know exactly which shares to short sell.

Investment management companies were subject to the same shareholder pressures as all the rest. One of their "solutions" to the task of increasing profits in their sponsored splits was the addition of a further layer of capital, in the form of bank debt. The exact terms of the debt of a public company are not always disclosed publicly.

In 1999 a few splits were launched with a significant amount of bank debt. In 2000 and later, indebted split launches became common. Suddenly, the zero was less safe. The bankers had the first rights when the split reached its term. The zero owners came second. Whether this change was important or not depended on the size of the bank debt. It should have been obvious to an IFA that he should take a look at the ratio of the various capital sources to the total, to see whether the zeros were still safe, as he had previously thought, or whether they were now a bit shaky.

There are several technologies available for assessing the "safeness" of a given share. A crude one would involve working out how much the assets had to fall in value before a given capital tranche started to be endangered, and also how much it had to fall before that capital tranche was completely erased. More sophisticated measures are available, as discussed by James Clunie in Chapter 6 of this volume.

It should, however, have been totally obvious to all IFAs that a split with debt had to be riskier than a split without, if the asset portfolios were similar. An IFA who performed some check on each new split with zeros would clearly be in a better position to assist his clients than one who did not. Such a check would establish the amount of senior debt capital. If the banking covenant were breached, the bank could call in the debt whenever it felt its capital to be at risk. The holders of the zeros, however, could not close down the company until its normal expiry date.

An IFA who told his client about the risks associated with a zero that was partially debt financed would not be behaving unethically if he told the client about the debt (and its implications) before investment. An IFA who found that the debt finance was, say, 10% or less of the total capital, and who therefore felt the zeros to be safe, and who said so to his client, would not be behaving unethically either. An IFA who found the same, and did not tell the client before investing his funds in the zeros, would not be behaving unethically either, unless the client had specifically prohibited investment in shares of companies with debt. Such a prohibition would be very rare, because very few companies are totally debt-free, and even fewer would guarantee to stay debt-free for eight or so years.

If the debt element in the capital of a split was a high proportion of the total capital employed, and if the IFA did not explain the situation clearly to his client, I believe the IFA was at fault, ethically. If the IFA invested the client's funds without explaining that the risk was materially higher than "old zeros" risk, the IFA was certainly at fault.

If the debt element was moderate, the situation is not clear. It is an ethical grey area. Ethics always has grey areas. In these situations, you have to look at what the other features of the situation are, before arriving at a conclusion.

The ethical motto on which the above argument rests is the concept of duty, as promulgated by Immanuel Kant ([1785], 1946). We have an obligation to treat every person, including ourselves, as an end in their own right, never only as a means to an end. In the context above, failing to inform the client/shareholder that his security is carrying a substantial burden of debt would be to treat them as means to the end of making our sales numbers for the year, not as a person who has the right to our best endeavours. At the same time, if it is a discretionary relationship, the client is not expecting to be phoned up for every triviality. If we follow the writings of Baruch Brody (1988), we have an obligation to defer to the other party's desired end state. When he has formulated an objective for his investment portfolio, we have an obligation, in taking on the job, to aim toward that objective. We may not hit the target exactly, but we do have an obligation to aim at it. Putting the client's money into a heavily debt-laden split when the client specified a high level of safety is a clear ethical failure on the part of the investment counsellor.

12.3 PRESSING THE PRESS

When a product becomes fashionable, the first producer has an advantage, and all the other producers scramble to catch up. If some of the other producers are big enough powerful enough and rich enough, they may be able to overtake the first producer. When you are selling a financial product, the inherent beauty of the product is usually lost on the average buying client. Your version looks pretty much like the ones made available by your competitors.

How, then, can the fifth (say) producer get his version of the fashionable product of the moment to the attention of the investors, or (perhaps more importantly) that of their IFA? One way is to get Victoria Beckham to buy it. Perhaps even better would be for her to buy one for Brooklyn's next birthday. Not always an applicable approach, and rather expensive, given her appearance fees.

Another way is to get a newspaper's finance editor to write an editorial about the fashionable product of the moment, and to give your particular manifestation of this a more favourable comment than he awards to the remainder. This is relatively simple if your version has some distinguishing feature which is clearly positive, and which the finance writer can understand. Neither of these can be guaranteed, however.

So, the promoter of the split may have to resort to brute force. "My investment company spent £125,000 on advertising in your newspaper last year. You are going to write our product up favourably, aren't you? Or should we just advertise in the Daily Blot instead next year?" Subtler versions of this approach are available. I was subjected to the version in this paragraph while serving as editor of a small journal in North America. My response was unprintable. It transpired that we did not lose the advertising, but it was reduced in size. It has been alleged that some variant of this approach was employed by at least one investment trust promoting company during the splits boom.

It is clearly unethical for the investment trust promoter to make such a threat. It would be similarly unethical for the newspaper to change its opinion of the share because of the threat. The right to advertise an investment product is clear and desirable. This right depends on the advertisement being truthful and current, and on the availability of a more detailed document which displays the more detailed information the investor and/or his IFA will require. But using threats like the one above is unethical, unequivocally.

If the promoter makes no threat, but simply refrains from subsequent advertising in a publication in which nasty things have been written about his product, no ethical violation would have occurred. Nobody has a moral obligation to continue to trade with his enemies, unless there is a contract to do so.

Plato, for instance, decreed that we should "do no harm" (*The Last Days of Socrates*, Crito X 49). The possession of power is not a reason for using brute force to achieve an immediate goal. In part, this is self-interest. Using force would simply bring about our own destruction in a relatively short time, as those we attack or their descendants take their revenge. Thinking through the sequence of future events that are likely to happen, following on our first action, a procedure advocated by Grotius (1625), is much safer.

Many newspaper articles have appeared since July 2001 which are seriously negative about the split trusts, and some of them have been written by journalists who may have been subjected to pressure at earlier times. Revenge is sweet.

Alternatively, we could invoke the ethical concept of honesty. In communications, a signal is significant if it would have caused a normal human adult to reconsider, but not necessarily to change, his previous opinion about the issue at hand. A newspaper article would be both significant and dishonest if it gives the reader an impression of the share which the journalist does not himself believe. In this instance, the journalist and the promoter of the split would be equally guilty, if the former seeks an erroneous endorsement and the journalist provides it. Nobody is ethically clean in that situation. Honesty is a virtue in the writings of almost every ethicist. Aristotle ([c. 330 BC], 1980) and

Confucius ([c. 490 BC], cited in de Bary and Bloom, 1999) were the most prominent early writers to articulate its importance.

12.4   PEDDLING THE PAPER

The independent financial adviser (IFA) belongs to a relatively new profession, effectively created by the Financial Services Act of 1986. This personage is to be contrasted with a tied agent, in that the latter was only allowed to sell securities created by his own group of companies, while the IFA was allowed to sell anything "that would be of benefit to his client". Unfortunately, it has been alleged that, in some cases, the last eight words of the previous sentence seem to have taken a walk.

If the client has specified in precise terms what he means exactly by "benefit", the IFA would have a clear picture of what was wanted and would have no excuse if he then failed to provide a set of securities which conformed to the investor's wishes.

Unfortunately, many investors do not have a realistic conception of what can be done. A client who specifies a minimum level of income return of 20% combined with a growth target of 15% may get lucky. In normal circumstances, however, this target will be totally unattainable. The IFA is in a tricky spot here. He may be inclined to say: "Look, you idiot, there isn't a hope in hell of getting a result like that. Get realistic. Specify about a third of that return and we are in with a chance!" However, this remark might well be considered poor marketing. The client, even if confronted with a very much softer edition of the remark above, might easily go elsewhere, to obtain guidance and advice from a different adviser with a smoother pitch. The second IFA would not promise any more than the first one, but might express himself hopefully for long enough to get the mandate form signed.

In any event, many clients signed up for guidance with IFAs, and many of them no doubt obtained, and continue to obtain, impeccable service. As always, however, allegations have been made that there were a few IFAs who did not seem to remember that they were working for the investor. It is difficult for an IFA to blot out completely, from his own memory, the commission rates paid for various financial instruments. Also, there were genuine difficulties in keeping up to date with the torrents of new investment vehicles being promoted from 1999 until about 2001. At the same time, the IFA does have a duty. He is holding himself out to be an expert provider of guidance on financial issues, albeit one who cannot "get it right" every time. The investor is entitled to be treated as an end, not as a means. He is entitled to have his interests protected and nurtured. He is entitled to assume that the IFA has read the more detailed features of many of the possible investment vehicles, and that the IFA will tell him about any features that make the vehicle particularly appropriate or particularly inappropriate.

What, then, were the clues available to the IFA industry? What, if any, were the oddities that he should have spotted and used as clues to protect his clients?

I have discussed above the issue of debt capital, and the IFA's duty arising from that. Now I want to consider the return expectations. If a security shows a yield of 10%, when others, which seem at least superficially similar, are yielding 6%, an expert in the field of investment should be wondering how this financial miracle has occurred. Some legitimate explanations exist, of course. A higher risk may explain, though it may not justify, the higher return.

In the case of split capital trusts, from about 1999 onwards, there might be four broad classes of capital suppliers to be provided for. The banks could look after themselves, and generally required a rather modest annual return. The other three groups were largely under the control of the promoter, subject to the overall performance of the assets. If the assets of the business seemed (in mid-year) likely to provide a return of, say, 8%, the promoter could make some choices. He might choose to provide a generous return to the income shareholders (11%?), while making formal provision for the zeros at, say, 5%. Or he could favour the zeros by over-providing for their entitlement, while trimming the return to the income shareholders. The capital shareholders would receive the residue, if any. The one thing he could not do was pay out more than 8% to everybody. During the bear market of 2000–03, 8% would have been a very good result, but −8% would have been likelier.

I find it hard to visualise how an IFA could have decided to put a safety-seeking investor into a new split capital investment trust during 2000 or later. Especially, if it had any significant quantity of debt. Any review of the balance sheets would have shown that they were not going to be able to fulfil everyone's expectations. The fact that they were yielding a high return should have been a source of worry too, with some zeros yielding higher than junk bonds. By definition, junk bonds are not safe investments. They are not even supposed to be safe investments!

There was a film many years ago about a character called Walter Mitty, who lived in a dream world of his own imagination. All sorts of wonderful things happened to him while he occupied his dream world, while most of the things that happened to him in his real world were rather unappetising. He grew fonder and fonder of the dreamworld, and eventually lost touch with reality altogether. Some of those involved in the splits saga were behaving just like him. The technical ethical failure which they exhibited was absence of integrity. This is a difficult virtue to define, but is generally regarded as the summation of uprightness plus honesty plus sincerity. The concept of integrity is well covered in Plato's *Republic* and in Alastair MacIntyre's (1981) *After Virtue*. The splits managers can hardly be blamed for not anticipating the collapse of the markets, a factual and largely external event. However, to react to the fall by attempting to bury the problem from sight would be ethically unforgivable.

12.5 FORCED SALES OF ASSETS

We have already looked at the impact of bank debt on the safeness of the other investors in split capital investment trusts, paying particular attention to the position of zero holders in the "pay-back queue". There is another aspect of the bank debt to be considered as well. A banker may become nervous about his investment, just the same as any other investor may become nervous. But the banker may be able to do something about it, while holders of zeros, income shares and capital shares cannot. The banker can simply force the manager of the split to sell assets and return the money to the bank when some agreed-on ratio of assets to liabilities has been violated. The assets that have to be sold to meet the banker's requirements may well be the best and most liquid holdings the split had in its portfolio. Some others may be illiquid, perhaps to the point of being completely unsaleable.

Perhaps I am oversensitive about liquidity. When I served as a director of a series of mutual funds in New York, one of our international funds was an active investor in eastern Europe. The manager had bought heavily into Turkish construction companies. Unfortunately, a substantial apartment building collapsed shortly after the investment was made, and we were all aware that there would be a loss, perhaps for quite a while. We were not ready for what actually happened, though. The Turkish market suspended all the construction shares, which meant that we had no accurate basis for pricing the units of our mutual fund for several weeks, nor any means of selling them. We got a severe ticking off from the Securities and Exchange Commission (SEC). I am very aware of, perhaps oversensitive to, the importance of liquidity.

In the case of the split capital trust manager and his banker, liquidity was of the essence. There is nothing unethical about the behaviour of the banker. He never said he would support the split through thick and thin, for richer for poorer, for better or worse. All he said was that he wanted a certain rate of interest and he wanted his money back if the relevant ratio fell below X.

The ethical problem arises in the management company supporting the split. The potential liquidity of the split might be deciphered from some of their balance sheets, but not from most of the ones I have been able to lay hands on. This liquidity feature compounds the risk we have already discussed, of being unable to meet the expectations of the zero holders. Every forced sale of a share by a split capital investment company eats into the cake that might have fed the shareholders.

The ethical concept that applies here is the Aristotelian warning on prudence (Aristotle, [c. 330 BC], 1980). This is the middle way between the twin vices of foolhardiness and the taking of risks just for the fun of it, on the one hand; and of timidity, on the other, where we avoid contact with almost everyone, so as to eliminate risk as completely as possible. This was updated by Grotius (1625) two millennia later. The world's first international lawyer advised all kings that they should "invariably study and consider what the other parties will do in response to the action we propose to take now, for thus we may still achieve much while averting their vengeance." The fund managers should have known that the bankers might force a sale, and should have planned and designed their trust accordingly. If half of the capital is debt, and the life of the fund is eight years, it just takes one short market dip to wipe you out. The managers should have known that, the IFAs should have known that, and the investors should have been told that by their IFA if they did not know it themselves beforehand.

12.6 CHARGES

Now consider the charges levied in some of the new issues during the splits boom. The corporate advisers raise some money for a new split, then they borrow about the same amount again from a bank. Then they levy charges based on the grand total of all the money raised, whether they raised it (which requires a certain effort) or borrowed it (which requires virtually none)! A remarkable way to make a living! Additional launch costs (for marketing, commission, etc.), as explained in Chapter 4, might boost the total expense at the outset of a new split to 5% of the shareholders' funds or more in some cases.

The annual fees would be generally charged on the basis of gross assets (funds under management). This was seriously costly for the equity investors. Other running costs were also generally quite substantial. A reasonably conventional 1% annual charge, based on gross assets, might suddenly blossom to 2% of shareholders' funds under this scheme. The problem is similar to the launch charges issue, being levied on the whole capital, regardless of origin. I note, however, that in answer to a question on this issue from Dr Palmer MP at the Treasury Select Committee hearings, Mr Tiner of the FSA said: "Now we could discuss whether the level of the fee was too high, that is an issue for the market, but levying the fee on the gross assets, i.e., the actual work they are supposed to be doing, seems to be reasonable" (HCTC, 2003a, Ev. 143).

The situation would become more complex if any of the split managers started to buy heavily into the ordinary income shares of other splits. If I buy shares in your split, using shares held by my own fund as payment, you have, suddenly, a larger empire, which brings in its turn a larger management fee. It would never do to let anyone think this was a circular back-scratching team, so I will not expect you to buy into mine. Someone else can do that. It will all come out even in due course. And the fees will go on rising. And rising.

The ethical problem in this instance is that of overcharging. The prohibition of such behaviour is present in many ethical writings. This time I will use the religions as a source; they could be used in several other places, of course, and there are secular writers who say similar things. For instance, the Koran prohibits traders from "devouring the inheritance of others with devouring greed, and loving wealth with a boundless love" (Arberry, 1964: Koran 89: 17; Ali, 1973) and states that these traders will suffer ferocious punishment. Al-Ghazali, one of the great Islamic ethicists, specifically instructs traders "not to exceed the normal profit margin, not to sell to the poor at high prices, but to buy from them at more than market" (Umaruddin, 1962). The Jewish and Christian Bibles similarly instruct traders "to deal honestly, to give full measure, to use accurate scales and weights, and never to adulterate produce or silver" (2 Corinthians 13: 7, Proverbs 16: 11, Amos 8: 4–6).

12.7 MUTUAL ASSISTANCE PROGRAMME

The companies involved in the management of split capital investment trusts are unanimously of the view (as reported in the Treasury Select Committee materials) that there was no collusion at all in terms of the mutual assistance programme allegations. The allegation that there was a "magic circle" of companies, who assisted each other by buying shares in each other's offerings, is consistently repudiated by all the companies whose comments I have seen. The people who are making these claims are reported to have admitted that they have no hard evidence that such actions occurred. My comments below on the alleged actions of mutual assistance are therefore hypothetical.

The Association of Investment Trust Companies (AITC) gave evidence to the Treasury Select Committee and this included (HCTC, 2003a, Ev. 28) a comment about certain rumours. The AITC confirmed that it had heard "numerous rumours and anecdotes about collusion where managers and sponsoring brokers were alleged to have agreed to support each other's new issues." The AITC evidence continued: "The charge is that the managers agreed to invest their client funds in each other's launches on a quid pro quo basis. In other words, the motivation behind certain investment decisions was not what was in the best interests of the investors ... but the best commercial interests of the fund management house. The purpose would have been to guarantee new funds for each new issue, which would then borrow against these funds, growing the assets under management on which fees would be paid." The AITC did not produce any evidence that this activity actually happened. They simply reported the rumours they had heard.

As I understand this allegation, the idea is something like this. If I buy a decent quantity of income shares in your split, and you buy a decent quantity of income shares in Rupert's split, and Rupert buys a decent quantity of income shares in George's split, and George buys into mine, we will all be hugely better off. All this activity may be used to persuade fund managers and IFAs that the splits are in demand, and may cause them to put some private clients' money into one or more of these groups of shares.

Another aspect of the mutual assistance allegation relates to restructuring deals in which the vast majority of the "income" securities were sold to other splits or other funds whose managers also managed splits. Many of these transactions were carried out by stock swaps. Apart from private client money, little real money changes hands. The value of the securities which are swapped is generally set by reference to the middle market price. So the last trade was a month ago. Not to worry. Isn't the capitalist system wonderful?

There are a couple of problems with this idyllic vision. First, the middle-market price may not be current. There is no doubt that the middle-market prices of the income shares of the early splits were accurate, or at least reasonable. The later ones, from 2000 onwards, were in many cases of antiquarian interest only. There were few trades being done. Once the music stopped, virtually no one was buying anything with real currency. Therefore, nobody was selling anything.

After the mutual assistance programme, there would be more paper about, but very little additional cash. Is this a problem? Well, yes. If you have more paper claiming to share in a fixed amount of real assets, the owners of the elderly segment of said paper would be upset if they found that the new paper was non-contributory. They would be even more upset if they learned that the result of all this paper shuffling was that the management fees were increased.

The second problem with this arrangement would be the extent of the discretionary investment funds. A private investor might give some capital to an IFA to invest for him. If the IFA trusted, and wanted to be supportive and friendly to, a fund promoter, and if the private investor had given substantial freedom to the IFA as to how he should invest it, then the private investor might well find himself the proud owner of a packet of income shares with a respectable middle-market value but no actual buyers.

Why does this jolly scheme not work? Or does it really work after all? We have to start by looking at the total value of the assets of the split. Let us suppose that the split had real assets which could have been sold in the market on 3 January 2001 for £50m. By 3 January 2002, it would be quite conceivable that they could have been sold in the market for £30m. Some of the natives would be getting restless by this time. If the total capital available has fallen, the investors will become inquisitive. The bank will check to see that its investment is still in good condition. The zero holders ought to make a similar check, and let us suppose they find reasonably good news. The income shareholders, and the capital shareholders, will by this time be going berserk. The income shareholders will be screaming for a colossal dividend, right now please. The capital shareholders will be contemplating suicide, probably quite quietly.

Unfortunately, it might not be as good as that. The zero holders might eventually find that there was nothing for them either.

It is difficult to find any heroes in this part of the saga. As is normal in a financial disaster, the problem starts in a small way. Someone tries to fix it by making a minor change to procedures. That turns out to provide a short-term repair, but makes it worse in the medium term. So, a month or a year later, the manager has to make a larger "fix", to repair the medium-term problem, and in so doing creates a worse problem for the new, additional, medium term. Occasionally, the manager (and his investment clients) are rescued by events. However, too frequently, it just spirals out of control. The really courageous action is to kill the problem at birth before it turns into a crisis. If there is a loss, declare it, say you will try to fix it and move on. If some shareholders abandon you, too bad, but that is a lot better than being heavily criticised in the newspapers.

Two of the most powerful of the maxims of ethics are the maxim of justice (Rawls, 1972) and the Kantian maxim of respect which we have already employed above (Kant, [1785], 1946). The concept of a just society is usually derived from the concept of equality of opportunity and that of equality of rights. In devising the structure of a split, the promoters are laying forth a structure of rights and obligations which they hope the investors will agree to and to which they also commit themselves. The investor has the right to walk away before investing, of course, but after entering into the deal he has certain obligations, usually involving paying money in. The promoter has another set of rights and obligations, governed by the Kantian obligation to treat the investors as ends in themselves rather than as means to an end, and also the requirement to treat people with justice. In this context, that means treating all the investors equally, within the terms of the agreed arrangement. If there is plenty, share the plenty as pre-arranged. If there is a shortage, then share the pain as pre-arranged. In most instances, the contract governing the split was fairly clear: the bank got interest; the income share got the incoming interest and dividends after bank interest, etc. had been paid;[1] the zeros got a predetermined amount at a fixed future date; and the capital shares got the remainder in the (now-laughable) event that there was anything left over.

The doctrine of rights does not allow you to change the structure unilaterally. The other party has rights and may choose to waive them, but if he does not formally do so,

---

[1] In certain cases, the Companies Act restrictions on dividend payments, and legal opinions about whether it was appropriate to pay dividends when zeros were uncovered, became relevant. These eventualities were not anticipated at the time the split was launched.

you cannot change the structure on your own. Justice means implementing the agreement you signed up for and sharing the results as specified. An allegation has been made that some of the promoters simply did not behave with justice in that they failed to conform to the original contract when reorganizing. An allegation has been made that some of the IFAs behaved unjustly, in that they were careless with their advice. Some members of both groups seem also to have failed to respect the legitimate needs and rights of their investors.

12.8   IT PAYS TO ADVERTISE

I have already dealt with the ethical issues if an advertiser exerts pressure on a newspaper for favourable editorial comment. Now, I turn to the content of some of the advertising. First of all, it is clearly right and reasonable that promoters of investment products should be entitled to advertise what they have for sale. They are entitled to assume that the reader is competent to make his own decisions about the products, or that he can hire the competence required. There is no obligation for an advertiser to lay emphasis on the weaker features of his product or the stronger points of a competitor's. The advertisement is a paid-for promotional document, and the reader must assess it in that light.

The advertiser has to be truthful. If there is any uncertainty about the veracity of the text, some elucidation in the small print should be provided, and it should be in comprehensible words, and in the same language as the remainder of the advert. Don't laugh: I have seen an advertisement for a Italian-made car with several asterisked sentences in the German language main text, each of which referred to small print explanations in Italian.

There were numerous advertisements placed for the splits offerings. Some advertised the whole range of securities available for purchase, including income shares, capital shares and zeros, and these usually stated that the whole thing was "geared" or "also anticipated bank funding". Other advertisements specified only one of the shares available.

A Jupiter advertisement, dated October 1999, offered ordinary income shares of the Jupiter Dividend & Growth Trust for a pound each. The expected 9% dividend might, the advertisement suggests, be enhanced by capital appreciation over the six-year life of the trust if the asset growth targets were exceeded. In smaller type at the bottom of the advertisement the dangers of the offer were listed. First, there may not be enough money to pay back the bank at wind-up in 2005. Second, there may not be enough to pay off the zeros. Third, even if these payments are achieved there is no guarantee that there will be enough to pay the ordinary income shareholders their (one pound) investment back. Readers were encouraged to phone for a "mini-prospectus", and to make their investment rapidly because the offer would expire in 40 days.

The paragraph you have just read is, I suggest, a neutral version of the content of their ad, with four lines of plus points, two neutral and five lines of minus points. The actual advertisement contained the same material in 22 lines of large type on the plus points and seven lines of small type on the minus points. Not neutral, but as stated above, they do not have to be.

However, they do have to be truthful. An advertisement may be untruthful by making positively untrue claims, which happens relatively infrequently, or by failing to mention some important aspect, which happens rather too often. In this situation, the omission is quite important. They do not tell the reader that the fund is a split capital investment trust. A reader who was familiar with the concept would be able to infer that it was a split by seeing the reference to the zero in the small-print section. A novice reader would not be able to make that inference.

The novice reader would certainly not be able to work out, from the text of the advertisement, that the bank claims and the preordained zero-dividend preference claims would be seriously likely to eat the entire resources of the fund, unless the assets of the fund appreciated at a very substantial rate. The advert states, truthfully, that the residual net assets of the trust after these claims were not guaranteed to be able to refund the income shareholders their initial investment. However, the advertisement does not make clear that the funds would have to make a very demanding return to recover the one pound per share investment. It seems to me quite inexcusable to omit these two significant items: first, that the organisation the reader was being invited to join was a split capital investment trust; and second, I think it unethical that the advertisement did not mention any quantitative investment return requirement at all.

A second advertisement has also been given to me. A supplementary leaflet by BFS Investments PLC to the January 2000 issue of *Select IT* displayed the asset allocation for their Geared Income Investment Trust (GIIT) by means of a pie chart. This sheet is quite clear, in that it states that 53% of the assets were invested in geared ordinary income shares, 15% in ordinary shares and 3% in capital shares. This means that at least 71% of the assets were in securities with the risk of equities, or a higher risk.

With 71% of the assets invested in shares which had the risk of equities or more, it would have seemed appropriate for the level of risk inherent in the shares of GIIT itself to be described as at least fairly high. The 100 million ordinary shares (valued at £75m) were described as "medium to high risk". The 120 million income shares (£66m) were described as "low to medium" risk, while the 39 million zeros (£47m) were low risk. The proceeds from substantial share issues, as well as an additional loan facility of £30m, were to be used to pay for a usefully larger dividend. When you have at least 71% of your assets in the high-risk category, it seems to me to be ethically hazardous to describe only 40% of the value of the shares you have issued in the same way. The new debt, together with previous loans, will make this discrepancy even greater.

One of the suppliers/promoters of split capital trusts advertised a unit trust that invested entirely in zeros by means of a compact disk. The visual text (but not the audio) makes the claim that this unit trust is the "one year old which lets you sleep at night." Having fairly recently acquired a grand-nephew of that vintage, I frankly do not believe such creatures exist. There is a widespread assumption that the company meant to convey the impression that the security was relatively safe. However, this statement does not seem to me to have any clear ethical meaning at all. Any literal study of the phrase establishes that the words are nonsensical; a zero-coupon security parchment with a built-in alarm clock would be exactly as nonsensical, albeit of the opposite function. We must therefore fall back on an allegorical analysis. It is a general feature of allegoric playwriting that they convey meaning by eloquence and inference rather than statements of hard fact. It would only be unethical to use such allegoric methods if there was any chance that a reasonably normal reader could mistake the allegory for hard fact. If the statement had been made that the security was "the one year old that multiplies your money by 1.23," we would find ourselves in a different philosophical realm. It so happens that that was the exact amount by which the Aberdeen Progressive Growth Fund outperformed the FTSE during its first year. It could therefore be judged true on its factual content. A claim that the security was "the one year old that doubles your money" could similarly be judged (to be untrue) on the same basis. An allegory cannot be so judged. It is ethically meaningless, because the reader must know, or certainly ought to know, that it makes no meaningful claim.

12.9   IF IT ISN'T WORKING, RECONSTRUCT IT

A number of Boards of splits decided, after mid-2001, to reconstruct the enterprise in the light of disappointing results. Nothing wrong with that, conceptually. But in some instances, it has been alleged that the restructuring has been done in a way that severely damages the rightful expectations of certain classes of investor. This arises because of sections of the 1985 Companies Act, notably section 265.

If an investment company's net assets fall in value to less than half of the value of its liabilities, section 265 bites. Several splits are actually groups of companies rather than stand-alone companies, and I have been advised that the zero-dividend preference shares have, in several cases, been issued by a subsidiary rather than by the parent. In that situation, the capital entitlement (accumulated so far) of the zero owners is classified as a liability of the parent company. If that liability, plus others, is big enough, the parent company cannot pay a dividend. The reasoning is that creditors are entitled to protection against the possibility that the directors might dissipate the remaining assets of a company to its shareholders instead of preserving them for the benefit of the higher ranking creditors.

I have been told that the Board of one split capital trust wrote to the shareholders and asked them to vote for certain technical changes to the operating rules of the investment trust. One of the consequences of one of these technical changes was that the shareholders cancelled the applicability of section 265. If this cancellation actually occurred, it would seem to be rather more than a "technical" change. It would enable the trust to recommence the payment of dividends to shareholders.

It is not clear why the Board of Directors was not advised against these proposed technical changes, or at least the one which killed off section 265. Presumably, they were informed of their consequences for the zero holders, who were one of several significant groups of people the directors were protecting to the best of their ability.

I find it difficult to understand how the Board arrived at the decision to recommend a change in the regulations that would transfer value from the zero holders to the income shareholders. In my view, there is no obvious reason to regard the income share holders as inherently more deserving of their dividend than the zero holders were of this value. Indeed, the fact that the income shareholders had been receiving dividends in previous years might be thought to tilt the moral balance, but not necessarily the legal entitlement, in the opposite direction. I hope the FSA will eventually throw light on this puzzle.

If any Board did in fact use the funds which had been accumulating for the benefit of the zero holders to pay a dividend to the holders of other securities, I have no doubt that they would make sure it was a legal transfer. I simply do not understand the basis for its ethical propriety.

This time, I will refer for ethical guidance to Moses ben Maimon, better known as Maimonides, who codified the rabbinical law in 1150 (Maimonides, [1150], 1949). His ideas have been amplified since, but not reversed. If you obtain something from another party and it is destroyed during normal use, then the owner is the loser. However, if you obtain something from another party and it is destroyed while being used for a purpose for which it was not intended, then the borrower must compensate for the loss in full. In the case of the splits, the object was money, and the use to which it was meant to be put was to pay the zero holders. It is alleged that the use to which it was actually put was to pay a dividend to the income shareholders. The "mis-users" in this case would be the managers and directors of the split, who would be morally liable to provide full recompense to the zero holders, out of personal funds. The income shareholders would, in my estimation, be innocent beneficiaries, unless it turns out that there was a collusive link between various groups of such shareholders.

12.10   WHY DID THE SHAREHOLDERS NOT REBEL?

As the storm clouds gathered over the split capital investment trust industry, there was no real sign of reaction by the shareholders. A valuable paper on zero pricing by Philip Middleton of Smith New Court explained the hazards and advantages very clearly, back in 1992, but his remarks seem to have been forgotten thereafter. Regrettably, many investors seem to take the view that they can completely forget about their money, from the moment they pass it over to an IFA or equivalent. There were virtually no protests or complaints until John Newlands' paper of May 2000 in which he questioned the safety of some of the more recent splits. Then, Adams and Angus (2001) weighed in with their "barbell" paper a year later. At this point, some people started to sit up and take notice. By mid-2002, everyone involved realised that there was a problem, and a growing number realised there was a crisis.

Why did so few notice this before? I suggest that the main problem is as stated above. A lot of people find managing money a distasteful task and want to "outsource" it. I hope these people will now realise how dangerous it is to do so. By all means hire an IFA to do the day-to-day work, but do not ever consider giving discretion to the IFA over broad matters of investment policy, sometimes referred to as asset allocation. It is bizarre behaviour, indeed it could even be called downright dangerous to allow an outsider to make such decisions.

One of the most regrettable by-products of this bizarre habit is that the citizen does not know what is happening to his money. Because he is trusting in the mistaken belief that the adviser is acting solely in his interest, he assumes that he can ignore the whole situation. Then, something like the splits saga happens and we start to complain bitterly. Too late, of course.

If any good is to come of the splits saga, surely it must come in the form of a certain amount of wising up on the part of investors, especially small investors. John Philpot Curran was speaking at an election event in 1790 when he produced the remark that "The price of freedom is eternal vigilance. If a man fails in this, servitude will be both the consequence of his offence and the punishment for his guilt." Surely the same can be said about investing one's own assets. We have a moral duty to exercise vigilance at all times and never to abandon our possessions to others, though we may entrust them to another's care for appropriate purposes and for appropriate periods of time.

12.11   CONCLUSION

There are few who come out of this episode with an ethically intact reputation. When shares are going up, everyone seems to assume that they will continue to do so indefinitely. Castles in the sky are constructed, and basement flats in them are sold to the poor, the maimed, the halt and the blind. We have had South Sea bubbles, Ponzi schemes, chain letters and the like for centuries.

The split capital investment trust saga gives the appearance of turning into one more sorry example of the same kind of thing. Every 20 years or so, a new generation of financial managers succumbs to the same temptation as last time. They assume that the growth of share prices is linear and will continue on that upward line. In reality, a growth trend in share prices will almost certainly follow a Gompertz curve, shaped like an elongated letter S, which many natural processes also follow. A Gompertz curve starts going upward very gently, then quite steeply, then eases off again to a very slow upward tilt. The subsequent decline will follow a similar S-shaped pattern.

The people who did come out of it ethically well included: the bankers, who did neither more nor less than they said they would; the promoters of the early splits, who had no debt in the structures; and the promoters who stuck to the contracts as originally devised, and did not participate in collusive agreements to arrange restructurings to their own benefit (maybe nobody took part in such agreements, so that the allegation is absolutely false). Many IFAs did everything that could have been expected of them. There are other groups who behaved impeccably. Unfortunately, it has been alleged that quite a few *did not* put their clients' interests first, but instead worked actively to protect the management company's interests at the investors' expense. No doubt the official bodies will get to the bottom of it in due course.

One tiny suggestion to conclude. Try putting these three maxims up on your screensaver and those of your colleagues if you can arrange it:

- We have a duty to treat people as ends in themselves, not as means to some other end.
- We should never do things to people if we would not want those same things to be done to us.
- We learn the reality of ethical living by repetitive practice, not by reading a book.

If we take heed of these three, by Immanuel Kant, Confucius and Aristotle, they will pretty well keep us, and everyone, on an even keel, so there won't be any more sagas like the splits saga. The long list of financial crises, occurring regularly since the beginning of recorded history, may leave you feeling that there is only a moderate chance of success. But it is certainly worth a try. A careful, vigilant and persistent try. And screensavers are persistent reminders.

12.12 REFERENCES

Adams, A.T. and Angus, R.J. (2001) For whom the barbell tolls. *Professional Investor*, **11**(3), April, 14–17 [see Appendix 1 of current book].

Ali, M.M. (1973) *The Holy Quran* (6th edn). Speciality Promotions, Chicago.

Arberry, A.J. (1964) *The Koran*. Oxford University Press, Oxford, UK.

Aristotle ([384–322 BC], 1980] *The Nichomachean Ethics* (transl. by D. Ross). Oxford University Press, Oxford, UK.

Brody, B. (1988) *Life and Death Decision Making*. Oxford University Press, Oxford, UK.

de Bary, W.T. and Bloom, I. (1960, 1999) Confucius' *The Analects*. Chapter 3 in *Sources of Chinese Tradition* (vol. 1, pp. 41–63). Columbia University Press, New York.

Curran, J.P. ([1790], 1948) Speech on the right of election. Page 112a in Sir Gurney Benham, *Benham's Book of Quotations* (Posthumous edition). Geo. Harrap, London.

Goldziher, I. (1910) *Introduction to Islamic Theology and Law*. Princeton University Press, Princeton, NJ.

Grotius, H. ([1625], 1738) *The Rights of War and Peace* (notes by J. Barbeyrac). Innys, London.

HCTC (2003a) *Split Capital Investment Trusts* (Third report of session 2002–03, vol. 2, minutes of evidence and appendices). House of Commons Treasury Committee.

HCTC (2003b) *Responses to the Committee's Third Report* (Fourth special report of the session 2002–03). House of Commons Treasury Committee.

Kant, I. ([1785], 1946) *Fundamental Principles of the Metaphysic of Ethics* (transl. by T.K. Abbott), Longmans Green, London.

MacIntyre, A. (1981) *After Virtue*. University of Notre Dame, IN.

Maimonides, M. ([1150], 1949) *The Code of Maimonides: Book 13: The Book of Civil Laws*. Yale University Press, New Haven, CT.

McCosh, A.M. (1999) *Financial Ethics*. Kluwer Academic, Boston.

Middleton, P. (1992) *Noddy Buys a Zero*. Smith New Court, London.

Newlands, J.E. (2000) *Split Capital and Highly Geared Investment Trusts*. Williams de Broë, London.

Rawls, J. (1972) *A Theory of Justice*. Clarendon Press, Oxford, UK.

Umaruddin, M. (1962) *The Ethical Philosophy of Al-Ghazali*. Aligarh University Press, Aligarh, India.

13

Reputational Risk

PIERS CURRIE[1]

> *History is put together from what people want to say or to remember: but how little of what is written seems to do with what an individual on the spot has experienced.*
>
> (From *Hopeful Monsters*, a novel by Nicholas Mosley, p. 367, Minerva, 1990)

13.1 INTRODUCTION

Dr Adams' invitation to write this chapter is a welcome opportunity to draw back from on-the-spot experience to a wider examination of reputational risk in the splits drama. This chapter explores the role of reputational risk, fears of contagion and communications conflict between different communities as the response to events.

13.2 REPUTATIONAL RISK

It is difficult to define corporate reputational risk, although we all know intuitively what it is. Roger Miles of Repute Limited, a London-based consultancy specialising in reputation, neatly describes it as "other people's opinion of you, what this costs you and the extent to which it limits your options for action."[2]

Beyond the City of London, multinationals and consumer industries are increasingly expected to develop sustainability strategies that move beyond the maximisation of shareholders' wealth, to engagement with and responsibility to the wider community, valuing reputations and broader stakeholder bases as well. These also move beyond book and market values to social values including reputation, intellectual, human, social and environmental concerns (di Florio, 2000).

Judy Larkin's (2003) *Strategic Reputation Risk Management* identifies major trends that have driven corporate reputation to the top of the anxiety lists for many chief executives. For them, these include the erosion of traditional authority; a decline in trust among employees and customers alike; a more intrusive, simplifying and sensational media; the emergence of a victim culture and the growth in corporate social responsibility and governance.

---

[1] Mr Currie has arranged for the fee to be paid for his chapter to be donated to the hardship fund for splits investors established by the Association of Investment Trust Companies (AITC).
[2] Interview with Roger Miles, August 2003.

Securities firms and local investment management companies can find themselves in a quandary when considering their responsibility to a wider community than shareholders alone, unless they are specifically mandated to adopt social policies. The culture and function of the investing community in institutional markets is clinical rather than sympathetic; it inspects, values and trades securities primarily based on their financial prospects. Socially responsible investing (SRI) is on the rise, but is not the mainstream investment process of fund managers and usually consists of an additional ethical filter applied to conventional financial criteria. As what is known as the "instividual" market (such as the changing pensions market where individuals carry more risk than employers) continues to grow, consumer and social values and expectations will continue to increase, presenting new reputational challenges.

The City of London is predominantly a market for institutional, that is to say, aggregated capital, with its own economies of scale, rules and margins. Michel Ogrizek (2002), in a forum paper exploring corporate social responsibility on the branding of financial services, summarised Control Risks Group's research into the City of London's conscience in 2000: "For investors and analysts, the head is still required to rule the heart … the City is reactive and not (yet) proactive." In the competing international institutional markets for global capital, this attitude is probably inevitable. However, as these markets increasingly touch people's daily lives, a different picture will emerge.

Risk management is now a key feature of corporate life. Furthermore, reputational risk is the most fashionable risk for global firms and localised City firms alike, because it is the most worrying and the least easy to anticipate and manage. In financial services, reputational risk is difficult to quantify and manage through a modelled risk management process or compliance system alone. In fact, the new risk-based regime for overseeing regulated firms adopted by the regulator mainly sidesteps reputational risk. The Financial Services Authority's document *The Firm Risk Assessment Framework* (FSA, 2003) does not cover reputation risk as a specific risk. The European authorities, through the proposed New Basel Capital Accord (the EU risk-based regulatory model for 2005), consciously exclude reputational and strategic risk from their parameters. One Luxembourg official has described reputational risk as a "subjective and social notion".

There are models for evaluating operational risk generally, defined as the failure of operations or systems, and insurance can be acquired for such events, but reputational risk is different. Unlike other forms of risk, it cannot be transferred. Being non-transferable, it is sticky and potentially lethal, as Arthur Andersen discovered to its cost after the Enron affair. It is also difficult to put its value on a balance sheet (likewise even as a potential liability) as accountants currently represent it only as "goodwill" on acquisitions or latterly as "goodwill impairment", or potentially not at all in future. Like fears of a virus or rumour, reputational risk may summon defensive responses from others, through fear of contagion, or critical responses, from those seeking to take commercial advantage, or from those who are immune from it.

In the US financial markets, reputational risk is more visibly argued than in the prudential-based regulatory regimes of Continental Europe. The US, similar to the UK, generally shares a values-based system drawn from common law. The Indiana Department of Financial Institutions (2003) defines reputational risk as "the potential that negative publicity regarding an institution's business practices, whether true or not, will cause a decline in the customer base, costly litigation, or revenue reductions."

One characteristic remains true for affected organisations, or industries by association. Angus Maitland argues that "it is important to have something in the bank with stakeholders"[3] (described by others as a "reservoir of goodwill") so that when disaster strikes, as disasters invariably do, an organisation is prepared and can mitigate the risk thrown at it. Otherwise, a communications vacuum is easily filled with rumour that is harder to control or manage. Because of the specialised nature of the investment trust sector, few in the splits saga had maintained a dialogue or banked goodwill with outer stakeholders. As a result, contagion fears fuelled rumour and communications risk for the investment trust market.

13.3 THE DOWNWARD SLIDE OF REPUTATION

Reputation and shared values today are not as yesteryear. The reputation of institutions generally has declined over the last quarter century with a corresponding fall in deference, diminishing faith in authority and loss of faith in experts, particularly engineers, scientists and politicians, as rail disasters, BSE and the Hutton inquiry have all demonstrated. The same can now be said of financial analysts.

Lucian Camp, Chairman of financial advertising agency CCHM, has recently argued that a "loss of trust" is not unique to financial services: "even the briefest search of the memory banks reveals a cross-section of recent 'crises of trust' that includes British beef, the police, Sunny Delight, the royal family, politicians (always), estate agents, post-Enron accountants, the United Nations, the oil companies, the Roman Catholic Church, makers of cars that topple over, the French, A levels, the pharmaceutical industry, the European Community, the media and Blue Peter presenters. Trust we can safely say is not exactly in at the moment. Indeed trust is out. The financial services industry is a bit part player in a long-running global trust drama, not a victim of a special and terrible fate" (Camp, 2003).

Nonetheless, financial services have special characteristics that make them prone to crisis, reputation shock and regulation. Financial services are seen as different from other industries; the core differences being information asymmetry (sellers have more information than buyers); the weaknesses of the principal–agency relationship (separation of ownership and control); the "market for lemons" (fear of contamination of products) and the natural propensity to attract bad characters, because they tend to follow the money. Carol Sergeant, formerly of the Financial Services Authority, has tidily distilled failure in financial services into one of four areas: incompetence (including failure to evolve), excessive risk appetite, integrity issues and misguided remote control. Life companies tend to lead the way in the UK in the finance hall of shame, given high-profile failures and their mass consumer distribution profile. Equitable Life is the most visible symbol of corporate reputational loss. Recurring disgraced products in the personal finance headlines include guaranteed annuity funds, endowment policies, private pensions, with-profits vehicles, split capital trusts and now "precipice" bonds.

The split capital trust story at its peak in 2002 ignominiously captured both the City press midweek and the personal finance pages at the weekend. Internet editions and the

---

[3] Interview with Angus Maitland, Maitland Consultancy, June 2003.

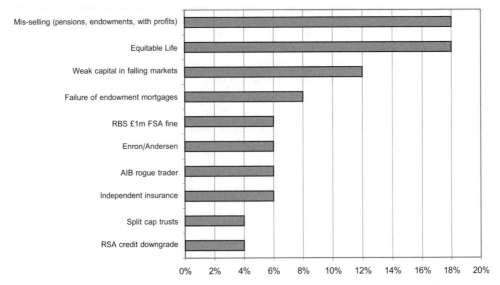

Figure 13.1 Significant factors drawing attention to reputation risk in the last three years. Source: *Argent*, **1**(4).

Reproduced with kind permission from Repute Limited, original research May 2003. Interviews with 50 heads of compliance in major insurers. © Repute Limited, *www.reputationrisk.com*

weekly trade press filled in any available gaps. Scottish media followed with interest from arguably the birthplace of the split capital investment trust sector. There was some disparity between the media focus and inner market opinion. To the inner constituency of investment analysts and stockbrokers interviewed in July 2002 by KRC Research, an opinion research organisation, just 2% on an *unprompted* basis felt that the split capital issue was one of the most important factors affecting fund managers today. By contrast, 57% stated falling markets as the most important issue (KRC Research, 2002).

Separately, in a poll conducted by London-based consultancy, Repute, in May 2003, 50 compliance officers in the wider context of the insurance industry were interviewed and asked what reputational risk items most concerned them. Repute (Figure 13.1) asked the question, "Have there been significant factors drawing attention to reputation risk in the last three years? If yes, what were the top three?" Split capital trusts, to the mainstream compliance community, scored 4% compared with the double-digit scores of falling markets and mis-selling scandals. Successor crises meanwhile have already been lining up: high-income or precipice bonds, store cards and the ongoing endowment policy crisis generally are in today's headlines and under the political spotlight.

Unlike the Lloyd's of London disaster, the split capital fall-out did not prove quite as systemic or as contagious as some commentators feared. What characterised the splits saga was its apparent suddenness, a City profile, the incessant drip of painful Stock Exchange announcements and finally fund failures.

It was the failure of certain funds in the split capital affair in 2002 that gave the story its political dynamic. In terms of timing, it also touched wider ongoing concerns about governance with a long legacy of Cadbury, Greenbury, Turnbull, Gower and now

Higgs reviews wrestling with best practices in corporate behaviour. There has also been a contemporary reflex to international accounting and securities scandals in the US, where the new Sarbannes–Oxley Act has introduced tough personal penalties for directors in the wake of the Enron and Worldcom scandals. Not surprisingly, politicians were inexorably drawn to the perception of "rewards for failure" and executive pay at a time when shareholders were nursing severe losses.

2002 proved to put investment and corporate behaviour generally under the spotlight of media and political attention. To some, the split capital saga achieved symbolic status in such a sensitised climate. Alan Ray, investment trust analyst at Credit Lyonnais commented in its *Investment Trust Companies Year Book 2003* "... without in any way denying that investors have lost a great deal of money, the treatment of the sector has been used by the media as a symbol of the whole bear market and the collapse of faith in stockmarkets, and therefore generated more column inches per pound of market capitalisation than probably any other symbol of the bear market. If the splits scandal had happened in the US, the movie would already be in production." (CLS, 2003).

13.4 THE RISE AND FALL OF EQUITY FUNDS' REPUTATION

Bernstein (1984) argues that the image of any individual company or sector is seen through a number of filters, "in particular the industry the company forms a part of". This positions the predicament of split capital trusts as a function of equity markets. Rising stock markets meant equity investments, particularly unit trusts (or mutual funds as they are known in the States), had been the ascendant star in the financial services firmament during the longest bull run in living memory leading, with hindsight, to unrealistic expectations of long-term returns. As it continued, advocates of equity-based funds, including investment trusts, extolled the generic virtues of product transparency, lower costs, clarity of charges and individual choice. These attributes were compared favourably to endowment policies, life assurance products and similar actuarially based products, often associated with high upfront sales costs and the mis-selling of private pensions.

A key driver of the ascendancy of equity-based vehicles over life products has been demographic change; one observer quipped in the late 1990s that nowadays people are not worrying about dying too early, they worry about living too long. There has been political impetus too; the welfare burden is shifting from the state and employers to individuals for investment portfolios designed to grow or preserve capital for retirement, backed with tax-deferred incentives. The difference between savings and investment has become blurred, abetted by demographic, political, corporate, industry, tax and regulatory change. "The savings shortfall", along with the pensions crisis, is a long-standing political lacuna; the Association of British Insurers has reported a £27bn "savings gap" in the UK (ABI, 2002). The issue of undersaving by the population as a whole has coincided politically with a loss of trust in equity investment and corporate management during the bear market.

The individualisation of risk means fund falls are borne personally, causing incumbent outrage and acutely painful personal tales of woe, particularly if investors do or did not understand their investment, mis-bought it, were mis-sold it or were struck by an unexpected event. With the stock market offering double-digit returns for nearly 25 years, massive investment falls, as the significant business risk, were lower down the anxiety scale in the late 1990s than today. Age is a contributing factor to this; few of the current generation of fund managers lived through the bear market of 1972–74. Likewise, consumers want not just low cost but ultimately low contributions that can only be funded by the equity risk premium relative to fixed interest instruments. Fixed income products are popular now, but require greater contribution levels and, with current low interest rates, annuitise at much lower fixed pensions than yesteryear. This equity bear market has however now wiped out billions of short-term value from stock market-related wrappers across Europe. A recent report (KPMG/Create, 2003) estimates an aggregate loss of €250bn for defined contribution plans across Western Europe. The charmed life of the equity culture has been severely dented.

The bear market has seen the reputation of fund managers generally take a knock. The KPMG/Create report highlights some of the fault lines within the fund management industry worldwide: the report catalogues "lack of focus", "unclear value propositions", "underperformance" as well as deeper cultural points including "inflated egos", "concealed tribalism" and "leadership vacuums". Consumers also come in for a pasting: "consumers were mesmerised by the relentless rise in equity prices and became undiscerning in evaluating many products." And, finally, the regulators: "regulatory and accounting rules came under scrutiny as investment risk became a real issue for the first time for many years."

The idea of equity risk for savers has now firmly entered the political arena; the proposal for low-cost Sandler products has recently prompted the FSA's Consumer Panel to warn about the inclusion of an equity-based product. Equity-based funds, rather than banking products, are now being reviewed in terms of suitability for savers as the assessment of investment risk has changed. This new political concern about equity-based funds means that splits cannot be divorced from the overall industry, political and regulatory arena.

13.5 REPUTATIONAL RISK IN THE REGULATORY FRAMEWORK

The newish unitary regulator, the FSA, has the task of managing consumer expectation while simultaneously supporting wholesale market confidence. The FSA as a brand is not just an enforcer, it is also a consumer champion and an educator, working under the watchful eye of the Treasury and Parliament. "Market confidence" is a popular regulatory phrase: but it can be used somewhat indiscriminately, blurring the line between consumer sentiment, the functioning of the stock market and a response to prevailing stakeholder attitudes, either separately or at the same time. With a multiplicity of roles, the FSA is not immune to reputational risk itself. It is dependent on maintaining political support, particularly as its role covers the management of consumer (therefore voter) expectation and perception, both subjective and relative measures.

The FSA's report *Financial Risk Outlook 2003*, a document that defines the risks to the FSA's own statutory objectives, recognises that there are potential future problems arising for regulated firms in retail space. They highlight the rise of the compensation culture among consumers: "It is concerning that 34 per cent of consumers believed they could claim compensation on the grounds that a policy has not performed as well as advertised. An additional risk is that consumers may receive compensation (on mis-selling grounds) but conclude this will always be available in the event investments underperform" (FSA, 2003). This analysis suggests that a third of all "consumers" expect compensation in a bear market if invested in equity-based products. It also underscores how perceptions of risk vary.

The FSA also identified in the same document that financial institutions in the main are poor at understanding and managing their reputational risk. *Financial Risk Outlook 2003* states: "Financial institutions are better at anticipating and understanding some type of risks than others. Processes and techniques for understanding insurance, credit or market risk are much better developed than those for legal, regulatory and reputational risk." This is well observed at a policy level; the combination of institutional ignorance and consumer expectation can create the perfect opportunity for reputational risk to breed.

As to regulated firms, fear of reputational loss should intuitively act as a check on bad behaviour. George Benston (1999) posits the view that this, along with competition, disclosure and legal redress, is a strong incentive in the good behaviour of firms. The fear of reputational loss in financial services is however believed by the authorities to be low or insufficient protection alone.

In the build-up to the Financial Services and Markets Act 2000 (FSMA), David Llewellyn, author of the FSA's *The Economic Rationale for Regulation*, argued in 1999 that fear of the loss of reputation is an insufficient safeguard on its own for consumers: "Reputation, competition and information disclosure are necessary ingredients of consumer protection. The question is whether they are sufficient ingredients" (FSA, 1999). It was clearly not sufficient for Parliament; self-regulation and existing regulation were seen as inadequate and led to new primary legislation represented by the FSMA 2000.

13.6 AN INTROVERTED FAÇADE: "THE BEST KEPT SECRET IN THE CITY"

Being introverted, investment trust companies can be their own worst enemy. The stylised reporting mechanism of quoted investment companies is dictated by the Listing Rules, which define minimum disclosure rules (and de facto communications *constraints*) for the companies themselves. Paradoxically, the rules surrounding the dissemination of analysis and opinion by institutional brokers can prevent, in many cases, private investors having access to topical analysis, a case where the desire to protect may in fact be self-defeating. In the past, investment trusts have been dubbed the "best kept secret in the City", an expression that conjured the image of a hidden gem, but also neatly captures the introversion of the sector to those outside the mechanisms of the regulatory reporting systems.

By the late 1990s, older constituents of the investment trust sector looked to a wider investor base to buy shares at a time of institutional divestment. The life cycle of some older vehicles ceased to serve a historic institutional constituency. By 1997, analysts argued openly that the sector needed to do more to promote its generic virtues more widely. Michael Hart, Director General of the Association of Investment Trust Companies (AITC), felt it important that investment trust companies must start "shouting from roof tops" (Newlands, 1997).

Introversion can suit institutional businesses or professional services with a narrow client base. But there are consequences to introverted behaviour in a more public sphere. Charles Fombrun, an American reputation expert and author of *Reputation: Realizing Value from the Corporate Image*, recognises that introversion can involve reputational peril: "Lacking information about introverts, outside constituents are likely to ascribe arrogance and elitism to them. The result may be an inclination to resent the arm's length relationship and to deplore the impermeability of the introverted company's activities. A possible conclusion is that the introverted company and its managers have something to hide" (Fombrun, 1996).

Investment trusts are traditionally less vocal than unit trusts and, thus, sometimes dependent on others to explain them. Many of the operating characteristics of the vehicle are legally externalised functions: its governance, its pricing as a quoted security on the Stock Exchange and its corporate structure. A legal and regulatory perspective, rather than a consumer one, dominates the governance system, particularly as directors' risk has become increasingly personalised. Such emphasis has historically led to corporate and structural solutions to trusts' business strategy rather than a marketing perspective of matching policy to a real or desired shareholder base.

As split capital investment companies announced dividend cuts or breaches of bank covenants on the Regulatory News Service during 2001, non-executive directors, as a group rather than as individuals, came under fire. The FSA's report into the split capital sector commented, specifically, on multiple directorships and fund manager representation on the Boards of investment trust companies. In reputation terms, Boards appeared faceless to opinion-formers and media commentators.

A cultural focus on structural solutions and restricted communications channels contributed to reputational risk. Perceived taciturnity allowed freer commentators latterly to allege incompetence or argue loudly directors' supposed lack of independence. It also highlighted the need to assess whether further sectoral reform was appropriate.

13.7   TENSIONS: BARBARIANS WITHIN

The last few decades have witnessed the well-documented decline of gentlemanly capitalism, ably covered by David Kynaston's fourth volume of the history of *The City of London* (Kynaston, 2002). On changing values, he records veteran commentator Christopher Fildes announcing in 1997 the City's obituary and its relaunch as "Hong Kong West". Elsewhere, reflecting on his earlier Report of 1990 into corporate governance, Sir Adrian Cadbury stated in 1998 that the self-governance mechanisms of the City had indeed changed. Drennan and Beck (2001), advocates of statutory regulation, refer to his reflection: "the gap in the framework of rules, which arose in the much enlarged City, was that nothing was put in place of the personal links with the heads of firms. There was no consistent means of passing on business values to newcomers and ensuring that they were adhered to."

As with many other City institutions, the 1990s did not see an investment trust sector at ease with itself. Traditional institutional shareholders had evolved and mandates for pension funds, insurance companies and local authorities were increasingly concentrated in the hands of third-party asset management groups. Relationships between institutions, fund managers and brokerage houses changed. Looking at share registers today, the institutional profile of investment trusts is more complex with diversified needs: institutions can comprise equity proxy holders, discount players, arbitrageurs, governance activists, proprietary traders and market makers and hedge funds as well as legacy pension funds, insurance companies and local authorities.

Talking primarily about conventional trusts, analyst Robin Angus (1991) predicted in the 1985 NatWest Investment Trust Annual Review a breakdown in the sector: "I believe that this polarisation between specialists and generalists will continue and become ever more clearly apparent, to the extent that the concept of an 'investment trust sector' at all will cease to have much meaning." The larger, older generalist vehicles stood at one side of the industry, hoping for a new congregation, as smaller, newer fashionable specialists worked the current appetite.

Globalisation during the last two decades changed the cultural face and continuity of many brokerage firms as well as the fund management groups. By the late 1990s, with reduced trading volumes and fewer corporate fees, the economic rationale for many investment trust desks in brokerage houses ceased to exist. Former broker Simon Colson (2002) explains, "the reason cited by Deutsche Bank, Merrill Lynch and CSFB for withdrawing from the sector is the sheer inconsequentiality of those earnings to the firm or their lack of strategic importance as a result of an internationalisation of the institutional client base." As the sector has come to terms with diminished importance to global capital providers, the traditional institutional investment constituency has continued to mutate. Margins were poor and some brokerage desks have abandoned the sector, reinventing themselves to serve higher margin, specialist products, such as hedge funds, private equity or derivative instruments.

During the mid- to late 1990s split capital investment trusts were flourishing against this trend of decline, becoming increasingly popular with institutions and specialist brokers alike. The rise of split capital trusts, from a relative backwater of the sector, coincided with a period of relative unpopularity for many conventional investment trusts. The sector was pulling in two directions at once, with innovators and guardians at each end of the rope. Observers could be understandably frustrated that the merits of conventional investment trusts should be so resoundingly ignored. Unit trusts had successfully tapped the distribution network of independent financial advisers and the retail market as a source of demand, and splits catered for the income-seeking fund manager and private client broker portfolios.

The sector had long argued within itself as to its failure to appeal to and reach a wider investor base, as seized by the rival unit trust industry. This resulted in a £27m consumer image campaign, known as "**its**" (Fluendy, 2002). John Newlands, author of *Split Capital and Highly Geared Investment Trusts* (Newlands, 2000), explained that the attractions of splits were grounded in undiminished demand for high investment returns in a low yielding environment. Commenting on the ambitions of the "**its**" campaign, he wrote: "while orthodox trusts were buying back their own shares, at the same time as

TV commercials for 'its' were being shown mid-way through that well-known private investors forum, *Police Camera Action* [a reality television programme about police chases] split capital trusts were being launched, expanded or reconstructed with a total asset value of more than £3bn in the space of a year."

With hindsight, all of the above collectively contributed to reputational fault lines in the sector. The business environment for trusts, fund managers and brokers had substantively changed.

13.8 RECOGNISING OUTSIDE STAKEHOLDERS

Investment trust companies, fund managers and stockbrokers have until recently been sheltered from consumer, regulatory and political activism, although institutional shareholder activism has led to dissolution, or change of structure, fund manager and Board members. Institutional activists, even fans of the sector, have been vocal about their frustration of the industry to respond to change. Peter Butler, chief executive of Hermes Focus Asset Management, said in early 2003: "the investment trust industry has a death wish. It is riddled with problems caused by poor corporate governance, excess supply of trusts and indifferent performance" (Burgess, 2003). The historic challenges presented have mainly been fought by shareholders through the *inner* constituency of the market mechanism, acquainted with the codes and rules of the sector and the stock market, rather than an *outer* consumer constituency of consumer opinion-formers, stakeholders and the media.

Stakeholders typically have an interest or a stake in an issue or companies but do not have to be shareholders. For example, Greenpeace is a stakeholder in Shell or BP. The stakeholders in the split capital saga have included: academics, journalists, broadcasters, trade associations, constituency MPs, regulators, HM Treasury, The Treasury Select Committee, class action lawyers, lobby groups and sundry advisers. Stakeholders are in effect the outer group who can impact on reputation without specific ownership rights. While they are generally immune from the same reputational risk, nonetheless they may face their own reputational risk to which they respond accordingly.

Shareholders by contrast are in theory different from "stakeholders" as a category; the term implies they have rights as owners and the mechanisms by which to air their voice. Consumer expectations and shareholder rights may however come into conflict. Some commentators fear that regulation, a typical response to increase consumer protection, can present a countervailing risk. Elaine Sternberg (2003) argues in a recent paper that regulatory involvement as a means of protecting investor interests may in fact be harmful: "In seeking to make equity investment 'safe', regulation tends in fact to make it more dangerous, by providing a perverse incentive for investors to be less diligent and less vigilant." This is what regulatory theory describes as moral hazard: a zero failure regime imposed through regulation could encourage inappropriately greater risk-taking by investors.

The loss of relevance of many trusts to traditional institutional investors led to the repositioning of the sector as a consumer vehicle. This shift carried with it reputational risks that were unforeseen. From a reputational viewpoint, the identity of the industry, firms and their external images need to correspond. Miles of Repute Limited states:

"you have to behave in a way that corresponds to other people's view of you." To ignore this can risk communications dysfunction, as authenticity is called into question, if consumer expectations are not met.

13.9   KNOWLEDGE, ROCKET SCIENCE AND DISCLOSURE

Sir Howard Davies, outgoing Chairman of the FSA, in a speech to the Securities Institute in March 2003, highlighted the gap between knowledge and expectation when it comes to equity-based products: "My view is that to the extent that the bubble was a classic case of overshooting, driven largely by psychological factors, there is little we can do about it. Except, and this is a big except, we should redouble our efforts to ensure that small investors are aware of the risks they run with unhedged, and especially leveraged investments in equities. That was the main mischief in split capital investment trusts and in precipice bonds and the like."

The structural difference of split capital companies also makes their analysis different from conventional funds. Such characteristics led to charges about lack of simplicity or suitability for consumers, chiming with the current political impetus for transparency.

The language of investment and industry jargon has been commonly attacked as bamboozling or distracting the "ordinary" investor from the earliest beginnings of the stock market. Satirist Jonathan Swift, in 1720, following the South Sea crisis, a genuine scandal of magnitude, wrote in the *Examiner*: "Through the connivance and cunning of stock jobbers there hath been brought in such a compilation of knavery and cozenage, such a mystery of iniquity, and *such an unintelligible jargon of terms* to involve it in, as were never known in any other age or country in the world" (Davis, 1940). Technical explanations do little to lower the outraged response to failures of certain share classes, representing an enormous culture gap.

Unlike unit trusts, the share price of investment trusts does not correspond to their net asset value. Investment trusts peculiarly carry equity risk at two levels: in their portfolios and in their price. Investment trust companies' shares, unlike unit trusts, are externally priced by the stock market, a price that can vary to its net asset value, incorporating sentiment as well as the balance of supply and demand in its pricing mechanism. Confidence is therefore more of a pricing issue for investment companies. Market operators saw negative publicity in 2002 help depress prices at the time when the sub-sector was already weakened.

Split capital investment trusts use their capital structure in a way that is unique to investment companies by gearing, which matched the appetite for higher yields. The analysis is also different; performance measurement for conventional investment trusts is typically *backward*-looking, examining relative past performance over different time periods against competitor funds and benchmarks. Split capital trust analytics however depend on a set of *forward* and absolute assumptions about markets or portfolios, in some share classes similar to fixed interest instruments. In terms of reputation, the language surrounding splits did little to commend it as an explanation, as this was seen as obfuscation. The design of splits, attractive when successful, exposed itself to suggestions of opacity in the downturn, particularly when seen through the prism of mainstream consumer funds, rather than as investment company shares. To some extent, controls over PR simplification of the message may have contributed to increased risk; however, all these factors compounded reputational risk for the industry.

13.10   GOSSIP, FAT CATS AND FAST CARS: THE PUBLIC GALLERY

Public relations consultants distinguish stakeholders from "publics", the main difference being that stakeholders are engaged and active; publics in the main are uninterested, which explains the role of retail public relations that attempts to engage or manufacture desire for a product or service. In the splits saga, to the public at large the storyline was presented as the well-trodden tale of City greed and nemesis.

John Bromfield, Global Leader of PwC's Global Risk Management Solutions, explains, in his preface to their report on reputational risk, the link between gossip and reputation. He quotes Robin Dunbar, author of *Grooming, Gossip and Evolution*: "[Gossip] performs a policing function: gossip ensures that 'free-riders' – those who take from society but don't give – get a bad reputation. By enabling us to exchange information about people, it short-circuits the laborious process of finding out how they behave and what they are doing."

"Fat cats", highlighted by the Greenbury report and more recently "rewards for failure" in corporate life are of recurring political interest. Angus Maitland of the Maitland Consultancy touched on this in a speech to pension fund non-executive directors, observing how distant corporate leaders can be from the floor of public opinion. He explains, "... had it not been for the growing feeling in Downing Street and the CBI that the political and media row over so-called 'fat cats' in the boardroom was starting to badly damage the reputation of British industry, there would have been no Greenbury committee in the first place" (Maitland, 2002).

At the end of 2001, the reported multi-million pound remuneration package to Aberdeen Asset Management's head of specialist funds Chris Fishwick provoked a media outcry as it coincided with large investor losses in some splits, some of them managed by Fishwick himself. Ten months later, the reportage of the split capital trust affair extended more widely than active stakeholders; it reached a more public circulation, including a TV documentary, with imagery as shorthand, drawing heavily on historic financial stereotypes.

With reputational issues in the political arena and contagion rising, reporting became increasingly personal; parody played an increasing role as events unfurled and developed. Displays of wealth became significant symbols; the photographs of the houses (invariably "mansions") of some of the leading split capital trust managers worked a strong allegorical message.

Another potent personal image of City life and excess were motor cars. It was alleged Chris Fishwick drove a purple Lamborghini Diablo "that changes colour in daylight" (*Daily Express*, 29 October 2002, then the *Scotsman* 31 October 2002). The FSA's managing director John Tiner is habitually described as "Porsche-driving" (before his appointment as Chief Executive of the FSA the *Daily Telegraph* headline on 22 May 2003 ran "Too Porsche for the post"). Class Action lawyer Stephen Alexander, described as an "ambulance chaser" by the FSA at one of the Treasury Select

Committee hearings, on learning of Tiner's vehicle of choice coyly revealed that he drives a "second-hand" Ferrari to *Money Marketing* (31 October 2002).

The increased polemic to wider media and publics, leaning on stereotypes, contributed to the damage for individuals and reputational risk leapt out of control. The public image of businessmen generally in the wider media is chastening: for example, John Blundell, in a foreword to a series of essays examining the representation of business in literature, tells a depressing tale of how business is seen through the eyes of television in the United States: "The Washington DC-based Media Institute tracked the portrayal of businessmen in 200 episodes of prime time TV programmes. It found that: over half of all corporate chiefs on television commit illegal acts ranging from fraud to murder; forty five per cent of all business activities on television are portrayed as illegal; only 3 per cent of television businessmen engage in socially or economically productive behaviour; hard work is normally ridiculed on television as 'workaholism' that inevitably leads to strained relationships" (IEA, 2000).

To date, the primary reputational casualties were those individuals put in the spotlight by mass media attention and the Treasury Select Committee. Chris Fishwick, formerly of Aberdeen Asset Management, cited media intrusion into his then employer and his family as his reasons for leaving the company; and broker David Thomas, formerly of Brewin Dolphin Securities, has left his firm as well.

13.11 IMAGE RESTORATION STRATEGIES

William L. Benoit (1997), Communications Professor of the University of Missouri, has developed a theory of image repair. He offers five broad categories of image repair strategies. These strategies include: denial; evasion of responsibility; reducing offensiveness; corrective action; and finally mortification.

Corrective action to investment trust companies through the market mechanism, the *inner* market, has been ongoing but too late for some 20 split capital trusts. Attempts by managers, boards and brokers to reduce debt, reconstruct and repair balance sheets were intermediated externally in an unfavourable light in a climate of uncertainty and loss.

If the legal and regulatory ingredients are complicated, with investment trusts as a separate legal entity to its advisers, broker and fund managers, explanations were viewed as shifting corporate responsibility or denial. Fund managers and corporate brokers explained that the depth and duration of the bear market was unexpected and, latterly, the fall in interest rates meant that break costs for bank loans were unforeseen and low probability, even if high impact. They stated that structures were stress-tested and that anything less severe than a 30% fall in asset values would have safeguarded zero-dividend preference shareholders. The personal finance press found any rationale for investor losses hard to accept, on the premise that failure alone is a sufficiently damning breach of consumer values.

The means of presenting corporate corrective action by the AITC was to introduce a hardship fund for distressed owners of individual split securities, similar to that designed for Lloyd's of London, to articulate an industry-wide response to the most vulnerable investors. The AITC has also recently published its own Code of Corporate Governance for non-executive directors.

Reputational threat even extended to the regulator, the FSA, with specific accusations being made as to its preparedness for the failure of certain zeros, as well as the risks involved. However, a perception of delay and lack of vigilance began to incense the Treasury Select Committee by November 2002. Chairman John McFall MP seemed to interpret the responses by the regulator and other witnesses as lacking sufficient contrition and in reducing offence.

The FSA therefore has found itself dealing in reputational terms with two competing aspects of its character: the conundrum of trying to regulate consumers and corporates in its bailiwick simultaneously and, at the same time, with the mounting pressure of a timetable and the expectation of a result loaded with political interest. Apart from ongoing investigations, it has now amended the Listing Rules in order to place more restrictions on geared "funds of funds" in future.

13.12   REPUTATIONAL CONSEQUENCES

It is too early to assess the full reputational consequences of the split capital trust saga. Reputations have been lost; however, the whole picture will only be revealed in the fullness of time. Public opinion is still out on the 400 or so directors of split capital trusts, the 34 different fund management groups who manage split capital trusts and the 11 investment trust brokers in the sector. Currently, fresh corporate actions or new issues in the sector have been depressed, although there has been some activity by arbitrageurs in the market as a signal of market change. Reactions to the sustained weakness in equity markets are breeding a new caution in fund managers: fund management groups are consolidating and many retreating from retail business. A low-growth environment and a fall from grace for equities will remain for a while longer.

The political machinery moves on, currently, in Autumn 2003, focusing on home equity release schemes, store cards and high levels of personal indebtedness. As a country, we are ageing fast, have saved too little and have seen our property assets rise (if we have them) and other investments fall. Half the population has no savings at all. As longer term policy, this is a problem. With compulsory saving seen as politically unacceptable, so the tactical political focus is to bring failure or perceived failings into the public arena. Even while the regulator argues that it does not look for a zero failure regime, it operates under the close scrutiny of politicians, while trying to balance market innovation and consumer protection at the same time, within a stock market still coming to terms with the end of its most recent bubble.

Historically, the political reaction to crises is to increase regulation. Stuart Banner, a US law professor, in an article in the *Washington University Law Quarterly* in 1997, explores the direct relationship between stock market crashes and securities regulation. Banner states that most of the major instances of new securities regulation in the past three hundred years of English and American history have come right after crashes with ramifications that were not always positive. Some argue, for example, that the legislation against "joint stock companies" after the South Sea Bubble delayed much of the entrepreneurial impetus of the Industrial Revolution by limiting risk capital.

Regulation has to balance the interests of innovation and investor protection. For the moment, fund managers are expressing caution in their investment decision-making and risk appetite. In a stimulating essay on behavioural risk, Arnold S. Wood (1997) of Martingale Asset Management eloquently questions rationality in fund manager behaviour and the dangers of the "Bad Dog Syndrome" in the principal–agency relationship. With a renewed emphasis on governance and heightened sensitivities, non-executives will need to be attentive to the behavioural risk in their relationships with fund managers that may or may not in turn lead to underperformance. Fund managers in return need to be attuned to recognising potential flaws in their own beliefs. If Boards and managers become too risk-averse, a consequence may be to offer low geared (or ungeared) investment trusts that merely hug indices, rendering the function and added value of active management redundant.

13.13   CONCLUSION

The splits saga has illustrated the impact of consumerism at the expense of a traditional common law system surrounding investment. The nuance here is delicate in contemporary culture. Equity-based funds are newer to a wider investing community, even necessary, yet the regulatory system, perhaps necessarily at present, adopts a legal and paternalistic response carrying incipient risks because of perceived investor immaturity. Even if possible, suitable or desirable, wider consumer status, to which investment trusts apparently aspire, will touch proportionately a greater reach of the population and a greater proportion of their absolute wealth. The investment trust industry needs to be aware of the supplementary reputational rules as a response to failed consumer expectation, reactions for redress, compensation culture, media intrusion, political interest, outside commentary and a different protectionist regulatory framework.

Acknowledgements

I am grateful to the following people for sharing their ideas, insights and comments while writing this chapter: Robin Angus, Director, Personal Assets Trust PLC; John Bocchino, Investment Strategist, Aberdeen Asset Management; Daniel Godfrey, Director General, AITC; Angus Maitland, Chairman, The Maitland Consultancy; John McFall MP, Chairman, Treasury Select Committee; Rob McIvor, Head of Media and Web Communications, the Financial Services Authority; Roger Miles, Founder, Repute Limited; Simon Morris, Partner, CMS Cameron McKenna; and Richard Plaskett, Structures Specialist, Aberdeen Asset Management.

13.14   REFERENCES

ABI (2002) The future regulation of UK savings and investment: Targeting the savings gap (a survey carried out by Oliver Wyman & Company). Association of British Insurers. Available at *http://www.abi.org.uk/oliverwymanreport.pdf*

Angus, R. (1991) *Haec Olim: NatWest Investment Trust Annual Review*, County NatWest, Edinburgh.

Banner, S. (1997) What causes new securities regulation? 300 years of evidence. *Washington University Law Quarterly*, **75**(2).

Benoit, W.L. (1997) Image repair discourse and crisis communication. *Journal of Public Relations*, **23**(2).

Benston, G. (1999) *Regulating Financial Markets: A Critique and Some Proposals* (Hobart Paper No. 135). Institute of Economic Affairs, London.

Bernstein, D. (1984) Corporate reputation and competitiveness. In: *Company Image and Reality*. Holt, Rinehart & Winston, Eastbourne, UK.

Burgess, K. (2003) Investment trusts do little to keep their houses in order. *Financial Times*, 7 June 2003 (p. 27, FT Money).

Cadbury, A. (1998) The future for governance: The rules of the game. *Journal of General Management*, **24**(1), Autumn, 1–14.

Camp, L. (2003) Put not your trust in me. *Argent Magazine*, June.

CLS (2003) *Investment Trust Companies Year Book 2003* (76th year edn). Credit Lyonnais Securities, London.

Colson, S. (2002) *Secondary Liquidity in the Investment Trust Sector* (p. 17). Association of Investment Trust Companies, London.

Davis, H. (1940) *Prose Works of Jonathan Swift* (Vol. iii, pp. 6–7 – 14 vols, 1939–1968). Blackwell, Oxford, UK.

di Florio, C. (2000) *Corporate Ethics and Sustainability: Building the Bottom Line Through (Good) Corporate Citizenship* (Management consultant report). Global Risk Management Solutions, New York.

Drennan, L.T. and Beck, M. (2001) *Corporate Governance: A Mandate for Risk Management*. Division of Risk, Caledonian Business School, Glasgow Caledonian University, Glasgow.

Dunbar, R. (1998) *Grooming, Gossip and the Evolution of Language*. Harvard University Press, Boston.

Fluendy, S. (2002) The man who put sex into savings that fuelled a scandal. *Mail on Sunday*, 17 November 2002.

Fombrun, C. (1996) *Reputation: Realizing Value from the Corporate Image* (pp. 163–164). Harvard Business School Press, Boston.

FSA (1999) *The Economic Rationale for Financial Regulation* (FSA occasional paper). Financial Services Authority, London.

FSA (2003) *Financial Risk Outlook 2003*. Financial Services Authority, London.

FSA (2003) The firm risk assessment framework. The Financial Services Authority. Available at *http://www.fsa.gov.uk/pubs/policy/bnr_firm-framework.pdf*

IDFI (2003) Risk Matrix Definitions. Available at Indiana Department of Financial Institutions' website.

IEA (2000) *The Representation of Business in English Literature* (foreword by John Blundell). Institute of Economic Affairs, London.

KPMG/Create (2003) Revolutionary Shifts, Evolutionary Responses: Global Investment Management in the 2000s, Professor Amin Rajan and Barbara Martin, CREATE; and David Ledster and Neil Fatharly, KPMG LLP, U, July 2003, p. 6.

KRC Research (2002) Aberdeen Asset Management Stakeholder Survey. KRC, Unpublished.

Kynaston, D. (2002) *The City of London IV: A Club No More 1945–2000*. Pimlico, London.

Larkin, HJ. (2003) *Strategic Reputation Risk Management*. Macmillan, Basingstoke, UK.

Maitland, A. (2002) *The Board, Strategy and Reputation* (Non-executive directors seminar series). National Association of Pension Funds, London.

Newlands, J. (1997) *Put Not Your Trust in Money* (p. 411). AITC, London.

Newlands, J. (2000) *Split Capital and Highly Geared Investment Trusts*. Williams de Broë.

Ogrizek, M. (2002) The effect of corporate social responsibility on the branding of financial services. *Journal of Financial Services Marketing*, **6**(3), 215–228.

Sternberg, E. (2003) *Competition in Control: A Shareholder-driven Alternative to the Higgs Proposals on Non-executive Directors*. Adam Smith Institute, London.

Wood, A.S. (1997) Behavioral risk: Anecdotes and disturbing evidence. *The Journal of Investing*.

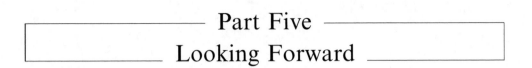

Part Five
Looking Forward

14

Product Innovation and Marketing

JAMES CLUNIE

> *In my attitude it doesn't matter how high the hurdle is, we'll cross it.*
>
> (George W. Bush, 9 February 2003)

14.1 INTRODUCTION

Splits offer enormous opportunities for financial engineering and tailoring of share class characteristics to meet client needs or desires. These opportunities suggest that product innovation and marketing have an important role to play in the splits industry. However, with financial engineering comes a redistribution of risks. Product innovation can lead to dangerous structures. It is important that investors have a good understanding of where the risks lie, and marketing can assist in this process.

14.2 UNDERSTANDING INVESTORS' NEEDS

Marketing a split means far more than selling shares to prospective investors. It involves identifying the needs of investors, creating products to meet those needs, promoting and selling those products, and managing client relationships after the sale. Integral to the marketing process is the need to understand investor needs, risk tolerances and expected returns. This stage of the marketing process requires either close, regular contact with existing investors, or some form of market research or investigation. Several product providers in the splits business had extensive client bases on which to draw. For example, at its peak, Aberdeen Asset Management (AAM) had over one million clients worldwide.[1] Such an extensive client base provided ample opportunity to gain market intelligence. Market research may involve the creation of focus groups or surveys of prospective investors. It may also take the form of contact with a third party with strong knowledge of the needs and aspirations of investors. Third parties willing to share such knowledge include investment banks, familiar with creating and promoting splits, or investment consultants, who identify suitable managers and investment products for investors.

---

[1] Strictly speaking, AAM had over one million client accounts: some clients may have held more than one account with AAM. This number includes as clients all shareholders of investment trusts managed by AAM.

The results from surveys of investors' expectations seem surprising at times. Generally, retail investors appear to expect returns considerably in excess of the long-term average equity return. As an example, the October 2001 UBS Paine Webber/Gallup poll of investor attitudes noted an expected long-term annual return from equities of 15%. Commenting on this, Dr Sushil B Wadhwani (a former member of the Bank of England's Monetary Policy Committee) stated that this was approximately twice the return implied by the mix of interest rates, equity risk premium and earnings growth expectations (Wadhwani, 2001). Even though investor expectations may at times be unrealistic, collecting information on those expectations remains a vital part of the marketing process.

Risk tolerances form another important part of the information set needed to understand investor needs. At times, investors' risk tolerances may appear to be inconsistent with their return expectations, and this will highlight where potential client-servicing problems might arise in future. If, say, a prospective client expects a 15% annual return, but is not tolerant of any more than one year of losses on his investment, it should be clear that satisfying the client's aspirations is difficult. Perhaps no product exists that could satisfy such a client consistently over the long term. Arguably, marketers should be rewarded for turning away prospective investors with unrealistic return expectations. The long-term benefit to the product provider from rejecting such clients might exceed the short-term gain in revenue from accepting them as clients. Section 14.6 considers a numerical basis for making such decisions.

14.3 MANAGING INVESTOR EXPECTATIONS

Prospective clients may have a set of expectations and needs that are already either partly or fully developed. Under these circumstances, it would be the task of the product provider to identify those needs and expectations, and design products to meet them. But how did expectations among investors develop? Expectations are unlikely to be formed in a vacuum. They will be related to a number of factors including: the historical (especially recent) returns delivered by existing or lapsed investment products; the returns suggested or promised by existing investment products or those in the process of being marketed; the "received wisdom" of financial commentators and analysts; and communications from product providers. Ahead of the splits crisis, all of these factors played a role in the formation of investors' expectations.

The historical returns delivered by investment products play an important role in setting expectations. A major feature of financial markets in the UK (and many other countries) during the 1990s was the general decline in interest rates. For example, annual returns on UK Treasury bills fell from 15.86% in 1990 to 6.22% in 2000 (Barclays Capital, 2002). There was a gradual reduction in deposit rates available from banks, building societies and National Savings. Redemption yields on bonds also fell during this period. But investors' desires were influenced by past interest rates, and in an environment of falling interest rates, this meant that the desired yields were too high. Manufacturers of financial products were aware that high "headline" yields would attract investors. A yield of 10%, in particular, had great appeal once interest rates had fallen firmly into single digits. Any marketing approach that offers an above-average headline yield in conjunction with some risk to capital, from either default risk or exposure to some volatile asset, represents an attempt to influence investor expectations. The headline yield *becomes* the expected return for less sophisticated investors. Expected return in the statistical sense, however, looks at all possible returns (including losses) and the probabilities associated with each possible return. In many cases, it will be below the headline yield. It could be argued that the promotion of headline yields that exceed realistic expected returns attracts investors but also increases investor expectations. So, product providers help to set investor expectations. They can choose to use this influence wisely, or they can seek to manipulate expectations for their own purposes.

In September 2003, a large UK bank received a £1.9m fine from the Financial Services Authority (FSA) and was ordered to pay £98m in compensation to investors. The bank had sold a product that appeared to meet an income need, but the risk features had been poorly explained and in some cases were misunderstood. The so-called "precipice bonds" offered a headline yield of over 10%, which was much higher than that available to buyers of government bonds or of high-quality corporate bonds. This higher yield, however, came with higher risks than that found with government or investment-grade corporate bonds. The risks were redistributed in such a way that there would be severe losses in some circumstances: namely, when an underlying basket of shares fell by more than a certain amount. The FSA determined that there had been failings in the training of the bank's financial consultants and ordered the compensation (and fines) after investigating the manner in which product risks had been explained to prospective clients. Precipice bonds were not splits, but the use of financial engineering to create high headline yields together with redistributed risks applies equally to the income-bearing shares and zeros of splits. Were those risks adequately explained to potential investors? Were suitable clients found for these products? These questions are examined in Section 14.8.

If financial service companies are able to influence investor expectations, do they have a role to play in the education of financial intermediaries, investors and prospective investors? Should product providers help in setting reasonable investor expectations? Whether or not they *should* play a role, financial service companies *do* play a role. From providing "sound bites" for financial news agencies, such as Reuters or Bloomberg, through to providing articles for specialist investment magazines, product providers influence the public's understanding of various investment products. With such a role comes a responsibility – to provide true and fair information. The Association of Investment Management and Research, in its *Code of Ethics and Standards of Professional Conduct*, states that its members "must not knowingly make any statement that misrepresents facts relating to investment analysis, recommendations, actions or other professional activities" (AIMR, 2003). Some firms have adopted a policy of engagement with the media and investors, via conferences for clients and intermediaries, quarterly client newsletters and press comments. Under most circumstances, informed engagement assists in the process of educating investors. Generally speaking, the provision of information through advertisements or communication is a form of marketing. The lessons for those involved in such marketing must be to note the role they have in influencing investor understanding and expectations, to assume the responsibilities that come with this role and to be aware of the risks they create in knowingly or unknowingly providing poor information to the public.

14.4 PRODUCT DESIGN

Designing a product to meet client needs is central to the product creation process. However, there is considerable danger in designing a product that superficially meets client needs (e.g., high running yield) but offers a potential "sting in the tail". The difference between running yield and expected total return only became obvious to many investors once they started to experience dividend cuts and cancellations, or sharp drops in capital values. Similarly, zeros were designed to meet certain client needs – the need for low-risk capital growth over a defined period of time. "School fees planning" was a typical application for zeros. However, as has been stressed elsewhere in this book, not all zeros share the same characteristics. Greater use of bank debt in a split structure increases the financial risk associated with a zero. Greater financial risk alters the nature of a zero, away from providing low-risk capital growth over a period of time, toward providing (capped) above-average capital gains with increased risk to capital. At what point did a zero fail to meet its original purpose of providing low-risk capital growth? As the redemption yields on some zeros rose to levels associated with junk bonds, the market pricing was indicating that these were "risky" securities. But if investors were buying these as low-risk investments, then either product designers were failing to meet investor needs and expectations, or marketers were failing to reflect the new characteristics of such zeros in their communication with investors. Where investment websites were not updated to reflect the new nature of some zeros, communication with investors became "stale". Also, "cut and paste" techniques meant that outdated perceptions on the nature of zeros found their way into new marketing communication, widening the gulf in some instances between investors' understanding of zeros and their true nature. The marketing of Aberdeen's Progressive Growth Unit Trust was perhaps a case in point. This fund of zeros was advertised up to the summer of 2001 as a low-risk fund, in accordance with the traditional perception of zeros. In fact, several of the fund constituents were highly risky and the fund's value fell sharply following the aggressive advertising campaign. After it became clear that the product should not have been marketed as a low-risk fund, AAM announced in 2002 that it was working toward providing an "uplift package" to investors, intended to take effect in August 2005.

Replicating or adapting a previously successful product is a popular path to take in product design. If a rival's product is successful, why not launch a similar product yourself? In the near term, this is likely to be successful, as the success of an earlier product indicates demand for such products. A new product might even have one or two special features, to differentiate the product from previous launches. But there are risks in replicating or adapting previous successful products. Risk analysis must be carried out on the new product. It is not sufficient to argue that analysis was done on a previous product and that no analysis is required for the next launch. Market conditions may have changed since the previous launch, or improvisations on a product may have introduced new risks. Additionally, the impact of a new launch on the price of the assets to be acquired should be considered. Could demand for those assets be artificially high because of a series of product launches targeting that asset class?

Typically, splits were marketed and launched before the Board of Directors had attended their first meeting. The involvement of directors in the product design process might well have highlighted some of the more serious risks or potential design flaws in advance of launch. This issue was highlighted in the article "For whom the barbell tolls ..." (Adams and Angus, 2001).

14.5 STRESS-TESTING NEW PRODUCTS

With financial engineering comes a redistribution of risks. It is important that all parties, including the product designers, understand where the risks lie in re-engineered products.

A standard undertaking ahead of any new product launch is "stress-testing" – the process by which the product is subjected to various market scenarios under "lab conditions", and its behaviour under these conditions is monitored. Information gained from this process may be used to redesign the product. For example, if the product was seen to fail under conditions that might arise with a greater than accept-able probability, the underlying portfolio might be redistributed into less volatile assets, or gearing might be reduced. Stress-testing should consider a number of scenarios that might be expected to occur with reasonable probability but should also consider the equivalent of the "one-in-a-hundred year flood" and beyond. It is, after all, *stress*-testing. It is the role of those involved in the stress-testing process to model extreme events and to report on the expected effect on the product. It is also the role of the product designers and sponsors to take note of this information. It could well be that a product provider launches a product, knowing that it will fail under certain extreme conditions. However, if this is fully declared and explained to prospective investors upfront, buyers of the product have no cause for complaint if they lose money under those extreme conditions.

A typical feature of the prospectus of each split was a table showing the impact of various market projections on the performance of certain classes of share. A typical example can be found in the prospectus (9 April 2001) for BFS US Special Opportu-nities Trust. The table on page 14 of the prospectus shows the impact on redemption values for the capital shares of compound annual growth in initial gross assets of +5.0% p.a., +5.5% p.a., +7.5% p.a., +10.0% p.a. and +12.5% p.a. This table is interesting in that it includes only *positive* market projections. But any observer of financial advertising in the UK is familiar with the phrase: "The value of your invest-ment can go down as well as up." This standard thinking has been withdrawn at a critical stage in the analysis – namely, when showing the impact on the fund of various market scenarios. It is likely that the stress-testing procedure involved some negative projections.[2] Why, then, were these not included in the above table? Might the inclusion of negative scenarios have influenced investor expectations?

Another weakness with the type of analysis above is that it considers a constant rate of growth of assets. In practice, assets exhibit varying degrees of price volatility. This matters considerably for splits with bank loans, where covenants are associated with those bank loans. Assets may grow by 5% over the period of a year, but if they fell by, for example, one-third at some point during the year, the impact of loan covenants may be significant. If covenants are breached, assets may need to be sold at depressed prices,

---

[2] It could be that, for the capital shares in question, the 5% growth produced a 100% loss; so, showing negative growth or even 0% growth is unnecessary.

jeopardising the long-term prospects for the portfolio. This suggests that a Monte Carlo simulation approach rather than a constant growth sensitivity analysis approach is required in stress-testing. Monte Carlo simulation was discussed in Chapter 6 in some detail. It is a particularly useful technique for analysing risks in splits as it can take account of such features as loan covenants.

One area in which stress-testing can have limitations is for complex investment products that are difficult to model accurately. If an asset return model failed to mimic the behaviour of the asset to be modelled, the results could be inaccurate or even misleading. Split capital investment trusts with bank loans and significant cross-holdings fall into this category. Modelling a web of cross-held investments presents a significant problem. Representing cross-held investments as high-beta securities offering high yields is a start, but still a significant simplification of their behaviour. The complete modelling of even limited universes of two or three cross-held investments contained within geared splits structures (using Monte Carlo simulation) requires considerable work. As shown in Chapter 6, the risks arising in such structures can at times be surprising. It could be argued that such product innovation represents a step too far. Stress-testing these products is extremely difficult and crude attempts may give misleading results. Were risk managers reassured by analysis that might have been flawed?

Interestingly, some of the structures created just before the splits crisis were hardly innovative at all, but bore a striking resemblance to products that collapsed during the Great Crash of 1929 in the USA. UK split capital investment trusts with bank loans and significant cross-holdings were similar to the highly geared, cross-held US investment trusts launched in 1929. Examples of such US trusts include Goldman, Sachs & Company's Shenandoah Corporation and Blue Ridge Corporation, both of which lost 97% of their value between 1929 and 1932 (Galbraith, 1975). Perhaps product designers should have been more aware of the long-term lessons of financial history (see Chapter 2).

14.6   A DECISION-MAKING FRAMEWORK FOR COMPLEX INVESTMENT PRODUCTS

In deciding on the launch of a complex or potentially risky investment product, there is one key process that any product designer, marketing professional or risk manager should follow. They must evaluate the expected benefit to the product provider from creating, promoting and selling the product. They must take into account the possibility that the risks become fact and that the product does not meet client expectations. They must evaluate the potential damage to their brand in terms of lost future sales, the costs in management time coping with client problems and the potential cost of meeting any compensation claims. They must then compare the benefits from launching a product with the risks and contingent liabilities that this creates. Finally, they should determine whether the "net present value" of the potential product is positive or negative. Only then should they decide whether or not to launch such a product. Of course, such an evaluation is difficult when a risky product is launched. But if it is too difficult to evaluate even approximately, is the product provider merely speculating with its own shareholders' money? This might explain why some fund management firms did not launch splits.

Above is a classical net present value approach, used by professionals who assess projects in any type of business. But in assessing the launch of a complex, new product, there is often one structural problem in investment management companies that prevents an appropriate decision from being taken. That structural impediment is the compensation structure of those charged with taking new product launch decisions. If the decision criteria are to be based on the interests of shareholders, the compensation structure of the decision-makers must be aligned with shareholders' interests. If decision-makers are compensated on marginal increase of revenue or on new assets gathered, there is a misalignment of interests. There will be a temptation to put personal interests ahead of shareholder interests – a classical "agency risk" problem. If a successful product launch can generate a personal bonus (payable within a year or possibly deferred for a number of years), would a contingent liability that might transpire (and which, if it did transpire, would do so many years into the future) be taken properly into account?

Risk managers have a vital role to play in advising on product launches, as they can provide technical expertise and a degree of independence. The nature of their relationship with the decision-makers on a new product launch is key. Product providers can choose to hire independent risk consultants to assess and report on the risks associated with new products. The risk consultant can also suggest means of altering the risk profile of a product ahead of launch. He or she should report directly to the Board of the product provider, or, if the Board of a split meets before the product design is finalised, should report directly to the Board of the split. The consultant's report should not be "filtered" by an in-house manager or "product champion", as they may be influenced by internal political or compensation structures. An alternative to using an external risk consultant is to have an in-house risk manager, together with some experienced technical expert in a strongly independent role. This expert might be a former risk-manager or product specialist who understands product structures but is either incentivised by long-term shareholder value or else is paid a fixed salary. This individual would report directly to the Board and would be independent of the marketing process. He or she would also act as a check and balance on other technical issues, including prospectus disclosures or the suitability of client communications. If the Board finds it difficult to understand a product, or impossible to evaluate the merits of launching the product, it should be rejected as a project.

In choosing to launch a complex new product, some firms establish contingency plans for product failures, offering a predetermined "compensation formula" for retail clients following adverse events in complex products. For example, in October 2003, UBS AG's Credit Portfolio Collateralised Debt Obligation Notes offered a fixed 40% recovery rate after each "credit event" among portfolio constituents. This technique has two benefits: it shows that the product provider has thought about adverse market outcomes; second, it clarifies where the client stands following such adverse events. This technique was never applied to splits, but it is certainly something for splits manufacturers to consider in future.

14.7 NEW LAUNCH DOCUMENTATION AND RISK WARNINGS

The launch prospectus sets out the permissible investments, investment process, rules for allocation of assets at wind-up and certain policy statements as to dividend policy. It also serves to highlight the risk features of the investment product. In theory, it is the primary document used by investors, prospective investors, directors and the investment managers in understanding how the split should be run. In practice, however, many professional investors rely on marketing information shown to them.

In describing the process for managing the underlying assets, the prospectus should provide a framework that gives the required flexibility to the investment manager, while offering clarity to the investor. This is a delicate balancing act, but one with which most investment managers and their clients are familiar. To highlight one such balance, the prospectus (8 December 2000) for Britannic Global Income Trust states: "At launch, approximately 55% of assets will be allocated to the Income Portfolio and 45% of assets to the Growth Portfolio." Additionally: "The Growth Portfolio may be invested in any economic sector. The primary focus will be on large capitalisation quoted stocks, however the Manager will have the flexibility to invest up to 10% of gross assets in unquoted stocks." Problems may arise with thematic funds, where the theme has been chosen on the basis of positive price momentum or current popularity. A good example was the launch of a flurry of TMT (technology, media and telecommunications) funds toward the end of the 1990s and in early 2000. Such funds included Technology & Income, European Technology & Income and Framlington NetNet.Inc. Any popular theme runs the risk of becoming exhausted or turning sour during the life of the fund (split trust lives typically run for between six and ten years). If the prospectus is constricting, the investment manager has little opportunity to reallocate assets toward a more appropriate theme or market segment. Shareholders could become trapped in a stale market segment, with little escape other than to sell or lobby for a change to the investment policy governing management of the fund. From the product provider's perspective, funds based on popular themes might be an "easy sell" at launch, and thus find approval from individuals in an organisation motivated by near-term growth in assets under management or growth in revenue. However, they might lead to future issues including poor performance relative to more generalist funds, future use of management time to address consequent problems, disaffected clients and consequent erosion in the value of the investment manager's brand. Perhaps such behaviour will be seen as self-defeating in the long term, and firms that launch fashionable funds will find that their long-term performance does not justify this type of launch. However, the short-term incentives can be strong enough to attract new entrants to "marketing-led" launches. If investors continue to buy fashionable single-theme, single-sector or single-country funds at launch, it appears likely, given human nature and the possible incentives on offer, that such funds will continue to be launched.

For some trusts, there has been ambiguity in the rules governing the distribution of assets among the various classes of shareholder at wind-up. Prior to launch, clear rules should be established governing how the revenue account and capital account will be apportioned at wind-up. Without clear rules, it is difficult for analysts and investors to assess the risks or price each security. Generally, prospectuses give clear and simple rules on this matter. However, in some cases, ambiguity arises. This might be due to poor wording in the prospectus, or to an unforeseen situation arising. For example, if a significant decline in the total assets of the fund led to an uncovered zero, but the revenue account held considerable assets approaching wind-up, which class of shareholder would have rights over the revenue reserve? Income shareholders might normally expect the right to the revenue reserve, but zero holders would expect priority at wind-up over income shareholders if their redemption value had not been met. For several trusts, including Jove and Murray Global Return Trust, it has not been clear from the prospectus how to distribute the revenue reserve in the approach to wind-up if the zero shareholders' final redemption value is unlikely to be met in full. In Jove's case, this ambiguity led to a ballot of shareholders in 2003. Each class of shareholder was asked to vote, confirming that the revenue reserve belonged to the income shareholders at wind-up. Unsurprisingly, zero shareholders voted against the resolution. An alternative to putting a resolution to shareholders is to seek a legal interpretation of the prospectus. Generally speaking, informed legal opinion would recommend that, when directors have discretion, all classes of shareholder be treated "fairly" if ambiguity arises on issues such as this. It is imperative that any future prospectuses set out the rules governing distribution of the revenue reserves at wind-up, so as to leave no ambiguity, regardless of the investment outcome.

Clear guidance in the prospectus on dividend policy would also be helpful. This would assist the Board in deciding on dividend distributions when, say, the zero is uncovered. Income shareholders and zero shareholders should both be treated fairly, but when is it prudent to cut dividends to income shareholders so as not to prejudice the interests of the zero shareholders?

The offering document for a new split (or any investment product) should clearly explain the risks to prospective investors. Prospectuses for splits did indeed provide comprehensive risk disclosure. For example, LeggMason Investors American Assets Limited provided 17 paragraphs of risk disclosures on pp. 15–17 of its prospectus (4 October 2000). Was the interpretation of these risk statements a straightforward task for potential investors? Generally speaking, misinterpretation appeared difficult: each prospectus gives clear messages to potential investors. One criticism of risk disclosures for splits, though, comes from Daniel Godfrey, Director General of the Association of Investment Trust Companies (AITC). It concerns information on the wipe-out hurdle rate for a security: the annual percentage change in asset value for the underlying portfolio that will lead to "wipe-out" or elimination of all value in a particular class of shares. He argues that the disclosure of a wipe-out hurdle rate for income shares and for capital shares, but not for zeros, could imply that wipe-out is not a possibility for zeros. Several zeros have subsequently been "wiped out" and so it would be misleading to suggest that wipe-out was impossible for zeros. Stating the "wipe-out" hurdle statistics, both in growth rate and total return terms, for a zero would enhance risk disclosure in the prospectus.

Further criticism of prospectus risk disclosures for many splits and barbell trusts came from Hamish Buchan, now a Deputy Chairman of the AITC. Although agreeing that much (but in many cases not all) relevant information was disclosed somewhere in each prospectus, he is critical of the fact that some important information was buried deep inside "this grey and legal document". Mr Buchan suggested to the FSA in February 2001 that key factors should be found in roughly the same area of each prospectus. He argued that all investment trusts should state a benchmark against which the investment manager's performance could be measured (most barbell trusts mentioned no benchmarks in their prospectuses). Mr Buchan also suggested that fund expenses (including launch costs, running costs and costs other than management fees) should be quoted not against total assets, but as a proportion of the assets attributable to ordinary or capital/income shareholders, as these shareholders pay the costs of the fund.

14.8   RISK AWARENESS AND CLIENT SUITABILITY

How aware were investors of the risks that they were taking in buying zeros or income shares of splits? If investors could identify a higher running yield, were they at the same time aware that such a higher running yield generally came with a higher risk? An investor who knew that there was higher risk would not be shocked by a capital loss. Where would a prospective investor learn about the higher risks associated with higher yields? He would learn either from the prospectus, where such risks should be clearly detailed, or from a financial intermediary who advised on the purchase of such a security. Any financial intermediary would be expected to understand the traditional trade-off between risk and expected return, and to make clients aware of this simple relationship.

Income shares were largely sold to investing institutions. Splits were major buyers of the income shares of other splits, thus creating the web of cross-holdings seen in the sector. In its evidence to the Treasury Select Committee enquiry on 11 July 2002, the AITC said: "as much as 70% of the income shares issued in 2001 were bought by splits funds and other funds whose managers also managed splits" (HCTC, 2003, Ev. 31). As an example, the prospectus (25 May 2001) for New Star Enhanced Income Trust states that directors expected over 92% of the ordinary income shares to be held by ten investment management companies immediately following the initial placing. These ten investors included LeggMason Investors, BFS Investments, Aberdeen Asset Managers and Morley Fund Management, all of whom managed splits. Such investors should be expected to understand the risks associated with high headline yields, and would thus be "suitable" clients from the perspective of the product provider. The ultimate purchasers of zeros were more diverse and included many smaller, retail investors as well as investing institutions. If made aware of the risks associated with each zero, these buyers can have little cause for complaint. If, however, buyers took investment advice but felt that they were not made aware of the risks, they may have cause to seek compensation from whichever party they believe "mis-sold" the investment. Such parties might include some independent financial advisers and private client stockbrokers. Product providers, however, might point to the split's prospectus as offering clear risk disclosures and are thus in a stronger position to defend themselves against accusations of mis-selling.

14.9   CLIENT SERVICING

Investors who purchase shares in a split can expect annual and semi-annual reports from the company. Additionally, net asset values are regularly released to the London Stock Exchange and published in various sources, including national newspapers. The

AITC encourages clear and comprehensive communication from investment trusts to shareholders, and identifies leading trusts in terms of their annual reports, newsletters and websites in its "Best Information to Shareholders Awards". In 2003, for example, JP Morgan Fleming Income & Capital Investment Trust PLC was identified as the split with the best annual report & accounts. Major investors may also receive periodic visits from the product provider's client-servicing team or from the investment manager, thus gaining the opportunity to learn more about the investments in the portfolio. Shareholders can also attend annual general meetings, and many splits now have websites.

If portfolio performance disappoints investors, they may demand better client servicing. Greater disclosure on portfolio holdings or detailed information on the investment process would typically be requested. During the splits crisis, transparency over cross-holdings became an important issue. Investors wanted to increase their understanding of the impact of cross-holdings. Unfortunately, as mentioned in Section 14.5, the risk managers themselves might have struggled to understand these implications. The AITC collected a data set in 2001 listing all holdings for all splits. The data were collected with the aim of unravelling the impact of cross-holdings. The information provided to the AITC came in varying formats and degrees of detail, and proved difficult to piece together. No clear conclusions were obtained, and the AITC published neither the data nor its analysis of the data.

A number of changes to the Listing Rules came into effect from November 2003 (these were detailed in Chapter 9). They require greater disclosure of significant portfolio holdings and of investments in certain other investment companies. These changes will provide new information to many investors, and it is likely that client servicing will improve as a result.

14.10   CONCLUSION

The role of marketing has been considered in a broad sense, from identifying investors' expectations and needs, to product innovation, stress-testing, deciding on product launch, risk disclosure and client servicing. A number of problems in the process have been identified that should be addressed. These include the role of the industry in educating clients, so that their risk tolerances are appropriate to their return expectations, and improved stress-testing. If stress-testing cannot cope with the complexity of the product, product designers should realise that innovation has gone too far. Appropriate incentive structures should be adopted, encouraging product providers to take decisions in the best interest of shareholders and clients. Risk managers should be independent of the marketing process, or external to the company, and should report directly to the Board. A number of weaknesses in prospectus documentation have been identified, and means of dealing with these problems have been suggested. Splits remain a potentially excellent means of meeting client needs, given their flexibility, but risks remain and should be addressed now before any further splits are launched.

14.11   REFERENCES

AAM (2002) *Annual Report and Accounts 2002*. Aberdeen Asset Management PLC, Aberdeen.
AAM (2003 *Interim Report and Accounts 2003*. Aberdeen Asset Management PLC, Aberdeen.

Adams, A.T. and Angus, R.J. (2001) For whom the barbell tolls ... *Professional Investor*, **11**(3), April, 14–17 [see Appendix A of current book].

AIMR (2003) *Code of Ethics and Standards of Professional Conduct*. Association of Investment Management and Research, Charlottesville, VA.

Barclays Capital (2002) *Equity-Gilt Study 2002*. Barclays Capital, London.

Galbraith, J.K. (1975) *The Great Crash 1929*. Pelican Books, London.

HCTC (2003) *Split Capital Investment Trusts* (Third report of session 2002–03, volume II: Minutes of evidence and appendices, February). House of Commons Treasury Committee.

Wadhwani, S.B. (2001) The stock market, capacity uncertainties and the outlook for UK inflation. Speech delivered to the Edinburgh University Economics Society.

15

Some Implications for the Fund
Management Industry

DAVID HARRIS

> *Keep the Ronseal promise – offer funds that say what they will do on the tin and do what they say they will do on the tin.*
>
> (Alan Burton, May 2003)

15.1 INTRODUCTION

The above words were spoken by Alan Burton, the outgoing Chairman of the Investment Managers Association, in his final speech to the industry. As I sat and reflected on his simple premise, it occurred to me that in one short sentence he had inadvertently identified the major reason behind the split capital investment trust crisis. Unfortunately, some investors in splits were given the impression that the tins they purchased were full of top-grade caviar only to find that they had stumbled on a can of worms. The fault lines in the fund management industry have, in short, been cruelly exposed by the failure of some splits to deliver on their promises.

15.2 WHERE DID THE INDUSTRY GO WRONG?

The warning signs had been there for some time. Investors had become both complacent and greedy. They had become accustomed to double-digit returns from the equity market and in some cases double-digit running yields. They had benefited from the dot.com explosion in which share prices soared and investment logic nosedived. Unfortunately, the fund management industry did little to inform investors that, as the market cooled and the excesses of the 1990s unwound, they must expect lower equity returns in a low-inflation environment. Instead, they developed ever more complex and inherently more risky structures that were greedily gobbled up by institutional and retail investors alike.

Splits were originally designed in the mid-1960s to meet the needs of investors subject to a UK tax regime that is now firmly in the past. Investors could generally rely on the simple traditional splits (with income shares and capital shares only) to deliver in line with their expectations. Some were better than others, of course, but that is where the art of fund management comes into play. However, the unprecedented boom in launches of splits and highly geared funds that took place in the late 1990s and early 2000s (around 100) dwarfed the number (only about 60) issued in the previous two decades. Many of the new splits were very complex structures and gave rise to increased levels of financial and investment risk, about which the majority of investors were unaware. It is true that the original launch prospectuses for these new splits gave considerable attention to the complexities of gearing, cross-holdings, charges to the capital account and barbell structures. But is it reasonable to expect financially uneducated individuals to read and fully understand these legal documents, given their own levels of education and experience? While *caveat emptor* must still apply, I believe that the fund management industry should have put more emphasis on educating and informing individuals about the true nature of these vehicles.

The sheer momentum of investor demand caused a section of the fund management industry to depart from sound practice. It is this and not the split capital concept itself that produced unstable structures. With clear investment objectives and sound advice, splits have the ability to offer something worthwhile to a wide range of investors. However, the fund managers' interests often lie in simply launching more and more trusts to increase assets under management and hence their fees. This, they might argue, is their job. They have their own shareholders to serve. In the splits boom, this resulted in a proliferation of vehicles with high costs and illiquid assets, which in some cases have collapsed altogether. In others, returns will be substantially less than was originally anticipated by investors.

It was the combination of gearing and cross-holdings that proved to be financially lethal. The effect of gearing is simple. It amplifies any gains or losses in the underlying investment portfolio. History shows that gearing has generally added considerable value for shareholders and is a main contributory factor in the longer term outperformance of investment trusts compared with other forms of collective equity funds. High levels of gearing, properly disclosed, need not be cause for concern, provided investors fully appreciate the underlying risk as well as the potential reward. However, assessing the risk of a trust that has significant investments in other geared investment trusts is extremely complex. In the recent crisis, this problem became particularly acute when highly geared trusts of trusts invested in other highly geared trusts of trusts. The overall level of gearing rises significantly in this type of vehicle, so the lack of transparency within the underlying investment portfolio was all the more important.

In his evidence to the House of Commons Treasury Select Committee (HCTC, 2003b), David Thomas, one of the main architects of the modern split capital trust, said, "It is nonsense to think that the designers of this kind of trust were wilfully dangerous. You would not have designed a product like this if you could have foreseen what was going to happen." Many investors were rightly appalled by this statement. Surely, an investor has the right to expect that the fund management industry and their advisers, to whom they entrust their money, will be diligent in ensuring that the structure of the product is sound and will survive stock market turbulence without total collapse.

Stress-testing, the mechanism by which managers test how the shares of a split will react in different market conditions, has always been fundamental in the product design process. Given the speed with which the prices of shares in so many splits collapsed, it must call into question the efficiency of the stress-testing methodology that was used.

The Association of Investment Trust Companies (AITC) has quoted the example of a theoretical split capital trust, with no external bank borrowing, invested in the FTSE 100 and issued in December 1999 when the index reached an intra-day peak of around 7,000. The AITC calculated that, if the index had then fallen to its lowest level (3,287 in March 2003) and remained at this level throughout the remainder of the theoretical seven-year life of the trust, zero shareholders would not have lost money (although they would not have received the full predetermined wind-up value for their shares). This startling conclusion suggests that when both bank debt and cross-holdings are in place, more sophisticated stress-testing methodology must be used.

Having said all this, it would be wrong to place all the blame for the splits crisis on the fund management industry. Despite the problems alluded to earlier regarding the disclosure of investment risk, it is not this, in isolation, that lies at the heart of the problem. The reluctance of successive governments to include the subject of personal finance as a compulsory subject in schools underpins the ignorance of the majority of consumers with regard to investment products and financial affairs generally. This is the catalyst for the scandals that have occurred. It leaves the fund management industry, and those advisors who distribute their products, with the unenviable task of attempting to explain a complex subject to investors with little or no financial education. This remains a recipe for problems and scandals in the future.

15.3   A ROLE IN EDUCATION

In his eponymous July 2002 report on the financial services industry, Ron Sandler noted that there was evidence of arbitrary regulation and excessive caution in the giving of investment advice (Sandler, 2002). This was, in his opinion, a direct result of the absence of any definition of the term "mis-selling". This must be a matter of great concern. In a more recent (July 2003) article, Geoff Kangley, Managing Director of Kangley Financial Planning, sought to interpret how and why mis-selling might occur (Kangley, 2003), citing the views of Austrian economist and Nobel prize winner Professor Friedrich Hayek in support of his argument. Professor Hayek maintains that a perfect selling and marketing relationship can only exist in a perfect market. This is because equality of knowledge between the buyer and the seller is assumed. But if that equality of knowledge did exist, there would be no need for advice or information. Buyers would know exactly what they wished to purchase. Such a market tends only to exist when there are regular buyers (e.g., food), and in the case of splits there was certainly an inequality of knowledge between buyer and seller.

The lack of understanding of the complexities of investment products among private investors is made worse by a number of factors. These include the complicated tax rules and the use of jargon that, while common in the investment industry, is totally alien to most investors. The designers of marketing brochures and documentation are often more interested in portraying the product's benefits rather than informing investors of the true nature of the product and the risks involved. Add to this the plethora of small print required by financial regulators, which most investors do not have the time, inclination or knowledge to read and understand, and it is, sadly, easy to generate a scenario in which mis-selling is likely to occur. The sale of certain split capital invest-ment trust shares since 1999 is but one example of this.

Some commercial organisations, such as the high street banks, do spend a substantial amount of money on financial education. However, there is a suspicion that their underlying objective is not to educate but to sell products and attract future customers. Education must not be about selling products. It should be about ensuring that poten-tial consumers are in a position to identify their financial needs and to find their way through the maze that is the current marketplace. The government and the Financial Services Authority (FSA), perhaps assisted by trade bodies, such as the AITC, are best placed to provide a suitable framework to enable future generations to understand and carry out their own financial planning.

The AITC has spent many millions of pounds over the past ten years or more on explaining, both to the general public and to investment advisers, the workings of investment trusts and how they can sensibly be included in investment portfolios. It has developed a number of investor fact sheets, which serve as an introduction to investment trusts. AITC conferences and seminars have brought together leading industry experts and fund managers to explain and update what is happening within the sector. At these forums "investment question time", in which a panel of leading names answer questions from an audience of both experienced and novice investors, has always been a popular feature. These events should continue to be an important aspect of the industry making itself available to the general public.

The AITC was early in introducing a floppy disk-based information and training programme in 1993, which was superseded by a more comprehensive and interactive CD-ROM version in 1996. This CD-ROM has subsequently been further upgraded and reissued in 2003. The AITC's much trumpeted and sometimes criticised "**its**" marketing campaign in 2000–02 also generated a variety of new investor information sheets and contributed to the transformation of the trade association's website *www.aitc.co.uk*. This site now contains a comprehensive base of technical information and statistics for anyone who is considering the purchase of investment trust shares. Add to this the upgrade of the AITC's statistical data service, available either online or in paper format, and it is clear that the AITC is taking on board the message that all those involved in financial services must produce comprehensive and relevant information for investors.

There is an incentive for the fund management industry to assist in the education process. The reputation of the industry has suffered in the wake of the splits *débâcle* and many investors see the managers as being greedy, arrogant and uncommunicative. Often the managers appear unwilling to accept responsibility when things go wrong. Whether or not this criticism is fair, if investor confidence is to be restored the industry must create products that the investor needs and understands. Managers must be seen to explain what they are offering and to ensure that potential investors actually under-stand what it is they are being invited to invest in.

One view of a savings product is that it is essentially a "piggy bank". Investors put money in the top and at some time in the future, when the money is needed, they take it from the bottom. What happens to the money while it is in the piggy bank is the responsibility of the managers. This is what they must seek to explain clearly. The marketing department and the fund management team must co-operate, despite the tensions that are bound to exist. They must not offer false promises. Risks to both income and capital must be identified and fully explained. Likewise, if the word "guarantee" is either used or implied, investors are entitled to know with absolute clarity which aspects of their investment are guaranteed.

A number of fund management groups in the past few years have attempted to educate investors and bring the investment trust sector to greater public awareness. Despite the criticisms levelled against it, Aberdeen Asset Management (AAM) has made strenuous efforts in this area through its own website, which includes online interviews with a number of leading fund managers, and through initiating and helping to develop the splits industry website *www.splitsonline.co.uk*. JP Morgan Fleming, ISIS Asset Management and other fund management groups have toured the country with the AITC, offering educational seminars to both independent financial advisers (IFAs) and private investors. Unfortunately, too much of the industry's marketing material is much less consumer-friendly. Investor newsletters are often bland and uninteresting. Investment reports that accompany biannual statements are often written with the professional, rather than private investor, in mind. These uninspiring documents are generally incomprehensible to the financially uneducated investor.

Investment trusts, with their often low-cost base, independent boards and diversification benefits should play a vital role in personal financial planning. But too many IFAs do not understand how investment trusts can assist in the planning process.

Marketing departments within investment trust fund management groups are too often the poor relation of their unit trust or open-ended investment company (OEIC) cousins. More resources are needed to ensure that the profiles of investment trusts under the fund manager's care are simply and properly explained.

15.4 STAKEHOLDER INVESTMENT PRODUCTS

The fund management industry does, unfortunately, have a reputation for selling products that are in line with current trends or fads rather than producing what the investing public really needs. How can this problem be addressed? Would a change in the regulatory regime surrounding product design and distribution help?

The splits crisis is symptomatic of some of the underlying problems that have caused the government to push ahead with plans for a suite of new, consumer-friendly, low-cost "stakeholder" products, first outlined in the Sandler report (2002) on the future of financial services. This government initiative is driven by the belief that, unless the fund management industry changes its current image of greed and high cost, public faith in its products will continue to erode. Is the UK government being simplistic in believing that a new era of cheap and cheerful products will give the mass of private investors what they want and need, thus narrowing the savings gap?

At the time of writing, these proposals include a suite of three stakeholder investment products:

- A short-term investment that will essentially replace the CAT (cost–access–terms) standard cash individual savings account (ISA).
- A medium-term investment fund. This will be a middle-of-the-road product with two investment options, each of which will permit a maximum exposure to the equity

market of 60% of the overall fund value. The first option will be a pooled investment fund that will resemble a unit trust, OEIC or unit-linked insurance savings contract. The second will be a new investment fund designed to "smooth" returns over time in a manner similar to the objective of with-profits policies.

- A longer term investment plan. This will have many of the existing features of a managed fund. It will be linked into the government's Stakeholder Pension regime and offer the facility for assets to be moved gradually from equities toward fixed interest and cash alternatives as investor requirements demand.

The government's aim of producing an investment product that is straightforward, flexible, low-cost and risk-controlled may be laudable. However, many in the fund management world do not consider a 60% equity weighting to be a suitable component of a risk-controlled, low-risk fund.

With regard to costs, the Sandler report urged a cap on charges of 1% p.a. The majority of the fund management industry thought that this figure should be higher and that some form of initial charge was also required. The Government listened to these concerns and announced that the charging cap should be set at 1.5% p.a. but made no move on initial charges. The debate will continue and, whatever the final outcome on administrative costs turns out to be, it is essential that any new range of product allows room for the proper level of advice to be given to potential investors. The splits crisis has demonstrated just how important appropriate advice is when purchasing investment products. I believe that there remains a real danger that those investors with sufficient financial knowledge will gain additional benefit by having access to a low-cost investment while for those with inadequate knowledge (i.e., the majority of the population) the problems of the past will remain.

Such a situation leaves the government and regulator with a real conundrum. In the idealised world of the politician, investors will rush to buy these new low-cost, straightforward investment products in the belief that the "Ronseal promise" is built in. In the real world, of course, this will not be the case. Moreover, it is quite likely that by the time a formal go-ahead is given for this brave new investment product "stable", few fund managers will feel that they are in a position to offer them.[1] Even if they could scrape by on the low management charge, it will leave them with insufficient profit to market their new product range. Without marketing, how many investors will buy the new products? The government has not mentioned this. It seems to me that politicians and the regulator are simply seeking the moral high ground. They will claim to have succeeded in offering investors what they need. The reality is that they have not provided investors with the tools to understand the products nor have they allowed the fund managers sufficient scope to provide both service to the investor and profit to themselves.

15.5 COMPENSATION AND THE AITC FOUNDATION

Investors who have been adversely affected by the splits crisis are, understandably, looking to the industry for compensation. Many have written to the Financial Ombuds-

---

[1] There might also have been a change in government leading to yet another round of change and maybe even a return to the PEP with a simplicity so lacking in its successors.

man Service (FOS) for adjudication on the merits of their particular claim. However, fears remain that, where the FOS finds in favour of an investor, there will be occasions when the concept of voluntary compensation will be tested. Understandably, some fund managers will refuse to comply "carte blanche" and seek to defend themselves vigorously, perhaps through the courts, against any unrealistic claims for compensation. In principle, I believe they will wish to co-operate fully with the FOS and the FSA regarding compensation. But as companies with their own stakeholders to consider, they will not allow themselves to become "fall guys" to anyone who is merely jumping on the compensation bandwagon.

The future of some fund management groups and IFAs will be at stake if compensation payments are high. In the event that the FOS establishes a case that sets a precedent for hundreds of similar cases, it will end up costing companies and their shareholders millions of pounds. To date, there appears no question of any obstruction to the mediation service. Indeed, managers have gone out of their way to provide data. But they are, naturally, cautious ahead of any final report from the FSA.

Many IFAs are also nervous. While they may insist that they have provided suitable and appropriate advice, given the information available to them, questions remain as to whether they were quick enough to pick up on the warnings within the sector that all was not well. These warning signs were fully highlighted in a recent compilation report from Newlands Fund Research (Newlands and Griffin, 2003). Suspicions remain of inadequate knowledge and research by financial intermediaries. It remains to be seen whether the advice given to investors contained satisfactory explanations of the risk involved. The IFA sector has already been accused of mis-selling pensions, endowments and so-called precipice bonds. They can ill afford to be implicated in yet another mis-selling crisis.

The AITC has taken a somewhat different approach to compensation by setting up the AITC Foundation, often known as the "hardship fund". Some in the industry see this as a somewhat cynical attempt to curry favour with the Treasury Select Committee, which made a strong call for compensation in its report on the crisis (HCTC, 2003a). The trade association strenuously denies this. When the hardship fund was originally conceived, the AITC hoped to raise at least £10m, but this has proved difficult. Without full and meaningful support from those firms that profited from the splits boom, it was felt by some that the hardship fund would be seen as a mere public relations exercise rather than addressing the real needs of investors. Despite these reservations, the AITC Foundation has been established and investors with savings or investments of less than £16,000 who have suffered losses by investing in splits are eligible to apply. The trustees of the Foundation are advised by an independent panel and, currently, the maximum amount of grant that is awarded is £10,000. I am sure that many will feel that this is insufficient, but, for now, this is all that is on offer. The fund has already helped a number of private investors who were left in distressed circumstances as a result of the splits crisis. Larger compensation claims will have to be dealt with on a case-by-case basis, either through the FOS or the courts.

15.6   CONCLUSION

There are a number of lessons that the fund management industry needs to learn from the crisis. I have seen the splits crisis described as "a problem in a sub-sector of a sub-sector rather than something endemic to the whole industry." In a narrow sense this may be true, but it would be folly for fund managers to ignore the wider concerns. These need to be addressed if the confidence of the investor is to return and the industry is to flourish.

The idea that the splits sector will expand, or even be maintained at its current level as current trusts reach their wind-up date, is difficult to envisage. Only new splits with a specialist investment remit will conceivably have appeal to investors and only then if their structures are straightforward. The overall market capitalisation of the splits sector is bound to decline, but it is unlikely to disappear altogether.

As this contraction of the splits sub-sector occurs, I believe that we will also see consolidation in the collective fund management industry as a whole. In 2003 we witnessed Rothschilds selling its fund management business, AAM taking over Edinburgh Fund Managers and the sale of AAM's unit trust business to New Star Asset Managers. Govett Investments has been forced out of the market by slow fund inflows and increasing costs despite improving performance figures. Their client contracts have been purchased by Gartmore Investment Managers.

I believe that pressure will continue to grow on fund managers in the future. The bear market of the early years of the 21st century has eaten into assets under management and hit both revenues and margins. Too many companies are left with a multitude of unprofitable funds. This situation cannot continue and we must see a reduction from the 2,000+ collective equity funds currently available in the UK. It is likely that consolidation will fall into two distinctive groups: the giant investment houses, with household brand names and full global coverage, and the specialist investment boutiques.

There will undoubtedly be resistance to such change. Banks, insurance companies and others see asset management as an integral part of their overall operations. They may be willing to withstand this bout of market weakness in the hope that they can rely on the strength of the remainder of their business to see them through to better times ahead. In addition, private investors are, for capital gains tax or other reasons, often slow to sell poorly performing funds, giving fund managers a breathing space in the bad times. As markets revive and investment performance figures improve, it is probable that investor confidence will start to return, bringing additional monies back to the fund manager coffers.

In the past it has been noticeable that consolidation has had little effect on bringing downward pressure on administrative fees. Apart from index-tracking, management fees throughout much of the unit trust/OEIC industry have remained stubbornly around 1.25–1.5% p.a. If the experts and analysts are correct and nominal future investment returns are likely to be in single digits in a low-inflation and low interest-rate era, managers will have to look hard at the fees they are charging their customers. Surely there is room for some economy of scale. For example, it does not take double the resources to manage a £4bn investment fund compared with one of £2bn.

Managers will also need to look closely at asset allocation processes and strategies. The days when asset allocation was reviewed on an annual basis are gone. The world changes quickly and economies change with them. The exuberance and greed typified by the technology bull run of the 1990s must be consigned to the waste bin and the forgotten art of asset allocation must return as a professional discipline.

The current practice of fund managers relying on performance records and investment processes in their brand messages has failed the consumer. A suite of stakeholder investment products, as suggested by Sandler and the government, may be a step in the right direction. However, most consumers need advice when it comes to making difficult and complex investment decisions. "Cheap and cheerful" may work in some industries but not, I suspect, in the investment world. It could be argued that these efforts would be better directed toward improving the quality of both investor and IFA knowledge, rather than interfering with the marketplace.

Recent sales figures from the Investment Managers Association (IMA) and the AITC show that, to date, too many investors have still not regained confidence in the fund management industry's ability to deliver on its promises. While this partly reflects continuing worries that the recent bear market may quickly return, the industry must ensure that, in the future, it moves away from sales hype and instead emphasises the true underlying characteristics of investment products.

The overall image of the investment trust industry has been hit hard by the splits crisis. I now doubt, with some regret, that the dream, as envisaged by Daniel Godfrey when he launched the AITC "**its**" marketing campaign, of an investment trust sector being as popular as its unit trust and OEIC relatives will ever come to fruition. In fact, investment trust managers must recognise that it will be a long haul simply to regain investor confidence. The successful application of the "Ronseal" promise will prove a worthwhile stepping stone in this direction.

15.7 REFERENCES

HCTC (2003a) *Split Capital Investment Trusts* (Third report of session 2002–03, volume I: Report and proceedings of the committee, February). House of Commons Treasury Committee.

HCTC (2003b) *Split Capital Investment Trusts* (Third report of session 2002–03, volume II: Minutes of evidence and appendices, February). House of Commons Treasury Committee.

Kangley, G. (2003) Education and mis-selling. *Financial Adviser*, 17 July.

Newlands, J.E. and Griffin, P. (2003) *Split Capital Investment Trusts – The Warning Signs*. Newlands Fund Research, Edinburgh.

Sandler, R. (2002) *Medium and Long Term Retail Savings in the UK*, July.

16

Lessons for the Future

ANDREW ADAMS

The underlying idea of a trust company, we have always conceded, is a good one, enabling an investor to spread his risk over a large number of securities ... [however] the operation of the new companies ... necessarily involved serious risk, and while they did for a time give handsome results, and create a temporary boom in the trust companies' stocks, they finally resulted in heavy losses. The directors, where they have not been ousted from office, have gained wisdom from the experience ...

(Trust Companies, *The Economist*, 19 March 1898)

16.1 INTRODUCTION

A range of opinion has been expressed in this book. Nevertheless, to me a number of clear recommendations have crystallised.

The last two chapters concentrated mainly on the lessons and implications of the crisis for the fund management industry. This final chapter sets out what I consider to be the main lessons to be learned from the splits crisis for corporate governance, the Association of Investment Trust Companies (AITC), financial advisers, financial education, the financial press and the regulators.

16.2 CORPORATE GOVERNANCE

This section looks at the key lessons for corporate governance, many but not all of which have been covered in the new Listing Rules and Conduct of Business Rules relating to investment companies (FSA, 2003a) or the *AITC Code of Corporate Governance* (AITC, 2003).

It is crucial that the chairman of the Board is appointed at an early stage and the directors then appointed before the initial marketing of a new trust. The Board would then be able to question the managers and the trust's advisers before it is too late to change the structural design of the trust.[1] By so doing, they could influence the capital structure, investment policy and details of the management contract. Competent directors involved in the product design process should be able to spot the more serious risks or potential design flaws in advance of launch. The directors should be

---

[1] The *AITC Code* Principle 10 states: "The Chairman (and the Board) should be brought into the process of structuring a new launch at an early stage."

paid for their work during the set-up period. If the Board did not feel expert enough on a particular matter, it could take independent advice from its own advisers. These would be different from the advisers to the trust, who normally work closely with the managers. In my view, the cost of such advice and the directors' fees during the set-up period should in due course be met from the trust's own funds once it was listed. These costs would, however, be underwritten by the managers so as to cover the risk that the launch did not take place.

There should be sufficient technical expertise within the Board.[2] It is vital that the Board of a split has in-depth knowledge of split capital structures including the consequences of gearing and cannot be "blinded by science". The splits crisis has vividly demonstrated that the managers and their own adviser/brokers may have on occasions appeared to be motivated more by fees than by best practice. Technical skill must be an important issue in the process of recruiting and training directors. However, Robin Angus expresses his doubts in Chapter 11 as to whether a technically competent Board can easily be achieved given the new Listing Rules on the independence of directors, saying: "This is one of the dilemmas that those legislating for corporate governance face: that those who are independent enough are usually not expert enough, while those who are expert enough are (at least as conventionally defined) usually not independent enough." Finding sufficient independent directors with the necessary technical skills will not be easy. Perhaps good accountants or retired fund managers might be suitable sources.

Directors should insist that fees be charged in relation to net assets (or market capitalisation[3]) rather than gross assets. Otherwise, there is an incentive for fund managers and broker/advisers to boost initial fees by arranging a bank loan before the launch of a new trust. And, thereafter, there is an incentive for fund management companies to put pressure on Boards to maintain or increase gearing regardless of the interests of trust shareholders. Many people believe there is also a case for variable annual management fees, based on investment performance, with a mid-point (e.g., 0.6%), a maximum (e.g., 1% of net assets) and a minimum (e.g., 0.2% of net assets). These matters concerning fees are not specifically covered in the *AITC Code* although Principle 14 states: "The Board should regularly review both the performance of, and contractual arrangements with, the manager."

The splits crisis demonstrated the need for a Board to establish the right relationship with the managers. This is reflected in the *AITC Code*.[4] The chairman should be paid to have regular contact with the managers but good governance should not be confused with interference in the day-to-day running of the trust. The *AITC Code* recommends that "The ideal relationship is where the manager effectively acts as the CEO of the Member Company, taking the initiative on all aspects of its operation, under the guidance and formal approval of the Board."

Shareholders should be provided with sufficient information for them to value and assess the risk of their shares. Before the splits crisis, it was possible for splits to have large numbers of undisclosed holdings in other splits, so there was a clear need for

---

[2] The *AITC Code* Principle 6 states: "The Board should contain a balance of skills, experience, ages and length of service."
[3] An advantage of using market capitalisation is that it aligns the interests of managers and shareholders. If borrowing lifts the share price, it lifts the fees.
[4] The *AITC Code* Principle 11 states: "Boards and managers should operate in a supportive, co-operative and open environment."

improved portfolio disclosure. This issue has been partially addressed in the new Listing Rules with the *AITC Code*[5] recommending more stringent requirements. Changes to the Listing Rules are also designed to ensure that there is sufficient information available on crucial matters, such as the cash position, debt and bank covenants. However, we still have the strange situation whereby basic facts about a trust may be unknown after its launch. Surely the Board should be required to announce through the public market, information such as initial net asset value (NAV), capital structure, details of debt and details of the underlying investment portfolio immediately after a trust is launched. These figures could be very different from those envisaged in the prospectus. Shareholders currently may have to wait six to nine months after the company is launched to receive this basic, yet important information.

Shareholder entitlements should be clearly laid down and adhered to by the Board. The splits crisis saw different legal interpretations concerning the rights and ranking of shareholders, with no consistency across the industry. Directors should ensure that articles of association and prospectuses clearly lay down the rules governing distribution of the revenue reserves at wind-up, so as to leave no ambiguity. There must also be clear guidance in the prospectus on dividend policy to assist Boards in deciding on dividend distributions when, say, zeros are uncovered. Without clear rules, it is difficult to value the different shares in a split.

Will there be better corporate governance in the investment trust sector as a result of the splits crisis? Peter Gardner and Geoffrey Wood offer an optimistic view in Chapter 9, even without the benefit of the new Listing Rules, *AITC Code* and *Combined Code*,[6] saying:

> *Better corporate governance, brought about by simply paying heed to existing best practice could have prevented many of the problems of the splits sector. The shock of these events may well ensure such improved governance for many years to come.*

Robin Angus offers a rather different view in Chapter 11:

> *I cannot see how a different regime of corporate governance could have averted the split capital crisis, although it might have lessened it to some degree and helped some of its worst excesses to be avoided. No amount of legislation can change human nature.*

However, even if this view expressed by Robin Angus is true, it seems to me that we are bound to see an attempt at improving corporate governance of investment trusts for many years to come in response to the publicity surrounding the splits crisis.

16.3   THE ASSOCIATION OF INVESTMENT TRUST COMPANIES

The AITC represents the interests of the investment trust industry. Its main purpose is the protection, promotion and advancement of the common interests of its member

---

[5] One of the recommendations within Principle 21 of the *AITC Code* is that "All holdings in other investment companies should be disclosed on a monthly basis and attention should be drawn explicitly to any material cross holdings."
[6] Boards can state in their report that on a particular point they may be at variance with the *Combined Code* but are following the *AITC Code*.

trusts and their shareholders. It is funded by the trust companies themselves and therefore by the shareholders, not by their investment managers.

Although the AITC is not a regulator, it must be quick to pick up on problems in the industry that may have a damaging effect on the interests of investment trust shareholders. It should be wary of new types of securities as demonstrated by the introduction of "geared" zeros ranking behind bank debt which have caused so much damage to the reputation of the industry. Marketing material sent out by the AITC right through 2001 treated zeros as a single low-risk asset category. It was also slow to realise the limitations of hurdle rates, asset cover and other traditional risk statistics as the new splits built up in the sector. In my view, the AITC should have spoken out earlier about problems in part of the split capital and highly geared sector. In particular, as late as February 2002, the AITC's response to the Financial Services Authority (FSA) Discussion Paper 10 did not take a sufficiently tough line.

However, the AITC's response to the deepening crisis from the spring of 2002 was open and honest, and this approach was clearly appreciated by the authorities. Evidence on breaches of regulation received by the AITC was passed on to the FSA. Many believe that the handling of the splits crisis by Daniel Godfrey, Director General of the AITC, saved the investment trust industry from a much stricter regulatory regime.

The splits crisis has emphasised the need for education and training, and the AITC has an important role to play here. It already has an information and education programme targeted at both independent financial advisers (IFAs) and private investors, and is a sponsor of the Personal Finance Education Group, a charity that promotes financial literacy. But it is the training of directors that is of crucial importance if the new *AITC Code of Corporate Governance* is to be implemented successfully. Principle 9 of the Code states that the directors should be offered relevant training and induction. It recommends that training should be offered to new directors about the company, its managers, their legal responsibilities and investment trust industry matters. Clearly, the AITC should be heavily involved in providing this. Until recently, there have been few opportunities for investment trust directors to receive formal training tailored to their own needs, but the AITC now offers two such training courses: "Governance and management" and "Accounting, tax and audit committees". It is to be hoped that the range of courses for directors offered by the AITC will be expanded to include such subjects as investment management and performance evaluation techniques.

The AITC must take a leading role in promoting good practice within the investment trust industry. The *AITC Code of Corporate Governance* is a good example of this. In my view, there is also a case for the AITC to produce a mock "best practice" prospectus as was done for Report & Accounts, despite the fact that the AITC is an association for existing trusts. This would reorder some of the less important material currently found in prospectuses and would provide clear summary information "upfront" in the document. It should clearly lay down rules for shareholder entitlements, including rules governing the distribution of revenue reserves.

The Chairman of the Treasury Select Committee, John McFall MP, certainly feels that the AITC has an important role to play in the development of the investment trust industry, saying in Chapter 10 of this book:

As the industry works to repair the damage of the scandal, Boards should play their part by supporting their trade association, by taking an active role in membership, and by demonstrating support for the code of governance.

16.4   FINANCIAL ADVISERS

We are concerned here with independent financial advisers (IFAs) and private client fund managers. Many of these financial advisers had chosen split capital trust shares for their clients in recent years. In some cases zeros were purchased as low-risk investments yet have fallen significantly in value.

I feel that the term "independent financial adviser" is misleading and is often misunderstood by private investors. IFAs are independent of any particular product provider (i.e., they can recommend any company's product). They are not independent in the sense that a doctor is independent, more in the sense that a shopkeeper is independent. Perhaps the term "self-employed financial adviser" would be a better title for the majority of them.

Financial advisers must now realise that traditional risk assessment measures for shares in splits, such as asset cover and hurdle rate, should not be used in isolation. Other factors, such as the quality of the underlying portfolio of assets, capital structure, sources of income and, critically, the amount of bank debt and details of bank covenants, must be considered. Sufficient information on these matters was often not available before the splits crisis but this should not be a problem in the future. The *AITC Code* Principle 21 recommends that the "wipe-out hurdle rate"[7] for each share class (apart from annuity shares) should be shown in the prospectus and recalculated in each annual report. This will be a useful statistic for assessing risk. "Total return to cover" (Chapter 6) is another simple statistic that could also be used (instead of hurdle rate) and compared with the expected return on the total underlying portfolio, to gauge whether or not the full redemption payment of a zero or an income share is realistic. These statistics could be misleading if the split held significant holdings in highly geared securities, so they have become more useful given the new restrictions on cross-holdings. But they should still not be used in isolation when assessing risk.

In assessing fixed-return investments, such as zeros, in my view financial advisers should assume that risk is reflected in the return (i.e., the gross redemption yield). So, if the gross redemption yield is sufficiently high, a zero should not be regarded as "low-risk". Is it possible to quantify what is meant by "sufficiently high"? The only yardstick with any theoretical foundation is the gross redemption yield on BBB— sterling corporate bonds, being the boundary between investment grade bonds and "junk" bonds.[8] But this may present difficulties because of a lack of familiarity with BBB bonds, particularly among less sophisticated financial advisers.

Many would argue that a simpler and more appropriate comparison is with gilts. Financial advisers must understand that a gross redemption yield of 9% on a fixed-return investment when gilts yield 5% implies a much greater risk than a gross

---

[7] "Wipe-out hurdle rate" is defined as "the rate of decline per annum in the portfolio that would cause total loss of capital value."

[8] In comparing the gross redemption yield of a zero with that of BBB— bonds, the minor effect of differences in tax treatment and in liquidity tend to cancel each other out. However, zeros may offer anomalously high gross redemption yields (which do not reflect risk) in certain market conditions (e.g., at the time of a new issue in that area of the market).

redemption yield of 9% when gilts yield 8%. Thus, advisers should consider "points over gilts" (i.e., the gross redemption yield of the zero less the gross redemption yield of a comparable gilt). Unfortunately, the "points over gilts" level which should be regarded as a warning signal is subjective.

Financial advisers have a responsibility only to recommend products that they understand. This was certainly not the case with some of the shares in splits. They should also be wary of complicated products that look too good to be true. They have a responsibility to the client not the product provider for determining suitability. But how can financial advisers hope to choose the most appropriate products for a client if they understand only a limited range of products available? This suggests to me that the FSA should be more particular about its approved qualifications and should require a higher minimum standard than at present.

It is clear that shares in splits are not mass market products. Only sophisticated fee-based IFAs should advise on them.

16.5   FINANCIAL EDUCATION

A major lesson from the splits crisis is the need for financial education of the consumer. I am not suggesting that the splits crisis could have been avoided with better financial education. Some would say that even the manufacturers of splits didn't understand the more complicated products fully themselves. But a better educated investing public asking more questions about yields and risk would surely have lessened the scale of the crisis.

One of the FSA's four statutory obligations is "promoting public understanding of the financial system." The aim is to provide individuals with the knowledge, aptitude and skills base necessary to become questioning and informed consumers of financial services and manage their finances effectively. In an interview in the *Financial Times* (24 November 2003), Callum McCarthy, incoming chairman of the FSA, said that educating the consumer was "a mammoth problem" but it was essential. He argued that the FSA could not achieve it alone, saying that: "The idea that the FSA, which is spending £6m or £10m against the £2bn that is spent by the state on primary education, is going to have an impact is risible." He would like to see different players – "employers, financial advisers, providers of financial products, the FSA, government, trade unions" – each making a contribution.

To me, the role that financial advisers and providers of financial products should play in educating the consumer is somewhat limited. The splits crisis has emphasised the need to be sceptical about the impartiality of these groups. The role of employers and trade unions would also seem to be limited.

The most efficient approach to the problem is to concentrate initially on schools. Personal finance education was introduced as a non-statutory part of the national curriculum in England in September 2000. Its aim is to develop financial capability among pupils of all ages (FSA, 2002b). However, I believe that basic personal finance education should be compulsory for all children. This is the most pressing need.

Apart from obvious topics (such as consumers' rights and responsibilities, different payment methods and a basic knowledge of compound interest) common sense rules such as the following should be taught to all children before they leave school:

- If a financial product looks too good to be true, it probably is.
- If a higher return is offered, automatically assume there's a higher risk.
- Higher gearing implies higher financial risk.
- If you can't understand a financial product, don't buy it.
- Question the motives of a financial adviser.
- If remunerated by means of commission[9] on products sold, financial advisers may be biased.
- Read comments in the press critically, be aware of the economic importance of financial advertising to newspapers and be aware that some journalists are higher quality than others.

The FSA recently published the document *Towards a National Strategy for Financial Capability* (FSA, 2003b). This concerns the education, information and generic advice needed by consumers to make their financial decisions with confidence. A steering group has been set up, chaired by the chief executive of the FSA, which includes representatives from government, financial firms, employers, not-for-profit organisations, consumer representatives and the media. It will develop a national strategy and oversee its developments. This is a welcome and long overdue initiative.

However, it will probably take decades before private investors generally have sufficient knowledge of financial matters to make informed decisions, even if the government gives financial education in schools a high priority immediately and increases resources accordingly. In the meantime, every attempt must be made to provide investors with a very clear and simple statement of product features and risks.

16.6   THE FINANCIAL PRESS

While there were a handful of warning articles, much of what was written in the press about splits up to the spring of 2001 was favourable. Many articles relied on information from product providers or others with a vested interest in promoting the benefits of splits and their shares. But, by the end of 2002, sentiment had swung completely in the opposite direction, fuelled by the Treasury Select Committee inquiry. Articles often tarred all splits with the same brush and on occasions the negative sentiment even stretched to comment on the investment trust industry as a whole.

The positive tone of the majority of media comment while mis-selling occurred followed by the very negative comment when the chickens came home to roost is similar behaviour to that of the press in other mis-selling disasters of the recent past. Over the years, the press was a vigorous promoter of endowment mortgages and Equitable Life policies. Journalists should be more sceptical about what they are told by product providers although this is clearly an area of difficulty because of commercial

---

[9] Most IFAs receive commission, a percentage of the amount invested by the client, rather than a fee based on the time spent working for the client. Many commentators believe that this distorts the advice given to the client, with some IFAs recommending financial products for the commission they can earn rather than suitability for the client. Indeed, the FSA found that the commission system acted to the detriment of consumers (FSA, 2002a).

pressures. If they are going to pontificate about a complicated product, they should at least attempt to understand the risks and costs involved. There is a need for thoughtful articles built on a conceptual grasp of the fundamental attributes of the product. But a real understanding of complicated products will require a significant increase in the level of expertise among financial journalists.

Is the introduction of a qualification devoted to financial journalism the answer? If that is not feasible, perhaps financial journalists should at least be required to take the Financial Planning Certificate exams, which the FSA describes as an appropriate approved qualification for IFAs.

Journalists need to be made to feel accountable for what they write. Misreporting rarely leads to negative consequences for the journalist. Concerns were certainly expressed about the standard of reporting of the complex issues involved as the splits crisis unfolded. One splits specialist likened the press coverage of the crisis to someone reviewing cars who did not have a driving licence. A City survey giving a "league table" of financial journalists might encourage higher standards. Genuine investigative journalism and balanced reporting would then be rewarded.

But how independent can financial journalists be? It is difficult to assess the extent to which press comment on financial products is influenced by advertising spend. The lack of unflattering comments about the unit trust industry (which has a substantial marketing budget for national press advertising) may be a case in point. Few people know the extent to which direct arm-twisting goes on. Furthermore, any pressure exerted by product promoters can be indirect and, indeed, not unethical. As explained by Andrew McCosh in Chapter 12:

> If the promoter makes no threat, but simply refrains from subsequent advertising in a publication in which nasty things have been written about his product, no ethical violation would have occurred. Nobody has a moral obligation to continue to trade with his enemies, unless there is a contract to do so.

One possible measure would be to require disclosure of any financial incentive for a newspaper or magazine to write positive pieces about a financial product.

16.7 THE REGULATORS

The FSA should try to anticipate problems rather than act after the event. Many analysts with expert knowledge of splits knew there was a problem from November 2000. The Guernsey regulator required health warnings, which talked of "systemic risk", as early as February 2001. In our article "For whom the barbell tolls ...", published in April 2001, Robin Angus and I argued that there was an urgent need for the significant risks and expenses involved in barbell trusts to be shown more clearly in their prospectuses and Report & Accounts.

It is perhaps not surprising that the FSA was slow to act in response to the problems building up in the splits sector. Investment trusts were never wholly under the control of the FSA or its predecessor regulatory bodies. Nevertheless, it must be an embarrassment to the FSA that zeros were treated as a single low-risk asset category on the FSA website as late as June 2002.

The FSA must have sufficient technical expertise to meet its objectives. As complexity increases, regulatory staff require more expertise to cope. More critical and expert assessment of prospectuses should be carried out by the FSA. In my view, the regulator should also make public pronouncements on the riskiness of products more frequently. The problems created by zeros ranking behind bank debt emphasises the need for the FSA to be vigilant about the term used to describe a security which may have "changed its spots".

One major problem, made worse by the regulatory response to the splits crisis, is the length and complexity of prospectuses. Irrelevant and unnecessarily complicated material should be dropped from the prospectus to make it understandable to a wider readership than at present. A clear "disclosure summary" should be included. The regulator should dictate where important information is to be found in the prospectus, or perhaps sub-contract this job to the AITC. Alternatively, a "mini-prospectus" could be issued, along the lines of those in the privatisation issues of the 1980s.

The Treasury Select Committee report (HCTC, 2003) recommended bringing investment trusts directly within the scope of investment product regulation by the FSA. John McFall MP writes in Chapter 10 of this book:

Following a recommendation of the Select Committee, the Treasury is currently considering the options for future regulation of investment trusts and will be consulting in due course. We await the results of this process with keen interest.

Should investment trusts become FSA-regulated products? It might mean that the regulator would be better able to consider marketing material in advance. But the process of change would be long and complicated. It would cause much upheaval. In my view it would be an unfortunate development, rendered unnecessary by the regulatory changes that have already been imposed. Investment trusts are not products, they are subject to company law, with a battery of protection. If investment trusts were FSA-regulated products, it would impose a significant burden on trusts, thereby increasing their costs and reducing their competitive advantage. It could lead to the erosion of benefits traditionally associated with investment trusts, so that they effectively became managed funds under a different name. It would be interference with the relationship between Board and shareholders other than by the ordinary officers of the law. The investment trust sector as we know it would be destroyed, a sector which has served investors by and large very well for over a century.

While the FSA and the Financial Ombudsman Service (FOS) are all too easily confused in the public mind, they are operationally independent and have distinct functions. The FSA is responsible for the operation of the regulatory system as a whole whereas the FOS investigates individual disputes between consumers and regulated firms, providing consumers with a free independent service. It does seem odd that the FSA and the FOS are conducting separate, very detailed investigations into the splits crisis. They obviously share information and consult when allowed to do so (FSA/FOS, 2002) but there is bound to be some degree of duplication.

In an interview with the *Financial Times* (24 November 2003) soon after taking over as Chairman of the FSA, Callum McCarthy expressed concern about overlaps between the FSA and the FOS, saying: "The question I think is really about whether the ombudsman, by making specific decisions, is actually making policy." He acknowledged the FSA's concerns, adding: "There's clearly an issue." Mr McCarthy was then reported as saying: "It's important that there is a proper understanding of any decision taken by the ombudsman on wider implications. It's quite difficult because the ombudsman has got legal duties and we've got legal duties ... There is a degree of untidiness."

The Treasury announced in November 2003 that it was to review the Financial Services and Markets Act, which sets out the respective roles and responsibilities of the FSA and the FOS. The review will look particularly at the FSA's relationship with the FOS. Should the FOS be subsumed into the FSA or is there a case for giving the FOS more power and more resources? I am not alone in having a preference for the latter. The FOS (unlike the FSA) is familiar to the consumer, who often assumes it has much more power and resources than it actually has and is accordingly surprised and disappointed to discover that it does not. We are concerned here above all with the protection of the consumer, and it is important to recognise that the FOS, not the FSA, is the interface with the consumer.

16.8 CONCLUSION

This chapter has tried to draw lessons for the future from the point of view of a number of parties involved in the splits crisis.

It is important that the Board is appointed before the initial marketing of a new trust and has sufficient technical expertise to understand the possible consequences of the structural design of the trust. Directors should insist that fees be charged in relation to net asset value or market capitalisation. They should also ensure that prospectuses contain clear rules for shareholder entitlements. However, as stated in the *AITC Code*, "Boards and managers should operate in a supportive, co-operative and open environment."

The AITC should place particular emphasis on promoting good practice within the investment trust industry. It must be quick to spot any problems building up and should be prepared to speak out at an early stage. It has an important role to play in the training and induction of new directors.

Financial advisers must only recommend products that they understand and should not rely too much on product providers for information. They should allocate sufficient time to assess the risk of products, using all relevant information. In assessing the suitability of fixed-return investments, they should assume that risk is reflected in the gross redemption yield. In my view, only sophisticated fee-based IFAs should advise on shares in a split capital investment trust.

There is a pressing need for the introduction of compulsory basic personal financial education in schools. This requires the government to supply sufficient funding. Even then the majority of private investors would, for the foreseeable future, have insufficient knowledge to make informed financial decisions. All parties involved should bear this in mind and be acutely aware that most consumers are vulnerable.

Financial journalists should only recommend products that they understand and should be made to feel accountable for what they write. Practical measures to help achieve this might include: the introduction of an appropriate qualification; a City survey which produces a league table of financial journalists; and a requirement for the disclosure of any financial incentive to write positive articles about a particular product.

The FSA should attach great importance to anticipating problems before they occur and should make pronouncements on the riskiness of products more frequently. It must have sufficient technical expertise to achieve its objectives as complexity in the marketplace increases. The FSA must monitor the use of generic names for securities and not allow "bells and whistles" to be added without proper risk warnings or an alteration of name for the changed securities. Hopefully, the Treasury's review of the Financial Services and Markets Act will clarify the roles of the FSA and the FOS, and will reduce duplication of work when a mess like the splits *débâcle* arises.

16.9   REFERENCES

AITC (2003) *AITC Code of Corporate Governance*. Association of Investment Trust Companies, London.

FSA (2002a) *Reforming Polarisation: Making the Market Work for Consumers* (Consultation Paper 121, January). Financial Services Authority, London.

FSA (2002b) *Personal Finance Teaching in Schools: Implications for Consumer Education of Research Carried Out by the National Centre for Social Research* (Consumer Research 11, February). Financial Services Authority, London.

FSA (2003a) *Policy Statement on Investment Companies (Including Investment Trusts)*. Financial Services Authority, London.

FSA (2003b) *Towards a National Strategy for Financial Capability*. Financial Services Authority, London.

FSA/FOS (2002) *Memorandum of Understanding between the Financial Services Authority and the Financial Ombudsman Service*. Financial Services Authority/Financial Ombudsman Service, London.

HCTC (2003) *Split Capital Investment Trusts* (Third report of session 2002–03, volume I: Report and proceedings of the committee, February). House of Commons Treasury Committee.

Appendix A
For Whom the Barbell Tolls ...[1]
ANDREW ADAMS and ROBIN ANGUS

> *The most notable piece of speculative [financial] architecture of the late twenties, and the one by which, more than any other device, the public demand for stock was satisfied, was the investment trust or company.*
>
> (J.K. Galbraith, *The Great Crash 1929*, Pelican Books, 1975, p. 72)

Attention-grabbing but slightly ominous words from J.K. Galbraith in a book all investment professionals should read. Investment trusts are, of course, still with us, and many of them are the souls of simplicity and caution. However, the public demand for investment trust stock in the UK is today being satisfied partly by the issue of trusts of a novel type – the so-called "barbell trusts". These are designed to offer their shareholders, at issue, the growth prospects of a fashionable investment area together with a good income. On the strictest definition of the term, three barbell trusts were issued in 1999 and 15 in 2000, raising £2.7bn of new money in all – a figure that would double were a looser definition of "barbell" to be employed.

Supporters of barbell trusts argue that they are an attractive way for income investors to gain exposure to growth sectors. We believe, however, that barbell trusts may be more costly and riskier than investors, especially retail investors, realise. As keen supporters of the investment trust sector our motive in writing this article is to increase investor awareness of the issues and risks involved.

A.1 WHAT ARE BARBELL TRUSTS?

Most investment trusts hold one single portfolio of investments as backing for all their classes of capital. By contrast, barbell trusts hold two distinct portfolios of investments – a growth portfolio and an income portfolio. In pictorial form this structure can look like a "barbell" such as is used in weightlifting.[2]

Figure A.1 illustrates the structure of one common type of barbell trust. On the assets side of the balance sheet are two portfolios, one of growth-orientated investments such as Japanese equities or technology stocks, and the other of UK bonds and high-yielding

[1] This article was previously published in *Professional Investor* (April 2001). Reproduced with permission from Professional Investor Journal, published by the UK Society of Investment Professionals.
[2] The term "barbell", in a financial context, originated in the bond market. "A spread or portfolio position made up of short-maturity and long-maturity fixed income securities with nothing in the middle" (Moles and Terry, 1997).

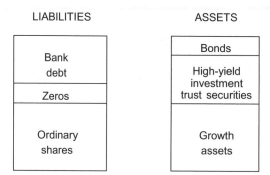

Figure A.1

investment trust securities. On the liabilities side of the balance sheet are bank debt and two classes of share capital. The zero dividend preference shares (zeros) are entitled to a fixed annual capital increment. The ordinary shares (often called "income & residual capital shares" in this type of structure) are entitled to all the trust's distributable income together with whatever capital remains after the bank debt and the zero dividend preference shares have been repaid.

The structure shown in Figure A.1 happens to be that of a split capital trust (split) (i.e., a trust with more than one main class of share capital). However, barbell trusts and splits must not be confused. While a good number of barbells are splits, most splits are not barbells. It is the division of the assets side of the balance sheet into two separate portfolios, together with a high level of gearing, which makes a barbell.[3]

A.2   HOW BARBELL TRUSTS EMERGED

The recent boom in new issues of split capital trusts is nevertheless bound up with the emergence of barbells. Why? One reason is that both splits and barbells typically offer at least one class of high yielding paper. While the yields available in both equity and fixed-interest markets have fallen sharply in recent years, investors continue to clamour for the high yields they have been used to for decades. So high-yielding equity securities such as those offered by barbells have found a ready market.

Furthermore, investors and fund managers alike have grown accustomed to remarkably high annual total returns from equities – 17.7% p.a. nominal and 10.7% p.a. real from the FTSE All-Share Index over the last 25 years (source: Datastream).

This has had two effects:

- Investors in and promoters of new trusts assume continuing high returns. While the past is not necessarily a guide to the future, 25 years is a lot of "past"!
- Investors in high yield securities, anxious not to miss out on what they see as freely-available capital growth, understandably are attracted to investments offering "high yield with a touch of equity", such as the ordinary shares of split capital trusts and barbells.

---

[3] For a lucid exposition of the split capital principle see Newlands (2000).

Lastly, banks have of late been eager to lend to the investment trust sector, whereas until recent years it was uncommon for trusts to have significant amounts of bank debt. The banks know their lending is safe because there is ample collateral. It is very unlikely that a bank loan to a trust would be defaulted on, because the bank ranks first in order of priority and the bank checks the covenanted cover on the debt each month. Therefore, although bank lending inevitably increases the risk of capital loss to holders of lower-ranking classes of capital, the banks cannot be blamed for making large sums of money available. The Boards, not the banks, are responsible for trusts' borrowing decisions and how these affect shareholders.

A.3   HOW BIG AND HOW MANY?

Table A.1 shows the number of new barbell trusts in recent years, their division into trusts with a conventional and a split structure, and the total amount raised by barbells for each class of capital. We have adopted a very strict definition of barbell trusts, including only those which have a non-UK geographical specialist portfolio or a sector specialist portfolio, and which therefore offer exposure to more volatile equities.

A.4   FEES AND EXPENSES

Initial and recurring costs to ordinary shareholders of barbells are much higher than may appear at first sight. First come issue expenses, which include a significant element of marketing costs. Issue expenses can be anything from 2% to as high as 4% of the gross capital sum raised by a new trust, including bank debt. So expenses expressed as a percentage of the starting net asset value attributable to the trust's ordinary shares will be very much higher:

- If ordinary shares represented 50% of the gross capital subscribed including bank debt (as is the case for the aggregate figures shown in Table A.1) and issue expenses were 4% of the gross capital subscribed, the expenses would approach 9% of the ordinary shares' starting NAV.
- If the ordinary shares were 33% of gross capital and issue expenses again were 4% of the gross capital subscribed, expenses would be nearly 14% of starting NAV.

These are startlingly high percentages. Perhaps it is not surprising that such trusts often do not put a starting NAV of their ordinary shares "upfront" in the Prospectus.

Table A.1   New barbell trusts with a conventional and split structure

Capital structure	No. of trusts	Amount raised (£m)			
		Equity	Zeros	Bank debt	Total
Conventional	8	481.9	—	393.5	875.4
Split	10	905.6	124.7	796.9	1,827.2

Then there are management fees. These are typically 1% of gross assets per annum. At first glance, the figure looks reasonable by today's investment trust sector standards and modest compared to the management fees for many unit trusts and OEICs. However, the key point is that again, management fees are charged as a proportion of gross assets rather than net assets. This includes assets financed by bank debt and zero dividend preference capital as well as by ordinary share capital. So the holders of the ordinary share capital may be paying management fees at the rate of 2% or 3% per annum of the assets actually attributable to them.

By contrast with unit trusts, total expenses may be significantly higher than management fees alone. Fitzrovia, a company that specialises in monitoring expenses of funds, estimates that on average two-thirds of total expenses for investment trusts are represented by management fees.[4] Hence, other expenses could boost the figures quoted above to an annual 3% or 4% of the assets attributable to the holders of the ordinary-share capital – a massive hurdle to clear before one even reaches the starting line.

Finally, most barbell trusts hold shares in other investment trusts. So there are management expenses upon management expenses.

A.5   ACCOUNTING – THE NEW FLEXIBILITY

The investment trust Statement of Recommended Practice (SORP) allows management expenses and debt interest to be allocated between income and capital in different ways. Hasn't this made the impact of costs and expenses less onerous?

Not quite. In fact, the SORP raises as many questions as it answers.

The SORP sets out the principle that management expenses and interest costs should be allocated in line with expected returns.[5] So if the Board expects 25% of a trust's total return to come from capital, one would expect that it would charge 25% of management expenses and 25% of interest costs to capital.

What, then, are we to make of those trusts, and there are many, which charge no less than 75% of such expenses and costs to capital? It is clearly unrealistic to expect that 75% of a trust's returns will come from capital if (as is not unusual) it has a total portfolio yield more than double that of the FTSE All-Share Index. We believe that the directors, whose responsibility it is to sign the Directors' Responsibility Statement in the Report & Accounts, should give this matter careful consideration.

If some Boards go against the spirit of the SORP in charging too much to capital, others are not subject to the SORP at all. 13 of the 18 barbells referred to in Table A.1 are not investment companies under Section 842 of the Companies Act and for them the SORP's writ does not run. Such companies tend to charge even more to capital than do Section 842 trusts – sometimes as much as 100%.

A.6   RISK FROM BANK DEBT

Universal to barbell trusts, whether conventional or split capital in structure, is a sizeable layer of bank debt. This is quite new in the trust sector, where gearing was traditionally in the form of debentures or preference capital.

---

[4] For unit trusts, on average there is roughly a 90%/10% split for management fees vs other expenses.
[5] Other (non-management) expenses in most cases are charged to revenue account. The uplift in zeros each year is taken to capital account.

The inclusion of bank debt in trusts' capital structures means that a major subscriber of capital to a trust now has the right to blow the whistle and demand either repayment or changes to the portfolio before the end of the game, regardless of the effect on the other subscribers of capital (the various classes of shareholder). This has already happened in the case of two barbells, European Technology & Income and Framlington NetNet.Inc. It could happen to others.

A.7   MISLEADING EXPECTATIONS

We remain nervous about some of the barbell portfolios underlying these funds. The growth portfolio is often highly volatile, while the income portfolio has more capital risk than many investors think. Not only could the proportion invested in other splits fall sharply if the underlying hurdle rates are not met, but the high yielding (née junk) bonds that are popular in some structures are quasi equity. The worst case scenario for investors is therefore a growth portfolio that does not grow and an income portfolio that suffers defaults and capital loss. In this instance high headline yields do little to mitigate the overall losses that will be suffered.

(Cazenove, *Investment Trust Companies Annual Review*, 10 January 2001)

These words, from one of the most respected brokers in the sector, are a reminder of the portfolio risks run by barbell trusts. The most obvious risk is that of investing in a fashionable specialist area like technology. Whereas traditional splits tended to invest in a broad UK portfolio with an income flavour, followers of TMT [technology, media and telecommunications] over 2000 know only too well how risky it is investing in a single "growth" area.

However, high-yielding split securities and bonds can be risky too. It is therefore important not to be misled by the illusion of conservatism offered by the two portfolios of barbell trusts – and legally, of course, there is only one portfolio anyway.

Assessment of risk for investment trust securities often involves looking at hurdle rates, which can be defined as the required annual growth rate of total assets to repay a given class of shareholder at the wind-up date. The hurdle rate does allow for the fact that the interest cost of part, and in some cases all, of the bank debt (and possibly other prior ranking capital too) is being met out of capital. However, a significant proportion of a barbell trust's assets will be held to generate income. Such assets may not preserve their capital value.

Because promoters' and investors' expectations of rates of return from equities have been shaped by the experience of the bull market of the last quarter of a century, the hurdle rates for the ordinary shares of barbells may be perceived as being less demanding than they actually are. Yes, there will have been "wealth warnings" galore. But how many investors in the ordinary shares of barbells really expect to receive back significantly less than the capital they have subscribed?

A.8   THE "MAGIC CIRCLE"

As reverse leverage did its work, investment trust managements were much more concerned over the collapse in the value of their own stock than over the adverse movements in the stock list as a whole. The investment trusts had invested heavily in each other. As a result the fall in

Blue Ridge hit Shenandoah, and the resulting collapse in Shenandoah was even more horrible for the Goldman Sachs Trading Corporation.

(J.K. Galbraith, *The Great Crash 1929*, Pelican Books, 1975, p. 145)

Translate today's so-called "magic circle" of split capital trust managers (i.e., those whose trusts hold shares in one another) back to the Wall Street of 1929 about which J.K. Galbraith wrote, and it is easy to see what the worries are.

To begin with, cross-holdings make it hard to disentangle the ownership of these trusts. It is also very difficult, if not impossible, to pin down where unit trusts managed by fund management groups within the "magic circle" hold shares in them.

So there is a problem of accountability and transparency. Who owns what?

But of even greater importance is what the interrelated structure of cross-holdings could lead to in a falling market. The risks created by geared trusts investing in other geared trusts are very real. Substantial price declines in the ordinary shares of some individual barbell trusts might all too easily become a self-feeding downward spiral as the net asset values of the ordinary shares of other trusts that held them fell in their turn.

Confidence in barbell trusts in general could thus ebb away, causing still further price declines in their ordinary shares. If this happened, many retail investors who were direct holders of such shares would be disadvantaged and it is inevitable that their confidence in the investment trust sector as a whole would suffer.

A.9   CONCLUSION

If barbell trusts started to unravel, confidence in the investment trust sector as a whole would be affected by the adverse publicity. The ordinary shares of barbell trusts are also more costly than some investors assume, in terms of fees and expenses deducted from net asset value.

Because barbells are complicated and difficult to understand, they should put more emphasis on communicating their investment characteristics to investors. In particular, there is an urgent need for the significant risks and expenses involved to be spelt out more clearly in their Prospectuses and Report & Accounts.

A.10   REFERENCES

Galbraith, J.K. (1975) *The Great Crash 1929* (p. 72). Pelican Books, London.
Newlands, J.E. (2000) Dual purpose funds. *Professional Investor*, **10**(7), September, 14–17.
Moles, P. and Terry, N. (1997) *The Handbook of International Financial Terms*. Oxford University Press, Oxford, UK.

Appendix B
Response to FSA Consultation Paper 164
ANDREW ADAMS and ROBIN ANGUS

Centre for Financial Markets Research
University of Edinburgh
William Robertson Building
50 George Square
Edinburgh
EH8 9JY

14 April 2003

Richard Emery Esq
UK Listing Authority
5th Floor
25 The North Colonnade
Canary Wharf
London
E14 5HS

Dear Mr Emery

FSA CONSULTATION PAPER 164 ON INVESTMENT COMPANIES (INCLUDING INVESTMENT TRUSTS)

The implications of Consultation Paper 164 seem to us to be very far-reaching – much more so, in our opinion, than may be immediately apparent. So, we feel it important to begin by reiterating that common sense (the foundation of all good corporate governance) and "*caveat emptor*" (the foundation of all successful investing) have served investors well in the past.

We therefore think that any new regulation resulting from what has come to be known as "the splits crisis" should be kept to a minimum. As we were the first to identify in print the structural flaws in many of the new trust structures, we feel a special responsibility to comment on which aspects of the proposed regulatory changes are necessary.

The recent problems started with barbell trusts getting into difficulties. Many such trusts do not have a split capital structure. We therefore accept that any additional regulation deemed necessary must be applied uniformly across the entire investment company industry. Indeed, we recommended this in our response to the FSA Discussion Paper on Split Capital Closed End Funds in February last year. Nevertheless, it would be most unfortunate if the regulatory response to the crisis had a permanent and significantly detrimental effect on the UK investment company industry as a whole, the vast bulk of which has not digressed from prudent practice.

In our opinion, this would undoubtedly happen if the recommendations of FSA Consultation Paper 164 as they stand at present were to be implemented in full.

In drawing up any new regulation in response to the splits crisis, it is important to keep in view the two main underlying reasons for that crisis, namely:

1   The aggressive pursuit of fees by certain fund management companies and broker/ advisers, which drove them to launch risky structures that exploited the retail demand for high yield in an environment of falling interest rates. This led in many cases to substantial bank debt financing, high charges to the capital account and investment in the ordinary income shares of other splits.
2   A lack of understanding of the true risks involved on the part of almost everyone from directors of splits to IFAs.

We strongly agree that investment companies should not become investment products regulated by the FSA. However, it is important to be aware of the UK regulation of other collective investment vehicles, such as unit trusts and OEICs [open-ended investment companies], to ensure that there is a "level playing field" for the wider collective investment industry.

    We urge that there is a need for standardisation of listing particulars, with key facts on risk and other important financial ratios being shown "up front" in the document.

We should be very willing to prepare for the FSA a checklist of what we believe to be the key risk factors and financial ratios of which investors and advisers need to be aware.

Our comments below relate to the specific questions raised in the FSA Consultation Paper 164, listed in Annex A of that document.

Q1   Do you believe that a limit should be placed on the amount of an investment company's gross assets that can be invested in the shares of other investment companies whose investment policies allow cross-investing? If so, do you believe that a 10% limit is appropriate?

We consider this to be FSA Consultation Paper 164's most controversial proposal. To begin with, the actual application of the proposed 10% rule is not clear and the terms "investment company", "fund" and "cross-investing" are not defined. This could mean that, in practice, investment company Boards might feel able to invest in other investment companies only if these had made a public statement that they would not invest in other investment companies. Many Boards would not want to make such a statement, however, as it would unjustifiably remove an effective way of diversifying risk and hence would not be in the best interests of shareholders.

    More generally, we do not accept that there is a need to restrict investment in other investment companies *per se*. Indeed, one of us (Robin Angus) is a director of an investment trust (Collective Assets Trust PLC) formed specifically for that very purpose, it being the Board's view that a spread of investment across a carefully-chosen selection of investment trust companies is ideal for the private investor.

We do agree, however, that such an investment trust should disclose information on holdings in other investment trusts (see our answer to Q10) and not only its own gearing level but also its underlying gearing level on a "look-through" basis with respect to the investment trust securities in its portfolio. Potential investors would then be able to make their own informed decisions in the light of the true underlying investment characteristics of such a "trust of trusts".

We briefly discuss a possible solution to the current problem of illiquid cross-holdings in the Annex (pp. 239–240).

Q2   What will be the cost, if any, of introducing a limit of this kind?

Genuine conventional "trusts of trusts" (often referred to as "funds of funds") would be unable to continue. This would reduce the range of choice available to private investors in an unnecessary and unacceptable way and would benefit no-one.

Another unfortunate consequence, that would have implications for the wider economic health of the country, would be that investment companies would be unable to use other investment companies as intermediaries for venture capital investment (something that a considerable number of investment companies currently do). The flow of funds into venture capital investment would thereby be reduced.

Q3   What are your views on the proposal to require an explanation of the risks associated with investing in investment companies to be included in listing documents?

We view it very favourably and would have been pressing for it very strongly at this time even had FSA Consultation Paper 164 not appeared. It is a prerequisite for any meaningful investor protection in this area that potential investors and their advisers should be given sufficient information to enable them to come to an informed decision about risks associated with individual securities in an investment company. We therefore agree that a clear explanation of the risks associated with investing in investment companies should be included in the listing documents. This section should be separate from the section on investment policy but should have equal prominence within the listing documents.

Q4   What are your views on the proposal to include an explanation of the specific risks associated with gearing?

We are strongly in favour. However, while better explanation of the specific risks associated with gearing is required, it is not enough by itself. It must be a part of the wider risk disclosure.

Q5   Are there any other issues that should be considered in the risk factors section of the listing document?

The risk factors section of the listing document should show the possible consequences of *negative* growth rates. The experience of the last three years has shown that these can reflect reality in the investment world in a way that both investors and advisers are inclined to forget during a long bull market.

Q6   Do you agree that limits should not be imposed on the amount of money that investment companies can borrow?

Yes. However, full information on borrowings (and on significant upward or downward changes in gearing levels, "significant" meaning perhaps 10% or more) must at all times be available. In particular, there is a clear need for the Listing Rules to require all investment companies to disclose the terms of banking covenants on a regular basis, together with information about cash holdings and the overall level of debt. The lack of this data has been a major problem for investors in attempting to determine the true position of many splits.

Q7   What would be the consequences of introducing a limit on the amount of money investment companies can borrow? Would such a proposal have significant cost implications and, if so, what are they?

Such a restriction would undermine the very existence of the investment trust industry, an industry that for well over a century has delivered very good long-term returns to investors at low cost. For this reason we find it astonishing that there should be any mention of "significant cost implications", as if this were just some mundane piece of fine-tuning regulation. Limiting the amount of money investment companies can borrow would strike a crippling blow at the sector's very existence and *rationale*.

Q8   What are your views on the introduction of a limit on the amount of an investment company's investment portfolio that may be invested in other geared investments?

This would not only be unwarranted interference with the proper responsibilities of Boards and managers but also would be so difficult to quantify that imposing a limit would be unworkable. Instead, the maximum effort should be directed at ensuring full and frank disclosure of the underlying gearing of such investments, so that investors can make their own informed investment decisions.

Q9   If you are in favour of introducing limits either on the amount of money companies can borrow, or on the amount of an investment company's investment portfolio that may be invested in other geared investments, how should borrowings be determined and what should the limit be? Should borrowings include amounts due under stock lending and repurchase agreements?

We are not in favour of introducing such limits.

Q10   Do you believe that it is appropriate for investment companies to disclose each holding that exceeds a certain percentage of the value of the portfolio at least once a month? If yes is 0.5% a reasonable threshold? If not what should the threshold be?

We agree that the FSA is justified in requiring a higher, more frequent and more uniform standard of disclosure of portfolio information. But we consider that the proposal put forward represents "information overload". It might well obscure, rather than clarify, the situation from the point of view of shareholders (which, in our view, must always be paramount). If implemented, it would also put a significant cost burden on investment companies. Furthermore, market makers would "see them coming" in potential trades if there were full disclosure, which would not be in the best interests of the shareholders. There is a need to strike a balance between openness on the one hand, and consideration of the legitimate interests of the managers and of the shareholders on the other.

A sensible way forward would be to require all investment companies to give full disclosure of their underlying investment portfolio holdings every six months, as is required for unit trusts. In addition, investment companies should be required monthly to disclose, one month in arrears, (a) their aggregate holdings in other investment companies, expressed as a percentage of gross assets; (b) any such individual holdings which represented above, say, 1.0% of gross assets; and (c) all holdings in investment companies run by a single management company, if there are three or more such holdings.

Q11   Is the scope of the changes to our risk warnings adequate or should it be drawn more widely to cover other geared investment products or services?

In our opinion, the scope is more than adequate.

We feel compelled, however, to add here a general note of caution. There is a danger that these new warnings and new restrictions will suggest to private investors that investment trusts are very risky investments indeed, constantly in danger of investing recklessly in other very risky investment trusts and hence of becoming insolvent. This would be a travesty. As investments, investment trusts are typically much less risky than are individual equities. Moreover, in our opinion a conservative and cautiously-managed investment trust investing in the shares of other well-managed investment trusts is one of the least risky types of equity investment imaginable.

The split capital trust *débâcle*, although distressing and regrettable, was nevertheless wildly out of character for the investment trust industry as a whole. Well-established diversified trusts (and, indeed, well-established geographical or sector specialists) were, broadly speaking, wholly unaffected from start to finish. It would in our opinion be a serious blow to private investors, as well as grotesquely unfair in itself, if good and responsible trusts of the type that form the backbone of the industry (a type that has given good service to private investors for some 130 years) were to be crippled and hindered by being punished for the sins of an errant few.

Q12   Do you think the measures proposed in paragraph 3.90 are appropriate?

It is extraordinarily difficult to generalise about this subject. We ourselves have personally known directors who fell into both the first two categories but were, in practice, utterly independent and single-minded in representing the interests of the shareholders, and directors who were even by the strictest possible criteria "independent" but who in practice were (by reason of personal character or social connections) no better than "yes men".

It is a source of great concern to us that regulators may confuse independence on paper with independence in practice. The two are not the same.

We believe that the matter should, as much as possible, be left in the hands of shareholders. The directors are elected to represent shareholders' interests and it should therefore be for shareholders either to extend their terms of office or to vote them off the Board. As a general principle, therefore, we deplore any attempt by regulators to restrict shareholder choice in the matter of the directors who represent them.

Moving from the general to the particular, the measures proposed in paragraph 3.90 may present Board recruitment difficulties, particularly at a time when indemnity insurance premiums are so high following the splits crisis. This would push up fees and, therefore, costs for investment companies, thus lowering returns to shareholders.

A special problem is presented by self-managed investment companies, which represent a long and honourable tradition within the investment company industry. In these companies there is no clear demarcation between directors and managers, and no explicit management contract. Hence, such investment companies would have to be excluded from the measures proposed in paragraph 3.90.

A particular difficulty also arises for companies in which the manager personally owns a significant stake in the company. He or she would rightly feel that in these circumstances a place on the Board would be appropriate.

Q13   Are there any other measures that you would like to see adopted?

There should be a requirement for management fees (and other expected expenses) expressed as a percentage of starting net assets attributable to ordinary shareholders to be shown clearly "upfront" in the prospectus.

Q14   Is twelve months a reasonable period to enable listed companies to implement these proposals?

It is our earnest hope that the more contentious of these proposals will not be implemented. Restricting the freedom to invest in other investment companies and further restricting shareholder choice in the matter of choosing directors would in our view seriously weaken the investment company industry and would thereby harm (especially) individual investors in the UK.

In other words, we believe they would harm the very people the FSA is seeking to protect.

Taking the proposals as they stand, however, probably 18 months to two years would be more appropriate given the significant changes required in Board membership in many cases and the difficulty there would be in recruiting an adequate number of suitable (in FSA terms) new directors at a reasonable cost to shareholders.

Q15   Do you agree that the decision to appoint the investment manager should be one that is taken by an independent board without reference to shareholders?

Yes.

Q16   Do you agree that the measures proposed in paragraph 3.90 above, together with those that currently exist in law, listing rules or other regulatory guidance are such that the board is deemed to be independent when making decisions that affect the interest of the investment manager?

Deemed to be independent by whom? As noted earlier, we believe generalisation to be impossible. We certainly wish to see no new restrictions on the right of shareholders to elect whichever directors they wish to represent them, and would welcome a significant reduction in such restrictions as are already in place. Shareholder democracy seems to us to be a good principle that should be interfered with as little as possible.

Q17   Do you agree that the directors should be required to explain to shareholders in the Annual Report and Accounts, whether the continuing appointment of the investment manager on the terms agreed continues to be in the best interests of shareholders, together with a statement of the reasons for this decision?

We welcome this. It should concentrate the minds of both managers and Boards. But the words "in the view of the Board" should be inserted in between "continues to be" and "in the best interests of shareholders ..."

Q18   Do you agree that, taking into account the other measures that are proposed, direct regulatory intervention in the terms of the investment management agreement, including severance arrangements is not warranted?

Yes.

Q19   Do you agree that material changes to an investment policy should not be made without prior shareholder approval?

Yes. But this is normally sought anyway.

Q20   Do you see any reason why the Model Code should not be amended to cover contracts for difference and spread bets? Are there any other instruments not covered by the proposed amendment that should be included?

We see no reason why the Model Code should not be amended as indicated.

Yours sincerely

Andy Adams and *Robin Angus*

ANNEX TO APPENDIX B

Given the poor liquidity that exists for many split capital shares at present, it is difficult for a trust to divest itself of many of its cross-holdings. One solution to this problem might be to encourage those trusts that have received shareholder approval for share buy-backs, to buy back their own shares from other trusts seeking to divest themselves of these stakes. Thus, an unwinding of the cross-holdings would take place, using the mechanism of a buy-back to create liquidity. Such unwinding exchanges should take place at fair prices. Given that the liquidity in many stocks is so poor, market maker-quoted prices may not represent fair prices. Thus, some form of independent valuation would be required to ensure that these unwinding exchanges are executed at fair prices.

Index